TOM JEFFREYS is a writer an[d]
in art that engages with enviro[nment]
has appeared in publications [in the]
Independent, Monocle, New Scien[ce]
is the author of *Signal Failure: L[ondon to Birmingham, HS2 on foot]*
(Influx Press, 2017) and editor of online magazine *The Learned Pig*. He lives in Edinburgh and is obsessed with cricket.

Praise for *The White Birch*

'*The White Birch* is a tightly packed hybrid of art criticism, politics, history, science, popular culture, internet scavenging and travelogue ... Wending his way among park benches, parochial museums and oligarch-funded arts centres, [Jeffreys] explores the relationship of birch to gender stereotypes, antisemitism and Soviet clichés ... stick with it and the oblique connections start to accumulate into a book of oddities propelled by the author's genuine curiosity ... genuinely revelatory'

Sophy Roberts, *TLS*

'*The White Birch* is a wonderful book: at once an idiosyncratic personal journey and an erudite and clear-eyed critical study. Jeffreys is a deeply human writer and a smart and honest critic who here, splitting the timber of the Russian birch, finds his way deep into the Russian idea of Russia'

Richard Smyth, author of *The Woodcock* and
An Indifference of Birds

A natural-political exploration of Russian relationships with the birch tree across past, present, and future. Moving from the Tsarina's garden to the Soviet Gulag, from Chernobyl to Lake Baikal, *The White Birch* is elegant and intrepid, like its subject'

Daisy Hildyard, author of *The Second Body* and
Hunters in the Snow

THE

TOM JEFFREYS

WHITE

A RUSSIAN REFLECTION

BIRCH

corsair

CORSAIR

First published in Great Britain in 2021 by Corsair
This paperback edition published in 2022

1 3 5 7 9 10 8 6 4 2

A CIP catalogue record for this book
is available from the British Library.

ISBN: 978-1-4721-5566-5

Typeset in Palatino by M Rules
Printed and bound in Great Britain by Clays Ltd, Elcograf S.p.A.

Papers used by Corsair are from well-managed forests
and other responsible sources.

Corsair
An imprint of
Little, Brown Book Group
Carmelite House
50 Victoria Embankment
London EC4Y 0DZ

An Hachette UK Company
www.hachette.co.uk

www.littlebrown.co.uk

'In five years, everything can change in Russia, but in two hundred – nothing.'

Svetlana Alexievich, *Second-Hand Time,* **2016**

'Nearly everyone who has ever travelled in Russia has become an expert, and nearly every expert cancels out every other expert.'

John Steinbeck, *A Russian Journal,* **1948**

And what kind of birch is that?
Who's to know or care? –
Only a prose inscribed on air,
Illegible; evanescent . . .

Osip Mandelstam, *Voronezh Notebooks,* **1936**

CONTENTS

DRAMATIS ~~PERSONAE~~ BETULAE

Betula pubescens	the white birch
Betula pendula	the silver birch
Betula alba	a phantom
Betula pendula 'Dalecarlica'	Ornäs birch, a cultivar, the national tree of Sweden
Betula nana	a low, shrub birch that carpets Siberia
Betula fruticosa	the dwarf bog birch
Betula gmelinii	another shrub, sharp-toothed, drought-tolerant
Betula dahurica	the rugged black birch, with shaggy, flaking bark
Betula ermanii	the stone birch, a white mountain tree
Betula utilis	the Himalayan birch, with bark that peels like paper
All the other birches	unnamed, unknown

INTRODUCTION

This book is a reflection upon Russia's surprisingly complicated relationship with birch trees. Inevitably, it also reflects my own relationship with Russia. Like any reflection, there will be distortions.

Once upon a time, a birch was just a tree. Then it became a material: its timber was burnt for warmth or carved into furniture; its bark was used for shoes and paper; its sap drunk fresh or fermented to make birch beer. Only much, much later did the birch become a symbol. And as it did so, it was represented and defined, imagined and redefined in folk tales and songs, paintings, photographs and the long, long memory of nationalism. This linear history of the birch is an alluring narrative: from tree to material to symbol. From simplicity to complexity: the story of how meaning was made. But alas, things were never so simple. The birch has always been (or always had the potential to be) all of these things – material, symbol, commodity – and, at the same time, a real tree out there in the world, growing and dying at the edge of the forest.

On a shelf in my study are nine little objects. Laid out loosely in front of novels and notebooks, magazines and postcards, they are relics from a journey, or rather from a series of journeys conducted through Russia and Eastern Europe. There is a short length of birch twig, a little longer than a pencil; three curling fragments of bark from different birch species; and three fragile birch leaves protected inside an A6 plastic sleeve. It once held a 'Happy Forest' greetings card that I purchased in Saint Petersburg, decorated with pop-up pine trees and cutesy deer. There is also a badge, made for me by my wife as a gift before a journey on the Trans-Siberian railway. Superimposed over a birch-bark-patterned background are three little words: *'berezki schitat' uslan'*, meaning something like 'sent to count birches'. It is an old Russian euphemism for being deported to Siberia.

Inside the plastic sleeve the first leaf is a healthy green, about the length of my thumb, with straw-coloured veins and just the faintest brown mottle. Its tip was folded over in my notebook as I travelled and it crumbles, now, as I pick it up. The second leaf is much smaller and rounder, its bowl maybe the size of a two-penny piece. It is sandy all over, its small edge serrations darkening towards tea. The third leaf is a leaf in flux. At its heart is a map of green, a leaf within a leaf, fingers stretching out from the central spine, around the veins, and out towards the tip. But the green meets sharply with a sea of autumnal ochre. The edges are a rich red russet. This leaf is more strongly serrated than the other two: like a child's drawing of a little fire. I don't know what species each leaf is from. I can't even remember where I found them all.

If what follows is an attempt to map these objects then I would not suggest you use the result for navigation. The map is full of holes. Too much remains unsaid, unwritten, illegible, caught between languages. Some interviews I recorded with a Dictaphone (like a real journalist); others I just scribbled into notebooks. The conversations you will read may be misremembered or misconstrued. I've accidentally deleted a series of photographs I took in Ukraine. I seem to have lost the two leaves I plucked from specimen trees in the garden of a Latvian castle. Only their traced outlines in a notebook remain. Their

Latin names are there too and a fading memory of a day-long bus journey.

I was a teenager when I first visited Russia. 'Russia is different,' pronounced a sweating, lank-haired history teacher in a special talk organised to prepare us for the journey to come. No other school trip necessitated such preliminaries. But Russia was the great beyond, even then, less than a decade after the end of communism, Putin in the early years of power. We flew to Saint Petersburg, took the overnight train to Moscow, and stayed in one of the Seven Sisters, those vast Soviet-era edifices that skewer the sky. The taps dripped into the night and the plug sockets sparked alarmingly. In Saint Petersburg, I spent a day in bed with food poisoning and missed the Hermitage. My wet hair froze in the winter air. I ate borsch.

It was not until living in Helsinki fifteen years later that my fascination with Russian culture began to develop in earnest. Russia was suddenly so close, just there across the border, increasingly erratic in its behaviour. Putin had only recently invaded Crimea. Might Finland be next? The border between Russia and Finland has not always been a stable one, and Karelia, the region either side of it, is of great symbolic significance to both countries. Compelled by geography to tread a diplomatic tightrope, Finland was once again discussing NATO membership, trying to gauge how Russia might react. Fear of the unknowable neighbour was rarely far away.

It was over coffee that Russia's lingering presence in my unconscious mind burst forth in unexpected form: the wolf. As my first Finnish winter drew closer, I met with artist Terike Haapoja and writer Laura Gustafsson to discuss a performance they were working on in response to heated public debate about the apparently illegal shooting of three wolves in rural Finland.

The subject of Russia kept coming up. For those who abhorred the shooting, advocacy of animal rights was a way to orient Finnish national identity progressively towards Europe and away from 'those brutal Russians'. But there was anti-Russian sentiment on the other side too: wolves continually range back and forth across the border between the two countries. 'Wolves in Finland are considered somehow intruders,' said Gustafsson. 'They don't respect the borders that humans have tried to draw between nature and culture.'

From this moment until I left Finland two years later, Russia rose like a wolf in my mind. All wolves carried the scent of Russia with them. If Finland represented civilisation, Russia was the wild. With its social democracy and trustworthy institutions, Finland felt comprehensible to me, its strangeness confined to the margins. Russia, meanwhile, loomed so vast and impossible. It is a simplistic opposition, but if Finland is a model, Russia is a monster: a huge place of huge ideas. Russia 'is a mewling, pulsating mass, full of mute madness, which needs perpetually to be described', wrote activist and writer Kirill Medvedev in the early 2000s. Russia prompts sweeping statements (like this one).

Gradually, Russia's birches began to speak to me. Birches are not the only symbolically charged tree in Russia. The oak or 'Tsar tree' is associated with Perun, the most powerful of the Slavic gods. The red-berried rowan is a symbol of life associated with luck and happiness. Fir trees and maples play significant roles too. By the same token, the importance of the birch tree is by no means unique to Russia. In the Middle Ages, English peasants would place green birch above doorways alongside fennel, a reddish-purple wild flower called orpine, white lilies and Saint John's wort in order to ward away devilry and witchcraft. In Scottish ballads the birch is associated with the dead. Samuel Taylor Coleridge famously described a 'weeping birch' as 'the Lady of the Woods'. Birch trees also have a powerful place in many indigenous North American cultures: the Pueblo people of New Mexico use the birch as a clan symbol; the Ojibwe people of North America believe that birches are immune to lightning strikes – making them a good place to hide during a thunderstorm.

The birch is a central symbol in the Nordic nations. A Swedish legend has it that Christ was scourged with a rod made from dwarf birch. Finland's national tree is *Betula pendula*, the silver birch; Sweden's is *Betula pendula* 'Dalecarlica', or Ornäs birch, a cultivar distinguished by its deeply indented leaves. Arguably, birch trees are even more significant in Scandinavian and Nordic cultures than they are in Russia. As I discovered first-hand while living in Finland, they are instantly identified with Nordic landscapes. In fact, it was precisely because I associated birches with Sweden and Finland that they stood out to me so clearly in a Russian context. Why did these Russians, I kept wondering, insist on thinking of this tree as their own? How could the birch be a Russian tree when it was already a Finnish tree, a Swedish tree? And yet ... Take the train across the border at Vyborg and I swear the birches change: the symbolism borne like heavy snow on their branches becomes darker, stranger, more resistant to any desire to understand. The birches change; the birches stay the same.

As a writer on art and landscape, I have continued to be enthralled by the complex story of our changing relationship with and conception of the nonhuman natural environment: from classicism to the picturesque, from romanticism to nationalism, modernism, postmodernism, and today's vexed discussions of psychogeography, media archaeology, climate crisis, the Anthropocene. As my fascination with Russia has developed, the question gnawing at me is how closely Russia's histories might map onto these predominantly Eurocentric narrative frameworks. What is nature to Russia? My aim is to connect the dots – between my work in environmental art and my growing obsession with Russia. Was my history teacher right – that Russia was irreconcilably different? As Russia once more dominates headlines in 'the West' and as the birch – a pioneer species – recolonises neglected estates or abandoned villages across Russia (and Europe and Asia), can a better understanding of the relationship between nature and identity either emphasise what we all have in common or reveal, once and for all, what makes Russia intractably unique?

For Russia's intelligentsia, the birch is an old cliché, something they would rather forget about. In the Soviet era, Beryozka (little birch tree) was a group of shops that sold luxury goods in exchange for foreign currency. In 1914, Russian lyric poet Sergey Yesenin (who was later briefly married to dancer Isadora Duncan) wrote a poem entitled *Bereza* ('The Birch Tree'), about a snow-covered silver birch visible beneath his window. During the late twentieth century, children had to learn this four-verse lyric off by heart. No wonder so many are by now half-sick of birches. Contemporary Russian poet and essayist Maxim Amelin has spoken despairingly of the general public's unconquerable enthusiasm for 'poetry about nice little birch trees'. In doing so, he places the birch at the heart of a bifurcation in Russian culture: between the kind of art and literature that is popular and the kind of art and literature that is good. This is a distinction that will not go away: my fascination with birches will force me to spend a lot of time with books and paintings that I do not like one bit.

As a non-Russian, I am coming to all this as an outsider. The symbolism of the birch is not overfamiliar to me but strange and new and I must pursue every last lead, wherever I may end up. Some clues I will uncover through painstaking research; others I will stumble across by sheer chance. Books will lead to other books; people to other people. There will be dead ends, pathways that peter out, roads that run in never-ending circles. I will get lost in the woods (not only literally).

As my research deepens, I will meet artists and curators, designers and architects, activists and ex-soldiers. I will travel the Trans-Siberian railway from Moscow to Vladivostok. I will visit palaces and museums and botanical gardens. I will climb mountains. Everywhere there will be birches – species I've never seen before, used in ways I had never anticipated. Sometimes I will be forced to wonder if I'm imagining the whole thing. Maybe I'm not discovering some deeply hidden truth about Russia but inventing it all as I go along. No symbolism, after all, is natural – especially a symbol of nature (like a tree). There is always a history. But in tracing such a history, how can I ever be sure what to trust? Maybe I'm simply seeing what I wish to see.

This unsystematic search for significance will encounter a multitude of different meanings and beliefs. Sometimes the birch will click sharply into focus; sometimes all these meanings will be little more than a blur. Over time, the symbolism of the birch tree has slowly merged with and come to stand in for certain ideas not only of Russianness, but also of femininity, purity and innocence. At times, the birch is a symbol of humility and suffering. At other times, it signifies honesty, authenticity, even reality itself. A Russian reality, in which Russia is always feminine – a youthful innocent, a cruel mother. In many ways it doesn't make any sense. And even though I'm trying to understand, I'm also aware that when it comes to nature and national identity and the power of symbols, there are limits to what rational explanations can achieve. I want to hold on to the random and the weird, the contingent, and the simply meaningless. Sometimes the irrelevant detail might be the most telling.

On one of a number of Russian journeys that inform this book, I stay a few days in Irkutsk in eastern Siberia. One of the largest cities in the region, Irkutsk is known for its fine wooden houses, built by prominent aristocrats exiled for rebelling against the Tsar in 1825. Early evening on a sunny September Sunday, I wander across to the Island of Youth in the Angara River that flows through the centre of the city. Established as a public park in the 1960s and further landscaped in 2011, the island is bustling with families and couples, teenagers on scooters and riverside drinkers. As I stroll down a winding path I look to the left where a teenage girl poses while her friend takes photographs of her. In a white top and black skirt, the girl is leaning back against a white birch. I want to stop and speak to them, ask them why: 'Why a birch tree? What does it mean?' Maybe its black and white bark just matches her outfit. Maybe it's simply because it's there. But I don't stop to ask: my Russian isn't good enough and I don't want to interrupt. I smile vaguely and walk on. Besides, I think to myself, perhaps they don't even know why they're doing what they're doing. Most of us don't.

Here in Irkutsk, as everywhere else, I'm on the trail of the birch. The birch has meant so many things to different people at different times. It has been hand-planted by Tsarinas and felled by foresters. It has been celebrated by peasants, worshipped by pagans and painted by artists. It has self-seeded across mountains and rivers and train tracks and steppe and right through the ruined modernity of a nuclear fall-out site. And like all symbols, the story of the birch has its share of horrors (white, straight, native, pure: how could it not?). But, maybe in the end, what I'm really in search of is a birch that means nothing: stripped of symbolism, bereft of use-value. The forests, surely, are not interested in human meanings. Somewhere, therefore, must stand a birch that escapes the great weight of significance that Russia has given it, that I will be giving it. A birch that is simply a tree in a land that couldn't give a shit.

I.

POSING

'Without the birch tree, crystal pure, I cannot conceive of my Russia.'

Viktor Smirnov, 'Once Again About Birches', 1968

Picture this: thirty Russian women, each alone in the woods. Wearing heels or high boots, bright, clinging dresses, lace or leopard print, each strikes a momentary pose now frozen: an arm across a stomach, a hand behind a head, one leg raised (calf muscle taut). Each photograph is a statement of individuality expressed through appearance and posture. But each is also a statement of collective identity: we are Russian; we are women; we are Russian women.

Each pose is struck for the camera, for the viewer. That viewer is you, whoever you may be. All of these photographs have been sourced from the internet by artist Maria Kapajeva, who was born in Estonia when it was still part of the Soviet Union. Originally the images appeared on some of the hundreds of dating websites through which foreign men look for 'mail-order brides' from Russia and the countries of the former USSR. According to the statistics compiled alongside the photographs, some twenty-five thousand Russian women per year sign up to these websites, but only around 6 per cent eventually find a foreign husband.

Maria has assembled the photographs into a short film. She has made only one change: the addition of a small oblong to conceal the eyes of each subject. It is an unusual gesture. As we sit and talk in her north London studio, Maria tells me that the oblongs are marks of respect. Concealing the eyes prevents artificial intelligence from effectively running recognition software and stops the images from being reused in other undesired contexts. Each oblong is a different colour, the exact tone (pink or turquoise, green or yellow) drawn from the photograph itself: a dress, a shade of make-up, the leaves of a tree. But in rendering the subjects partially anonymous, the oblongs also foreground the essential depersonalisation that takes place in any act of online self-presentation. The personalised colours ironically individualise the process by which one's individuality is concealed.

Birch Trees of Russia © Maria Kapajeva

Russia, your white birch trees

Maria has set the whole film to music. The song is an accordion-heavy pop chanson entitled 'Birch Trees of Russia' (Maria's work borrows the same name), performed with predatory folksiness by Russian singer Yevgeniy Ross. It is an apt choice, for next to every woman in every photograph, unwittingly draped over or leaned against or gently caressed, stands a birch tree – as if it were the most natural thing in the world.

Throughout its long history, portraiture has involved great sensitivity to symbolism. In portraits of monarchs, the orb and sceptre denote power. In portraits of landowners, the rolling hills of a landscaped estate communicate wealth and taste. A locket can be a token of love. Books are symbols of learning. Likewise, the dating photographs brought together in Maria's film would originally have been conceived to communicate to a specific audience by means of a limited visual language. Careful choices of pose and clothing are suggestive of certain characteristics thought to be valued by Western men: sexual availability, submissiveness, loyalty. These women must perform their individuality through a narrow, pre-existing aesthetic vocabulary. They are on show. But the birch tree? What could it possibly mean?

The birch tree is a symbol of Russia, but it is much more than that too. It is doubtful whether the middle-aged Western men trawling through these websites will have any idea of the complexity of this symbolism.

Like all national ideas, Russianness has been riven by ironies and contradictions. But rather than undermine its power, self-contradiction seems actually to reinforce it. Over the past two hundred years or so, Russian national identity has been consciously coupled to a specific idea of 'Russian' nature. My aim is to ask what the birch tree can tell us about this tenacious equation between nation and nature.

Today, Maria Kapajeva's film shows Russian women performing their proximity to the birch in order to signal their Russianness in public. But the irony that Maria's art draws our attention to is that the subjects of these dating photographs are performing this Russianness in order to appeal to non-Russians. They only strive to identify themselves with Russia in order to leave the country. The Russia that is evoked, therefore, is a highly generalised one: easy to communicate to foreigners but, given visa difficulties, fluctuating exchange rates, political suspicion and economic uncertainty, not so easy for Russians to escape from. What does national identity really mean if it is simply an escape route from the nation itself? If one must declare allegiance to a nation in order to leave it behind? And what might the birch tell us about all this?

The singer in Maria's film, Yevgeniy Ross, provides a first clue. Even his name is suggestive: Ross is an Anglicisation of *Pocc*, 'Russ', the first four letters and grammatical stem of the Russian word for Russia. Yevgeniy Ross also performs under the name Yevgeniy Chuzhoy (Yevgeniy 'the Stranger' or Yevgeniy 'the Alien'). At once the archetypal Russian and the archetypal non-Russian. Self and other, both at once. By contrast, the lyrics to 'Birch Trees of Russia' do not embrace such dichotomies. Instead, the song crystallises a narrow understanding of the role of birch trees within Russian culture. Ross harks back to an apparently timeless symbolism, one whose timelessness, in fact, has a history that I want to try to trace. Russia is not as ancient as some Russian nationalists like to claim. The birch tree's symbolic power, it turns out, may not be so old either.

'Russia,' the song begins, 'your white birch trees / keep your warmth and kindness.' From the start, the birch is evoked as distinctly Russian. Ross then sings of running away from his father's house (and in this one line situates himself within the entire tradition of Russian émigré art and literature with all its yearning, yawning nostalgia). But he will always be welcomed back, if not by his absent father (who disappears from the song as quickly as he arrives) then at least by the motherly birch trees: 'Birches are waiting me with womanlike patience,' he sings (according to the slightly idiosyncratic English subtitles that accompany Maria's film). The women in Ross's lyrics, not dissimilar to the women in the film, are like trees: patient, passive, ever-waiting for the man to return. 'They wave me with leafage like with a scarf.'

This is not an original analogy. Fifty years before Ross released 'Birch Trees of Russia' the shadow of a birch was likened to a woman's scarf in Boris Pasternak's much-loved novel *Doctor Zhivago* (1957). Each evening, the workers tasked with clearing snow from the railway line return to a ruined train station: 'just as the sun, as if out of loyalty to the past, set[s] at its usual place behind an old birch tree outside the telegrapher's window'. After an appropriately picturesque description of the interior of the ruined station, Pasternak, who in the same scene has acknowledged the influence of two great figures of nineteenth-century Russian literature, Sergey Aksakov and Alexander Pushkin, returns to the birch. Or rather, its shadow:

> As before the collapse, the setting sun brushed the tiles, brought out the warm brown glow on the wallpaper, and hung the shadow of the birch on the wall as if it were a woman's scarf.

In these lines Pasternak confirms a trinity of symbolic meanings around the birch: Russia, femininity and nostalgia for a lost past. This is the same trinity that Ross too will evoke. It is no accident that the opening credits to the 1965 film version of *Doctor Zhivago* starring Julie Christie and Omar Sharif also feature birches. Slow, stirring orchestral music and sonorous 'la la las' by French composer Maurice Jarre overlay a painted forest of expressionist birch trees by Spanish scenery painter Julián Martín. As a symbol of Russia, the birch tree was becoming international. If the birch does communicate an image of Russianness to all those men in search of mail-order brides, it may well be that it came to them in part through *Doctor Zhivago*.

(Prompted by both Ross and Pasternak, a question arises: could it be that every great Russian journey is actually a return journey? To childhood, to the family estate, to some authentic past . . .? This question of the return will itself return.) 'But I'll be back,' Ross continues, 'in winter, spring and summer.'

And then it starts to get just a little weird. Not for the first time in Russian history, the logic of the birch analogy is pushed to its limits. 'Then I'll come quietly to them, my darlings,' Ross sings of the birch trees, whose association with a feminine presence is becoming stronger. *Rodimymi* is a vital adjective. The internet translates it as 'dear'; Maria as 'my darlings'. But it has specific connotations: the verb from which it derives, *rodit'*, means to give birth, to give rise to, or, in the case of land, to yield (for example, a crop). *Rodimoye pyatno* means birthmark. *Rodit'* is also the root from which two fundamental Russian concepts both derive: *narod*, the people, and *rodina*, the motherland. These ideas will also return. For now, it is enough to observe how in Ross's song, this one little word evokes a complexity of affection that is at once patriotic, filial, sexual and nostalgic. All of this comes together in the song's final stanza:

> I'll embrace a birch tree as a bride
> Nestle my cheek to its cool bark
> My land, I will stay with you together
> In both: happiness and trouble!

Here, the man finds his home in Russia, in nature, and in the nameless, unspeaking bride to be. All of these are encapsulated in the birch. *'Zemlya moya'* is the key phrase here: 'my land'. The noun is feminine: the long, difficult history of associations between nature and femininity is not unique to Russia but it will nonetheless be vital to unpick. Here, the last two lines of each stanza are repeated and, as the crescendo rises into the subject of Ross's address, its zenith coincides with the second beat – the 'my' of 'my land'. For a song with such regressively patriarchal attitudes to gender, it is infuriatingly catchy. Then the accordion volume lowers and Ross's language echoes that of Russian wedding vows as he promises an eternal relationship with the bride, the birch, with Russia itself.

If this reads as downright bizarre, it should not be dismissed as simply the fantasising of some lecherous old pop singer. This kind of sentiment is surprisingly widespread. One of the best analyses I've read of Russian nationalism leant heavily on psychoanalysis. Psychoanalysis, I had always thought, was a way of reading the unconscious of an individual: surely the same techniques could not be applied to a nation of 144 million people? But what if it makes sense? What if a psychoanalytical reading can help us understand Russia just that little bit better? Maybe then we should start paying attention. That is certainly the argument made by humanities scholar Daniel Rancour-Laferriere, who has characterised Russian nationalists as pathologically masochistic, unable to move away from an obsessive conception of Russia as suffering parent. Russian-American writer Masha Gessen also channels psychoanalysis, but goes one step further, describing not only Russian nationalists but all of Russian society as effectively suicidal.

Following Russia expert Vera Tolz, Rancour-Laferriere argues that the 2014 annexing of Ukraine might best be

understood not by analysing possible geopolitical motiva-
tions, but by heeding the psychological impact of the shame
and humiliation that Russia supposedly felt over the 'loss'
of Ukraine following the fragmentation of the USSR in 1991.
Ukraine became an independent nation and Russia, according to Rancour-Laferriere, has never got over it. Gessen notes
bleakly that, according to one study, a scarcely believable 88 per
cent of Russians supported Putin's military action in Crimea.

A psychological or psychoanalytical approach is not that
new: Russia has long been conceived of as the motherland
and associated with a feminine conception of nature. But
it was not until around 1900 that artists and writers began
to associate Russia with, as professor of Russian literature
Ellen Rutten puts it, 'the more modern image of the female
beloved'. Rutten was writing mainly about the paintings of
Mikhail Nesterov and the poetry of Aleksandr Blok. But she
mentions in passing a strange work by Wassily Kandinsky,
best known for his pioneering abstract compositions, especially his work at the Bauhaus in the 1920s. In 1903, however,
he produced a little painting on cardboard: variously referred
to as *Russian Beauty in a Landscape*, *Woman in the Russian Land*
or simply *Bride*. The painting is owned by a public gallery in
Munich and its Russian title seems to be unknown.

Painted in a style known as divisionism, which separates
every colour into an individual brushmark, Kandinsky's painting depicts a pale-faced woman in flowing white dress and veil.
She is seated in a night-time landscape framed to the left by the
slim, white trunks of a pair of birches. The unusual painting
technique, which Kandinsky did not stick with for long, allows
for one especially interesting characteristic: with the colours all
separated, the white of the woman's dress gradually seems to
merge with the whites of the wild flower meadow in which she
sits. Her pale skin is nearly the same colour as the moonlit grass

behind her. Russians prized pale skin in the nineteenth century and women would undertake many procedures in order to lighten their complexion, including drinking water made from birch sap. The merging of women with birches is therefore not only metaphorical but molecular too. In Kandinsky's depiction, this merging operates in both directions: the woman is gradually becoming landscape and the landscape is becoming woman. Just as in the pop lyrics of Yevgeniy Ross, the Russian man – the presumed audience for such a painting – is encouraged to love both.

In his recent book, *Other Russias*, Brian James Baer, a US academic who specialises in Russian language and literature, charts a sexual history of Russia with a particular focus on the Soviet and post-Soviet eras. He describes the 'extreme normativity of Soviet society' which was silent on all sexual matters beyond the importance of marriage and reproduction. Homosexuality was criminalised under Stalin in 1934 and only decriminalised under Yeltsin in 1993. Despite such an apparent relaxation, Baer argues that in fact essentialist gender roles (strong men, submissive women) became even more rigid in the 1990s and 2000s.

Baer writes about a book entitled *The ABCs of Sex* written in the mid-1990s by Russian politician Vladimir Zhirinovskii, leader of the ultranationalist Liberal Democratic Party (neither liberal nor democratic), with co-author Vladimir Iurovitskii. In it, the pair argue that gay people have too much visibility and power in the US and that Russia ought to be more like Thailand, encouraging sex tourism. The pair champion what they describe as the 'enormous sexual potential of Russia, whose men are known for their sexual power and women for their beauty and attractiveness'.

In Baer's book, birches feature in two interesting ways. One is a homoerotic film by Canadian Steve Kokker entitled *Birch*, in which Kokker films a young soldier called Nikolai, who poses topless but resists the sexual advances of the film-maker. The other is the book's front cover: a photograph by Vyacheslav Mizin and Alexander Shaburov entitled *Epoch of Clemency*. Made in 2005, twelve years after the decriminalisation of homosexuality, the photograph shows two men in police uniform kissing passionately against the backdrop of a white birch forest. The title suggests that this should be seen as a celebratory image. But liberalism was short-lived: Russia under Putin has become violently repressive of any sexual minority. Homosexuality has been repeatedly equated in public discourse with paedophilia and gays slurred as American agents and a threat to the Russian birth rate. Beatings and murders have increased while the state looks on approvingly.

In Baer's introduction, he recalls the decision by the Russian government to remove the photograph, alongside sixteen other works of art, from an exhibition due to open in Paris in 2007. The episode garnered significant international news coverage, as censorship stories often do. Many pointed out the irony that the work had been permitted to be shown in the Tretyakov Gallery in Moscow but not abroad.

In the photograph the birch forest functions in several ways. It is immediately familiar both as a real place (a birch forest near you) and as a symbol of Russia. But the forest serves another function too: it creates an enclosed space, a world walled off from outside influence and imbued therefore both with freedom and intensity. In this respect, this birch forest differs from the 'mail-order bride' photographs in Maria Kapajeva's film, which usually show each woman standing by a single birch tree.

Mizin and Shaburov's image reminds me of a famous scene in Andrei Tarkovsky's 1966 film *Ivan's Childhood*. Set during World War II, the film follows the titular Ivan, a young village boy whose knowledge of the rural terrain enables him to run unofficial reconnaissance missions on behalf of the Russian army. Aside from Ivan, the film's other main characters are Captain Kholin, who cares, father-like, for the orphaned Ivan while sending him on dangerous missions; Lieutenant Galtsev, a young officer; and Masha, a young army nurse. Galtsev is in love with Masha but seems unable to tell her. Instead he represses his feelings and replaces them with petty irritability.

Ivan's Childhood. Image courtesy of MINISTERSTVO KINEMATOGRAFII/Ronald Grant Archive/Mary Evans

One of the film's most visually distinctive scenes takes place in a birch forest, very much like that in Mizin and Shaburov's photograph, nearly thirty years later. If the war necessitates a harsh existence limited to the carrying out of duties, the forest offers the fleeting possibility of freedom

and licentiousness, albeit within limits. For Kholin, the male
officer, it is a place in which to act without repercussions; for
the younger Galtsev, and in particular for Masha, it is a con-
fusing place of disorientation and doubt. It is far too easy to
get lost in the woods.

Wearing a military greatcoat, Masha takes a walk alone
through the birches, where she meets Kholin. She frequently
stands close to one of the birch trees, creating a visual parallel
between her pale skin and dark hair and the black and white
of the bark.

'Are you from Ukraine?' asks Kholin.

'Why?'

'You're beautiful and stubborn.'

'No, I come from near Moscow.'

She approaches and shyly retreats. He is teasingly dominant.
The scene cuts to Galtsev who hears that the two are together
and charges into the birch forest to find them. Meanwhile,
Kholin coaxes Masha to walk up a fallen birch trunk and back
down again. He is playing a game, aggressively. She is unsure
how to respond. Then he stands astride a trench, and as she
crosses it, he grabs her and kisses her, her body hanging lifeless
in the air. The camera dips down into the trench to look up at
the pair of them, soil and severed roots to either side, incessant
birches all around.

Kholin orders Masha away, and she retreats. Suddenly the
camera changes again, merging with Masha's point of view as
she rushes and stumbles among the birches. Is Masha, visually
equated with the birches and publicly confirmed as Russian,
here a symbol of Russia itself? Does she suffer domination (by
the military) or, in Tarkovsky's view, desire it? There is nothing visible beyond these trees, no sky above, and they seem to
crowd around her, offering no discernible route through or out.
There is a palpable sense of panic.

A man and a woman alone in a forest. A kiss. A fallen birch tree. All in the middle of a war. This is a scene laden with symbolism. For the man, the birch forest is a place of sexual possibilities. For the woman, it seems overwhelming, restrictive, inescapable. The birch forest is a world within the world, a self-contained (Russian) world.

As soon as I enter Maria Kapajeva's north London studio, I know I'm on the right path. We're meeting to talk about her film work, 'Birch Trees of Russia', but I'm very quickly distracted. On her desk is a small dark object, no bigger than a purse. I recognise it instantly. The object is a Soviet-era reproduction of a famous Russian landscape painting: *A Rye Field* (1878) by Ivan Shishkin. Large pine trees rise above a field of ripe golden rye. From the foreground, taking the eye towards the horizon in a way that was typical of nineteenth-century landscapes, is a winding track. The original is an oil painting, over six feet across, that hangs in the Tretyakov Gallery in Moscow. Maria's little reproduction has been printed onto paper and attached to a block of wood. It is dark and muddy under layers of age and brown varnish.

Maria hands me her latest work: a book incorporating family photographs that she found at her parents' home in Estonia and subsequently rearranged to suggest imaginary past narratives. There are images of grey apartment blocks, a woman glimpsed from a train window, groups of men turned away from the camera. There is sparse text too. The first line reads: 'But how to establish the exact moment in which a story begins?' Time and again, I find myself asking exactly the same question.

One of the photographs shows a nondescript Soviet interior. All that's visible is a rectangle of wall. A shadow of something unidentifiable, possibly a plant, flits across the geometric floral pattern of the wallpaper. Hanging in the top left, its frame just cropped out, is another reproduction of exactly the same nineteenth-century landscape painting that is sitting on Maria's desk. She is explaining some of the background to her work but the presence of Shishkin's painting – in the photograph, in the reproduction – makes it difficult for me to concentrate.

One unexpected discovery during my research has been the enduring popularity of nineteenth-century landscape painting under the Soviet regime. Many people I speak to mention a reproduction of some famous old landscape hanging on the wall of their parents' or grandparents' home. It's so unexpected to me because Russian art of the twentieth century is often generalised into two camps: on the one hand, the radical abstract work of the early twentieth-century avant-garde characterised by El Lissitzky, Kazimir Malevich, Liubov Popova and others; and on the other hand, once Stalin came to power, the rosy-cheeked workers of state-sanctioned Socialist Realism. Landscape painting is easily overlooked. But it played a surprisingly prominent role in the Soviet era. In the aftermath of World War II especially, a whole new generation of landscape painters emerged. The likes of Arkady Plastov, Viktor Ivanov and Vladimir Gavrilov each adopted their own approach to the landscape aesthetics established in the nineteenth century. All the while, those old paintings retained a powerful popular appeal.

The Soviet era is often understood as a radical break from the Tsarist past. But there were many threads of continuity from one regime to the next. The centrality of nature to national identity is just such a thread – one that has been woven through the art and literature of the twentieth century. In response to unprecedented social change in the 1930s, landscape became imbued with a powerful sense of nostalgia: mass urbanisation engendered a longing for a lost rural past. In the 1940s, this nostalgia was mobilised as state-sanctioned nationalism in the war against Nazi Germany, known in Russia as the Great Patriotic War. Then, with the Nazis defeated and much of Europe and Russia ravaged by war, many artists and writers sought to offer idealised landscapes as places of escape.

Socialist Realism has been widely derided by Western art historians. But the Russian landscapes summoned up by the poets and writers of the Stalinist era and beyond were not simply false. Rather, they intertwined with government policy in ways that were sometimes contradictory and sometimes mutually reinforcing. Their realism was the reality not of the present but of the future that was being built. As I shall soon discover, Soviet policies towards nature were much more complicated than I had been led to believe.

From the eighteenth century to the twenty-first, the Russian relationship to nature has been characterised by a shifting tension between love for an untouched (Russian) nature and the desire (and necessity) to harness the land in order not only to survive but to thrive. Across fields and forests, this dichotomy is neatly dramatised in Maria's photography book. The reproduction of the great Shishkin landscape is on a left-hand page, harking back to an apparently timeless past. On the facing page is another photograph: a figure in a long black coat and fur hat kneeling before a freshly felled pine. As this juxtaposition suggests, Russia's relationship with the natural world is much more complex than a simple opposition between Romantic nationalism and industrial efficiency. To start to sketch these complexities will take both time and care.

As we sit drinking strong black coffee, Maria tells me about her upbringing in Soviet Estonia and I continue looking through her book of photographs. Another image grabs my attention. It fits my search for birches so perfectly it's almost as if I put it there myself. The image depicts an unknown woman looking into the camera from the branches of a birch. She has climbed up a little and stands in a fork between two trunks. Her body curves in echo of the tree, her hand placed against the bark. Only the eyes separate this image from those Russian dating portraits. Here, the unknown woman looks off to the left; the camera is at ground level, below her. There is a suggestion of freedom, of independence from the (male) photographer that is not shared by those on the dating sites. But this is not an image designed to be seductive. My eyes are drawn to the way her tights wrinkle just below the knee.

'I associate Estonia with the smells of pine trees and the sea,' says Maria about the country of her birth. 'But birch trees have been so implanted in our consciousness. You can't avoid how important they have been. Maybe that's why these women are not questioning it – the birch tree is so present in Russian folklore that you are already thinking by default that, if you are Russian, this is your tree.

'I always say I'm a Soviet product,' Maria continues. 'I was a teenager when the USSR collapsed. Everything turned upside down. From being a member of a celebrated, dominating nation, we were turned into an occupied minority. That was the hardest challenge.' As Maria opens up about this past there is still confusion about exactly what happened, maybe anger too. 'But this unique experience, even though very traumatic, made me realise that what we know of history depends on who is the narrator. Nobody asked us questions. They just gave us new history books and said, "Now you have to study these".'

Erased, repressed or simply unaddressed, such traumas linger beneath the surface for many in Russia and the countries of the former USSR. After 1991 Estonia introduced new laws that required Russians living in Estonia to pass language and history exams in order to obtain citizenship. Capitalism threatens existing identities at the same time that it tries to sell us nationalism as a false solution. For many post-Soviet countries, the 1990s were marked, on the one hand, by a desire for those long-inaccessible, foreign-made consumer goods and, on the other hand, by a doubling-down of national or regional identity – a clinging to familiar symbols, like the birch perhaps, in the face of unprecedented change. For so long, a certain relationship existed between Russia and the West, one characterised by the apparently clean simplicity of a binary opposition. But suddenly everything changes. If nationalism attempts to root itself in the soil, what happens when the earth begins to shift? Boundaries are hastily redrawn. Russia splinters. But so too does that which is conceived of as non-Russian, foreign, other. No self-identity without an identifiable other. So many places become suddenly foreign: Estonia, Latvia, Lithuania, Azerbaijan … So many Russians become foreign in their own homes; their homes become foreign to them. No wonder the birch has returned as a powerful symbol of a simpler past.

II.

PLANTING IDEAS

'I'm sick of Crimea ... I want to go back to Russia. You
know, birch trees, mosquitoes, the nostalgia.'

Maria Baronova, quoted in Masha Gessen,
The Future is History, **2017**

The birch, a botanist once told me, is a 'cryptic species'. What
they meant is that various taxa within the species can be difficult to differentiate from one another. But 'cryptic' also carries
with it the sense of a hidden meaning. It is in crypts where
the dead lie concealed. Birches are cryptic in both senses. The
history of birches goes right back to the Upper Cretaceous, sev-
enty million years ago, before the extinction of the dinosaurs.
Today, birches span most of the globe and have been especially
widespread in the northern hemisphere since the last Ice Age.

The family *Betulaceae* is made up of six genera of deciduous
nut-bearing trees and shrubs: birches, alders, hazels, horn-
beams, hazel-hornbeams and hop-hornbeams. The birch genus,
Betula, was established by Swedish botanist Carl Linnaeus in
1753. Since then, the size and composition of the genus has
continued to shift as various taxa – such as common and grey
alder – have been reallocated to different families.

In 2013, Kew Gardens published *The Genus Betula*: *A Taxonomic Revision of Birches* by botanists Kenneth Ashburner and Hugh A. McAllister, billed as the most authoritative treatment of birches to date. The book, a kind of *catalogue raisonné* of birches, redraws a number of pre-existing taxonomic boundaries in light of new knowledge and new scientific techniques. Taxonomists are always redrawing lines, either lumping previously separate species together or splitting them apart. A species is a hypothesis, a suggestion to be tested (and potentially disproved).

The size and range of the *Betula* genus have generated a number of difficulties. In particular, it is the white-barked species that do not always like to be pinned down. To me it is perhaps this aspect of the tree, rather than its elaborate symbolisms, that makes the birch so well suited as an analogy for Russia: a tree of shifting boundaries, hard sometimes to distinguish from its near neighbours.

Today, *Betula* contains dozens of taxa: from the common (and commonly accepted) such as *Betula pendula* (silver birch) to the hyper-rare *Betula megrelica*, an endangered shrub species found only on Mount Migaria in western Georgia. Due to the region's political instability, Western botanists know little about this particular species. There may be other such rarities, but botanists do not always agree. One example is *Betula klokovii*, named by a botanist who believes there may be as few as fifty all living in one tiny area, under six square miles, in the Kremenets Mountains in western Ukraine. But *Betula klokovii* is not recognised as a separate species by Ashburner and McAllister. By email McAllister explains to me that to name a new species is to become the authority on that species, meaning that 'there can be a perverse incentive to describe species on rather little evidence'. In addition, he tells me: 'In some countries there is a nationalistic wish to have endemic species which only occur in that country – even though they may not be distinguishable from similar plants in neighbouring countries.' This botanical nationalism is therefore pitted against botany's historical proximity to colonialism. But that's another story ...

To me at least, there is something fascinating about botanical disagreements – as if you can see the apparent certainty of expertise unravelling right before your eyes. A common difficulty is distinguishing between *Betula pendula*, the common, silver or warty birch, and *Betula pubescens*, the white, moor or downy birch. *Pubescens* supposedly has silky or hairy twigs (downy) rather than the rough twigs (warty) of *pendula*. Of all the species of white-barked birch, it is only *Betula pendula* whose branches hang down vertically and allow the foliage to move easily in the breeze. Moreover, it is only the European populations that have these characteristically 'weeping' branches.

I'll be honest with you, though: I cannot always tell them apart. But then I'm not alone. When he named the genus *Betula* in 1753, Carl Linnaeus did not distinguish between *pubescens* and *pendula*. Instead, he named them as a single species: *Betula alba*, the white birch. Botanical boundaries have shifted in many ways since then, but if you look carefully enough, you can still track these changes on herbaria specimen sheets. The contradictory notes and botanical marginalia constitute a strange kind of argument that traverses the centuries. 'Appears to be *B. pubescens x verrucusa*,' reads one caption from 1923 that I'm delighted to discover on a specimen housed at the South London Botanical Institute. The label has been pointedly pasted over a previous one describing the same specimen by the Linnaean classification, *Betula alba*. It dates from 1884. Such classificatory problems have apparently been so severe that something called the Atkinson Discriminant Function was proposed in 1986 in order to differentiate mathematically between *pendula* and *pubescens*. It involves extremely detailed measurement of different parts of each birch leaf. Few outside the botanical profession have the energy for such precision, but somehow I can't help but be beguiled.

If Linnaeus himself did not distinguish between *pubescens* and *pendula*, then should I? Little of the art and writing I'll be looking at will show much interest in taxonomy. This means that the white birch of this book's title is a strange hybrid. It combines the species *Betula pubescens* with the Linnaean *Betula alba* and also a generic birch. In some ways then this book is a return to the science of the eighteenth century. Any birch will be important to me, as long as it is white and as long as it is Russian.

Scientists have been (justifiably) criticised for their often reductive approach to the complexities of the world. But when it comes to birch trees, it is artists and writers who have overlooked diversity far more than those in the fields of botany or horticulture. In both painting and poetry, the birch tends to be a generic birch. It is white or silver interchangeably. A birch is 'wet and bare ... like a roadside beggar' in Anton Chekhov's short story 'Dreams' (1886); a pair of them gleam white on a hilltop in Mikhail Lermontov's poem 'Rodina' (1841); a row of birches shines in the sun, with 'motionless green and yellow foliage and white bark' in Tolstoy's *War and Peace* (1867). No mention of the betulin that causes the whiteness of birch bark, even though it had been discovered in 1788. No mention of the species of birch in question. It is not important necessarily to know the botanical details. Indeed, sometimes the not knowing can be just as significant. As Osip Mandelstam writes in his *Voronezh Notebooks*, 26 December 1936:

> And what's that forest – spruce?
> Not spruce, a spruced-up violet –
> And what kind of birch is that?
> Who's to know or care? –

Only a prose inscribed on air,
Illegible; evanescent ...

Writing is ephemeral, fades in the air. The birch leaves just a passing impression.

But it is not simply artistic licence that has led to this generalised presentation of birches in art and literature. There are other reasons too, and they have to do, I'm beginning to think, with the biology of the birch itself. The first reason is that birch trees are comparatively short-lived. A grand old oak is a charismatic individual around whom meanings cluster, whose very presence becomes synonymous with the histories and mythologies of the place in which it lives. There are some ancient birches too: the oldest scientifically dated living birch outside the Russian Far East stands on the north side of Lake Torneträsk in sub-Arctic Sweden. In 2009, this mountain birch (*Betula pubescens ssp. czerepanovii*) was 258 years old. There may be an even older example in Kamchatka, easternmost Russia: a stone birch (*Betula ermanii Cham.*) reportedly 350 years old. But the dating methodology has apparently not yet been validated. Thirty years on from the end of the USSR, Western scientists can still be sceptical towards the claims of their Russian counterparts.

But these examples are outliers. The typical lifespan of a birch is often similar to that of a human. The birch grows with us, dies with us. 'Prolific and ephemeral' is Ashburner's description. Birch forests often don't last long either: as a pioneer species, the birch is one of the first trees to grow in disrupted land, its airborne seeds carried far from the parent. It can cope with the kinds of poor soils, difficult climates and high altitudes that other trees cannot. It grows fast, and produces seed fast too. *Betula pendula* has been induced to flower at less than a year old. Norway spruce, by comparison, takes about forty years before producing seed. Birches take over patches of disturbed or apparently barren land before preparing the way for other species. They can radically alter the chemistry and biology of the soil, transforming humus, the organic component of the soil, from 'mor' (acidic, low in nutrients) to 'mull' (neutral pH, much more biologically active), encouraging earthworms, and increasing rates of nutrient turnover. Within a generation, other, more demanding trees and woodland plants can grow up around them, the birches may die and a new birch forest may spring up elsewhere.

Nature is often viewed as forever fixed, a place of stasis. Russian nationalists in particular have long loved the idea of 'eternal Russia', characterised by the unchanging landscapes of forest and steppe. The birch, by contrast, represents something temporal, fragile, in need perhaps of protection. Yet it is also flexible, adaptable, and maybe even hardier than species such as the oak or elm more traditionally associated with strength.

In times of turmoil, nature offers us refuge. It conveys the illusion of an uncorrupted past, or the promise of a future when all of this – whatever *this* is – will finally have faded away. From the elegant yearnings of the émigré writers to the wholesome scenes of Socialist Realism, nature, especially Russian nature, is often understood as fixed: cyclical yes, but ultimately unchanging.

Today, nature seems anything but fixed. The natural world feels both fragile and dangerous. The world's temperatures are changing, a zoonotic pandemic has infected millions, and so many animals have died and species become extinct on account of humans. There are plastics in the deepest oceans, detritus in space. In countries such as the UK, it has become a truism in certain environmentalist circles to say that there is no such thing as the wild any more. In the age known to some as the Anthropocene, there is no place, no ecosystem, no animal or plant or tree that has escaped completely from the impact of humans. There is no pure nature now. For many, this is a cause for regret. Others, following feminist philosopher of science Donna Haraway, argue that relations between the human and the nonhuman have always been entangled (we share our lives with domesticated animals; our guts are full of bacteria) and that this could in fact be cause not for lament but for celebration.

For some people, if the wild still exists at all, it is not in space but in time: the wild is an imagined past before the industrial revolution, or before agriculture, or before humans existed at all. Or it is a projected future, a time after the apocalypse when humans have all but disappeared from the face of the earth. As temperatures and sea levels rise, the prophecies are grim: climate-induced mass migration, resource scarcity, war. And yet, in the privileged West, even in the middle of a pandemic, much of that can still feel so unreal. People live in cities, get their food from supermarkets. Many of us are more discon-nected than ever, in our day-to-day lives at least, from any conception of nature or the wild.

Russia, however, remains vast. The possibilities of unknown wilds still linger in the minds of many of those Russians I meet and speak to. Even those most attuned to today's global ecological debates still believe in the possibility of the wild as a place that can be visited. Is this wisdom or charming naivety? 'In Russia, we do still have native, untouched states,' one Moscow-based curator assured me. 'You'll see when you travel.'

Gatchina – thirty miles or so from the centre of Saint Petersburg – is by no stretch of the imagination a wild place. Here in Gatchina, Count Orlov, a favourite of Empress

Catherine the Great, ordered the building of a grand palace.
It was designed by Italian architect Antonio Rinaldi and built
between 1766 and 1781. Twenty years later, with Catherine the
Great now dead and her son Paul I in charge of both Gatchina
and the Russian empire, an artist called Semyon Shchedrin
came to visit. As professor of landscape painting at the Saint
Petersburg Academy of Arts, Shchedrin had forged his career
by operating obediently within the rules of classical landscape
painting. Whether painting cows, peasants and log cabins on
the outskirts of Saint Petersburg, or views over the ancient
ruins of Rome, his compositions remained rigidly classical.
Today's art lover might look down their nose at Shchedrin's
paintings. But, for me, they contain some significant clues and
I need to take a closer look.

Shchedrin painted *The Stone Bridge at Gatchina* between
1799 and 1801. Apart from the slightly unusual fact of being
a landscape painting in portrait format, Shchedrin's image
of Gatchina is typical of his work: trees serve as framing
devices in the foreground while the eye is led, by a road and
the titular stone bridge, gently into the centre of the painting,
where a distant obelisk provides the requisite focal point.
This painting is a doubly perfect encapsulation of the classical
landscape aesthetic: not only does it showcase Shchedrin's
own knowledge of the rules of composition, but it also – and
far more importantly – demonstrates that, finally, Russia had
landscapes that could be depicted as landscape paintings. The
owner of Gatchina, Paul I, could bask in the reflected glory
of a world precisely constructed according to neoclassical
aesthetics.

Once upon a time, all this was swamp. But in the seventeenth
and eighteenth centuries, Russia's elites, influenced by their
European counterparts, sought to imprint their names upon
the earth in ever more sweeping statements of preposterous

wealth and impeccable taste. The reign of Peter the Great, Tsar from 1682 until his death in 1725, marks the beginning of this kind of landscape design in Russia. This is, at the same time, the beginning of Russia as a modern nation state.

Following victories against Sweden in the Great Northern War of the early 1700s, Peter embarked upon a major programme of modernisation, which meant, effectively, Westernisation. Peter wanted to make Russia more like Europe. He swiftly set about augmenting his Baltic fortress with a brand new European-style city: Saint Petersburg, full of grand pastel-hued façades and Italianate stucco. He also reformed the civil service, introduced French as the language of the court, and raised significant sums for the treasury through taxation and trade reforms. During this period, as for centuries to come, Europe was associated with modernity, Russia with backwardness. Under Peter, modernity was the goal and Russia must therefore strive to 'catch up'. But in later years this position shifted back and forth many times. While 'Westernisers' continued to wish for Russia to become more like Europe, 'Slavophiles' came to reject Europe as corrupt and superficial, striving instead to return to a more authentic (but paradoxically imaginary) Russia that they believed had existed prior to Peter the Great's reforms. Those who looked West admired efficiency, modernity and an urban bourgeoisie. The Slavophiles built their beliefs on rural peasants and the Russian Orthodox Church. This was the great debate of the nineteenth century. In various forms, it continues to this day.

But long before these questions came to define Russian intellectual culture, Peter the Great began planting trees. Or rather the serfs did, and the army. Russia was still feudal then. In 1714, two years after moving the capital of Russia from Moscow to Saint Petersburg (also built on the backs of thousands of forced labourers), Peter set to work on a lavish palace and gardens for himself some twenty miles along the coast from the centre of the city. It would be called Peterhof.

Initially, Peter designed the pleasure palace himself. But his ambitions soon grew, and he needed something bigger. The model for the new Peterhof palace was, naturally, Versailles. European artists and architects were drafted in to take charge of design and to train Russian counterparts. In 1721, two thousand soldiers and peasants were working on Peterhof. Three years later this figure had doubled.

In this period, when the wild was still a place to be feared, the fashion was for tightly clipped borders and elegantly arranged parterres. These are not so much gardens to walk in as to look at: from a well-placed vantage point high up in one's château or through the windows of a carriage. With the forest a place of darkness and disorder, French painters Claude Lorraine and Nicolas Poussin provided order, their straight lines repeated by the designers of French-style formal gardens. And unlike the UK, where by the eighteenth century apex predators such as wolves and lynx had long since been hunted to extinction, in Russia the world did remain wild. There were real dangers lurking out there beyond the parterre. As John Busch, one of the garden designers at Gatchina, wrote in a letter to Lord Coventry after his arrival in Russia in 1771: 'It is dangerous in these woods to collect plants there being large bears and wolves'.

But this wildness was also symbolic and therefore political. Increasingly, Russia's rulers sought to tame what they saw as the wild places around them, to make them Russian. With these places under control, the garden too could begin to relax – aesthetically at least. The imperial policy of Russification involved imposing Russian language, culture and religion on recently conquered or long-subjugated peoples. It frequently involved violence and the forced relocation of huge numbers of people, from the interior of Russia to the edges of the empire, from the edges to the depths of Siberia. In 1764, Catherine II wrote a letter to Prince Alexander Viazemsky: 'Little Russia, Livonia, and Finland ... as well as Smolensk, should be Russified as gently as possible so that they cease looking to the forest like wolves.' But how to impose 'Russian' culture when it was still unclear what that really meant?

What Saint Petersburg was to the Russian city, Peterhof was to the Russian garden. In short, it changed everything. The gardens at Peterhof are monumentally grand: there are large ponds, elaborate fountains and myriad classical sculptures. It is, like Versailles, almost overwhelmingly ornate. Following Peter, Russia's aristocrats also sought to refashion the land and showcase their great wealth. Expressions of personal taste, however, were strictly limited: for a while, under Peter, it was compulsory to follow the designs laid out by the Tsar's Swiss-Italian architect Domenico Trezzini. This whole region was transformed by a string of vast new estates, mostly built by Peter or Catherine or their close allies. There was Strelna, halfway to Peterhof, built by Peter as a grand summer residence (today it is where Putin likes to host gatherings of global leaders); and Tsarskoe Selo, given as a gift by Peter to Catherine I but developed by her daughter, Empress Elizabeth, and extended by Catherine II (the Great); Pavlovsk, built by Catherine II for her son Paul; and Gatchina, built by Catherine II's favourite, Count Orlov.

By the close of the eighteenth century the road between Saint Petersburg and Peterhof was an extraordinary sight, as oversized dachas sprang up between the great estates. *Dacha* in Russian means 'given', and was originally used to denote a parcel of land bestowed by the Tsar. Many of these properties along the Peterhof Road were open to the public. 'More like a pleasure-ground than a highway,' was how Heinrich Storch, a Riga-born political economist and tutor to the Russian royal family, described the sheer diversity of the spectacle in 1802: 'Magnificent villas, Dutch villages, hermitages, ponds, islands, rural prospects, in ceaseless vicissitudes.' The Russians had turned the landscape into an art gallery, a place to drive through in wonder as the sights passed by. A 'fairyland,' wrote Storch, 'where nature and art dance in magical mazes about [the] carriage'.

And yet, although there is arguably something distinctly Russian in this great eclecticism of styles (for a long time this is how the country's architects defined 'the Russian style'), in the eighteenth century the question of what the Russian landscape ought to look like had yet to be answered. In truth, in an era of intense Francophilia, it had yet to be asked.

But, in time, the region around Saint Petersburg would disproportionately shape Russian attitudes to landscape. More than any other that I will visit, more than Moscow or Kyiv or Siberia or Karelia, it is the rulers of this region who have been so desperate not only to define Russianness as an idea but to move vast quantities of earth to make it a physical reality. Ironically, it is this desire to *represent* Russia that makes such estates so unrepresentative. Russian national self-awareness emerged, in large part, through a mutually confirmatory spiral of art and landscape aesthetics limited to a comparatively small area of a very big place. This idea that the 'real' Russia is to be found not in the cities but in the countryside, not in the centre but in the provinces, has returned, arguably stronger than ever, since the end of the USSR. I will return to it too, in Irkutsk maybe or Ulan-Ude. Somewhere in the east. But not yet.

In *Russian Parks and Gardens*, garden historian Peter Hayden tells the fascinating history of Russian landscape design. He begins under Peter the Great, and charts a shift in trend from the French formal gardens of the eighteenth century to the English-style landscapes of the nineteenth and through into the people's parks of the Soviet era. It is while reading Hayden, sitting in the grand top-floor reading room of Edinburgh Central Library, that the birches first begin to speak to me. But what are they saying? 'Birch groves,' observes Hayden of the early gardens of the 1700s, 'already provided by nature or planted, were particularly admired as picturesque features in the landscape.'

The more I read of Hayden the more the birch keeps cropping up. Confirmation bias – or something more? I re-read the entire book, making a note of every single time that Hayden mentions the birch, hoping it will all add up to something significant. But what?

I look again at the cover of his book. It shows a photograph taken by the author himself of one of the great estates. How had I not noticed it before? Four slender birch trees divide the image. Through their bare, wintry branches is an undulating, snow-clad landscape, a sliver of frozen lake. Atop a low snowy rise beyond, a pastel yellow palace beckons. The image is of Pavlovsk, but really it could be any aristocratic estate in western Russia. By the time of the book's publication in 2005, over two hundred years after the estate was first laid out, the birch had become shorthand for Russia itself.

In the first half of the eighteenth century, the French formal style predominated. In this context, if the native birch was used at all, it was in loosely planted peripheral areas that would emphasise the carefully delineated structures of the main gardens. At Tsarskoe Selo, for example, the palace and gardens fifteen miles south of Saint Petersburg that Peter the Great gave as a gift to his wife, the future Catherine I, a 'wild grove' was planted in 1718 with 738 birch trees. That same year, a further 935 birch trees were planted elsewhere at Tsarskoe Selo, in the so-called

New Garden. Over time these birches were replaced by oaks and limes. Whether this was a deliberate decision to replant, or whether the birches simply yielded in time, I'm afraid I do not know. Nor do I even know what species of birch they were.

If the French style emphasised man-made order in a world of chaos, the English landscape style that superseded from the late eighteenth century onwards signified very differently. Loose and flowing rather than rigid and straight, the English style created places not only to look at but also to spend time in, to take walks. Despite – or perhaps because of – the very natural-istic effects of the English style, it was often considerably more expensive than the French approach that preceded it. Under Peter the Great, the Russian nobility had been obliged to carry out compulsory service to the state and to the military. But this was repealed by Peter III in 1762 and the nobility were sud-denly free to travel or read or live lives of extravagant leisure. Twenty-three years later, the Charter of Nobility encouraged landowners to settle on their estates and develop industry and agriculture. Russia's aristocracy was returning to the lands (which they had long owned) in order to remake them anew. As Hayden writes, 'the English landscape style, emblematic of freedom, was the natural choice'.

The rise of the English style was inseparable from the rise of the British Empire. And the same could be said of Russia too: soft power writ large in plants and gardens. While the world's elites travelled to Britain to marvel at the latest gar-dening fashions, the British for their part made fortunes in selling these gardens across the world. Kew Gardens was then a global hub of colonial horticulture. Plants and seeds arrived from all over the world as the British adventure capitalists collected everything they could. At Kew, these plants were studied, cultivated and distributed far and wide, in particular across colonial plantations. The Russian aristocracy were also excellent clients. Many of Russia's chief gardeners were British. 'Anglomania rules my plantomania,' wrote Catherine the Great to Voltaire in 1772.

At the same time that she was adopting the English style of garden design, Catherine was strengthening the Russian Empire. The period from the 1770s to the 1790s saw the partitioning of Poland, in which Russia gained two thirds of its land, including all of Lithuania. This was understood in the official discourse not as a process of expansion but as a reclamation of lands that were rightfully – because historically – Russian. In his 2017 book *Lost Kingdom*, Ukrainian-American historian Serhii Plokhy tells us that, 'in Russian imperial historiography, the partitions of Poland were often referred to as the reunification of Rus''. The history of the Rus' – the medieval settlers of the lands that were to become Russia, Belarus and Ukraine – is bitterly contested. It is a history I will be forced to confront in more detail soon. In the meantime, it is sufficient to point out the significance of Russia's emphasis on *return*. 'I *restored* what had been torn away,' read a coin issued by Catherine II to mark the partitions of Poland. Then, in 1794, as she imposed Russian Orthodoxy on the Catholics, Jews and Uniates of Ukraine, it was communicated as a *return* (Plokhy's word) to 'the faith of fathers and forefathers'. Spoken of as a return to the natural order of things, Russification was invariably violent and repressive and not always successful.

As Russia flexed its imperial muscles, the design of Russian country estates had wide implications. For, unlike the formal garden with its self-conscious artifice, the apparently 'natural' style of the landscaped park would become a model upon which, in the eyes of the mighty, all of Russia ought to be based. In 1787, four years after the annexation of Crimea, Catherine the Great embarked on her own picturesque voyage to tour the new territory. The trip was arranged by Grigory Potemkin,

Catherine's lover and the newly appointed governor of the region. It is said that Potemkin hastily constructed fake villages along the route purely to impress the Empress. His men dressed as peasants in order to give the impression of a thriving rural community when in fact Crimea was still devastated by the recent wars. Each village was disassembled at night and then reassembled further along the route. Like many of the best stories, this one may well be a myth. But in the USSR, Potemkin villages, as they would come to be known, were very much a fact of life for Russian and foreign dignitaries alike. The wealthy and the powerful, it seems, are content to be deceived when what they see confirms what they wish to see.

Following Catherine's tour, artists were also sent to capture Crimea. Karl von Kügelgen, a Prussian landscape artist working for the Russian court, journeyed through the region in 1804 and again in 1824. Art historian Maria Shlikevich points out that, while von Kügelgen's preparatory drawings, produced in situ, were characterised by 'topographical precision', the resulting formal paintings were, by contrast, 'compilatory ideal landscapes'. These paintings were commissioned primarily to show to the court in Saint Petersburg. As such, they depict not Crimea's war-ravaged people but picturesque vistas of these recently captured lands. The violence of conquest and the labour of serfs were just two of the many things that such images relegated to the world beyond the picture frame.

As Russian contact with Europe grew (through trade and travel, culture and war), some were beginning to argue the need for a new Russian approach to gardens that would be different from both the French classical style and the English natural landscape. Andrei Bolotov, for example, a pioneer of Russian agriculture, advised against Russian landowners hiring foreign gardeners and designers. He argued that European formal and landscaped gardens were ill-suited to the Russian climate, especially for those without an unlimited budget. Aesthetically, however, it's hard to see how his preferences differed much from the prevailing English winds. It seems to be more a matter of designation: 'I have completely ceased to love formal gardens,' he wrote, 'and have acquired a taste for gardens in the new style, called irregular, natural, for it would be a sin to call them English'.

These Russian/English 'natural' gardens were to become some of the most spectacular that the world had ever seen. Peter Hayden describes the garden at Pavlovsk, laid out for Maria Feodorovna by Catherine II's architect, Charles Cameron, as 'the world's greatest "English" garden'. Cameron lived an intriguing life: he was born in London but pretended to be a Scottish aristocrat in part to smooth his passage into Russian society. His designs were conceived to recreate the tranquillity of classical antiquity. But, as fashions changed from the neoclassical to the Romantic, other designers and architects took different approaches. Among the grottos and avenues that proliferated in all these estates, among the canals and summerhouses, among the temples and classical statuary and the hilarious-sounding 'coasting hill' (a 582-yard-long, triple-track proto-rollercoaster known as *les montagnes Russes* that Catherine I had constructed at Tsarskoe Selo), there were also birches. At first, they encircled Catherine the Great's palace at Tsaritsyno to the south of Moscow. Then, Ian Munroe and Francis Reid, two Scottish gardeners who arrived in 1782, planted even more. But what did these birches mean?

As the eighteenth century gave way to the nineteenth, birches seemed to be gathering in significance. In the 1820s, Scottish botanist John Claudius Loudon described 'a natural forest of birch and wild cherry' at Gorinka, a seat of Count Alexei Razumowsky near Moscow. This natural forest 'clothes the park and harmonises the artificial scenes', wrote Loudon in his *Encyclopaedia of Gardening* of 1822. There were also birches planted at Petrowka outside Moscow, Tantsy (on the present-day border with Belarus) and Kachanovka (built by Catherine the Great's envoy Pyotr Rumyantsev); birches surrounded an arbour at Dvoryaninovo near Tula; and a mile-long

Tolstoy's Bench © Olga Koroleva

birch avenue, planted in 1888–9, was one of the major features of the park at Gorki, where Lenin went to recuperate in 1918 after an assassination attempt.

The birch avenue in particular became a common feature of Russian gardens: at Yasnaya Polyana, the country estate of the Tolstoy family, an elegant avenue of birches runs from the entrance gates right up to the house. Such planting mimics the way that birches habitually respond to the lines carved by humans through the land. As a species, they love disturbed ground. That's why they thrive by the banks of rivers or along footpaths or roads. A birch avenue, therefore, is a human reflection of nature's response to us. At Yasnaya Polyana, this reflection is doubled: there are two long parallel lines of birch trees on one side of the main driveway and two on the other. The main avenue creates a journey of familiar formality. On the left side is a narrow footpath that runs between one pair of birch lines. For me, walking this path fosters a more intimate relationship with the birches. Around us are young families taking photographs of each other. It's a popular place for weddings. To the left, as you walk, ponies graze among an orchard of low apple trees.

I'm visiting Yasnaya Polyana with Olga Koroleva, an artist I know from London. Her work frequently features wolves (I think that's why we were first introduced). She was born in the nearby city of Tula and returns regularly to stay with her grandfather. We wander the grounds. Olga has injured her knee so we pause to sit on a bench. Acorns drop from the oaks above as we discuss trees and time and her grandfather's war stories. Tula is a Hero City: its inhabitants resisted the German offensive in 1941. There is a Soviet armoured train at the station to greet new arrivals, to welcome locals home. Olga tells me about the idea of the 'mother tree' in German ecologist Peter Wohlleben's *The Hidden Life of Trees*. Wohlleben argues that trees talk to each other, and that mother trees feed their saplings with liquid sugar via an underground network of interconnected roots. Wohlleben implies that this is in some way intentional, but it need not be. Ectomycorrhiza is a form of symbiotic relationship that develops between the roots of certain plant species and the fungi that coat them. Birches are especially conducive to forming these symbiotic relationships: they enable the species to thrive in comparatively infertile soils. It is via a network of these ectomycorrhiza that nutrients can move between different plants. Carbon, for example, has been shown to move from paper birch trees into Douglas-fir trees. It is this, some argue, that promotes what is known as succession, the frequent, but not inevitable, development of one type of ecosystem to the next: say, from pioneer birch forests to the arrival of the evergreens.

Olga and I walk a little further. We pause as something wriggles away through the grass. '*Uzh*,' says Olga. An adder. And then, some way down a narrow path between a field and a pine plantation, is the reason I'm here at Yasnaya Polyana: a small, two-seater bench made from birch. Utterly unremarkable. Apart from one fact: it was, so I'd read, Tolstoy's favourite chair. Eight slim birch trunks form the seat. The bark is glossy from use. Surely none of the birch is original. If every individual component has at some stage been replaced, is this still Tolstoy's chair? The same question could be asked of every living being: neurons aside, our cells are fully replaced every seven to fifteen years. And indeed every nation: national myths must be told and retold over and over again, each time the same, each time a little different. Meaning, like benches, must constantly be reconstructed. I take a seat on 'Tolstoy's chair' and scribble half-formed thoughts in my notebook.

Some eighteen miles south-west of Gatchina is Pavlovsk. Here, birches seem to have been especially significant for Maria Feodorovna, a Prussian princess of the House of Württemberg, who was born in the Pomeranian city of Stettin (today Szczecin is part of Poland), and in 1776 became the second wife of Grand Duke Paul, son of Catherine the Great and future Tsar Paul I. Along with the various architects, gardeners and landscape designers that she employed, the Prussian-born Maria Feodorovna emerges as an unlikely figure in my attempt to understand what appears to be the increasing importance of the birch tree as a distinctively Russian element within the landscape garden.

The gardens of Pavlovsk already contained a ring of birches planted by Catherine the Great's architect Charles Cameron. But of more interest to me are the trees that Maria Feodorovna herself planted around the so-called Urn of Destiny, a large stone focal point in the garden. Initially, she planted ten birches, one for each of her children. But as they married and had children of their own, Maria Feodorovna personally planted another birch tree for each additional member of the family. By the time she died in 1828, there were forty-four birch trees around the urn.

Maria Feodorovna could have planted practically anything around the Urn of Destiny. The region's mild climate enabled exotic plants to thrive at Pavlovsk. Plants were ordered for the estate from all over the world as a way of demonstrating not only wealth but also taste and the global connectedness of Russia's ruling classes. Maria Feodorovna was a 'great plants-woman', writes Hayden, and yet, at key moments, for planting that had a particularly personal resonance, she chose birch. It is impossible to know exactly why but it nonetheless evokes a striking image: the Prussian-born duchess, ostracised to Gatchina and Pavlovsk because of the relationship of mistrust between her husband Paul and his mother, Catherine the Great, spending time alone in the gardens, planting birch saplings by hand, rooting the fates of her beloved into the earth itself.

This is not the last time that a non-Russian will be instrumental in the construction of Russian identity. Apart from the birches of Maria Feodorovna, the bulk of the landscaping at Pavlovsk was carried out first by Charles Cameron, the Englishman who claimed he was Scottish, and then by Pietro Gonzaga, an Italian theatre and set designer. Gonzaga's appointment draws my attention to the cross-over between the landscape gardens of this period and the theatre: like stage sets, these places were not quite lies but neither did they describe a truth. Pavlovsk, like all great landscape gardens, was a drama-tisation, a performance of the real. It created its own truth. With Alexander's return after the war against Napoleon, Russia was riding a wave of triumphalist patriotism which, I will soon learn, would have a huge impact upon the emergence of land-scape painting. Gonzaga's response was to create an area of the garden that looked just like an authentic Russian village. There, plays could be staged to celebrate Russia's military victory. National identity and war form a well-worn double act – and the landscape is so often the stage upon which they speak their lines together.

In Pavlovsk is a 620-acre area known as White Birches, after the ring of trees planted by Cameron, and later refashioned by Gonzaga. The landscape is modelled on the environments of northern Russia: a combination of meadow and forest with a range of native trees including pine and birch. Cameron's con-temporaries were delighted. Pavel Svinin, an artist, writer and diplomat whom architectural historian Dimitri Shvidkovsky has described as 'one of the first Russian art historians', wrote the following in 1816:

> If it is possible for art to approach nature, to replace it in all its games and appearances, terrible and agreeable, magnificent and simple, then it is, of course, at Pavlovsk that it happens. These sullen cliffs, these roaring waterfalls, these velvet meadows and valleys, these dark, mysterious forests seem to be original creations of graceful nature, but they are the work of human hands.

Svinin's writing, so full of drama and adjectives, comes twenty-six years after German philosopher Immanuel Kant published his *Critique of Judgement* in 1790. In it he states: 'Nature is beautiful because it looks like Art; and Art can only be called beautiful if we are conscious of it as Art while yet it looks like Nature.' European intellectuals had been discussing the relationship between art and nature for much of the seventeenth and eighteenth centuries. At the tail end of these debates, Kant emphasises a circularity between art and nature, each one to be judged according to values set out by the other. This circularity is precisely how landscape was understood in this period. This is the argument that Svinin is following. But there is one extra element: consciousness. The viewer must be a person of sufficient understanding to realise that what seems oh so natural is in fact not quite. This is Kantian connoisseurship.

What both Kant and Svinin draw my attention to is the role played by power. For the elaborate links forged between constructed and natural environments also serve a political role: the pre-existing Russian landscape echoes the aesthetics of the garden, which echoes the landscape in a mutually confirming circle. This not only situates each estate owner atop an unchanging and unchangeable hierarchy but also reinforces the impression of feudalism as a system of unending authority. The phrase 'eternal Russia' recurs in books and articles or in the titles of paintings as a way of evoking the timelessness of Russian thought and Russian lands. But 'eternity', I'm beginning to believe, was actually invented in the eighteenth century, while 'Russia' would not be invented until the nineteenth.

Autumn is creeping up on Gatchina on the day I visit and the fledgling ducks are learning to fly. They flap low and loud along the surface of a sheltered waterway, like clumsily skimmed stones, before thwacking face-first into the water. Each emerges, a little surprised, gives itself a shake, and tries again. They need to learn quickly: Russia in winter is no place for young ducks.

It's not hard to see why the Russian royal family loved Gatchina. To my surprise, I find myself easily succumbing to the effects that this garden has been carefully designed to induce. My awareness provides no immunity. Instead, I see the landscape as a confirmation of Shchedrin's depiction of the landscape: it gives rise to the satisfying Kantian consciousness of the trick being played upon me. Each curling path leads you through woods and meadows, by streams and lakes, takes you gently by the hand on little journeys of carefully managed discovery. The landscape is here its own guide. The sky is flat blue-grey and the tree leaves are curling to little copper crisps – exactly, more or less, as they would have done for Paul and Maria Feodorovna some 240 years ago. Autumn was when they most liked to visit too.

But my visit does not begin quite so auspiciously. Having misunderstood the online booking system for Russia's state railways, I arrive in Gatchina ridiculously early, and at the wrong station. With hours to kill before the park opens, I wander the town in the grey morning rain. It's cold and nothing is open. At a bus stop is a poster for a missing cat; ten paces onwards, a dead cat (the same cat?) lies like an abandoned duster on the edge of the pavement. In a nearby park, I think I spot the culprit: a dog attacking another cat as it tries to hide. The dog's owner looks on in silence, using a pocket knife to peel an apple with almost comic villainy. I sit on a bench, taking notes and trying to avoid eye contact.

Throughout the town, history crumbles. Money is rarely limitless and priorities must always be made; you can't conserve everything. But it's often revealing to see what is lavished with the lustre of restoration and what just gets left to rot. In Gatchina, it's all about the palace. A disused industrial building made of red bricks is half-buried by foliage; an old tower is boarded up and graffitied. A busy road runs between two 'centurion columns', each comprised of twin Ionic pillars topped with a suit of armour. Nearby is the Rotunda Riga, a circular eighteenth-century building once containing shops and a bakery and thought to be the oldest surviving stone building in the town. Today, despite the proud brown heritage sign denoting its significance (in English no less), the structure is barely supported by wooden scaffolding. It looks like it could collapse at any moment.

At the edge of the park one or two of Gatchina's once-beautiful hothouses have been repaired, but most remain dilapidated and unusable. Once upon a time these were used to grow grapes and apricots, plums and peaches. I eventually find a kiosk near the other train station (the correct one) and sit on a stool drinking scalding hot coffee. If I'd been in charge of the renovations, I think as I burn my tongue for the fourth time, these hothouses would have been top of my list. Instead, a fortune has been spent on the palace interiors. The result, I discover once it opens at 10 a.m., is sparkling: there are wood-panelled doors and floral tapestries, lush carpets and wallpapers, a *trompe l'oeil* floral cupola in some side room or other, and unbelievably elaborate patterned parquet flooring. One of the old women invigilating the room (there are old women in every Russian gallery and museum and I'm pretty certain they don't get paid) insists on listing every variety of wood in the floor as well as its country of origin. At least I think that's what she is saying. Unfortunately, restored like this, stripped of the patina of history, the whole palace feels as glossily pointless as the day it was built.

I head outside into the gardens. To the east of the park, not far from the road, set on a small elevated hillock within sparse wood and open grass is the major reason I'm here: an architectural folly of such unique silliness that it alone is worth the train ride from Saint Petersburg. Such buildings became popular among a rather elevated section of society during the eighteenth century. At Pavlovsk, Maria Feodorovna delighted in showing visitors her personal dairy, where milk was dispensed not from anything as vulgar or hands-on as the teat of a cow but from a Japanese porcelain vessel with a silver tap. Marie Antoinette would have been thrilled.

At Gatchina, the folly I'm here to see is a little square cabin made of birch. Although birch wood is not especially well suited to architectural use (being too fast growing and therefore too flimsy) it works rather nicely if you don't expect your building to be lived in, or even to last all that long. At Mon Repos, an English-style landscape park near the Russian border with Finland at Vyborg, plans were drawn up for a rather handsome prospect tower made from birch. Sadly, I don't think it was ever built. Catherine the Great had a little birch house built at Tsarskoe Selo. From the outside it was supposed to look like an ordinary peasant's hut, but one that contained a dining room, a sitting room, two studies, a divan room and a WC. In another echo of Versailles, its walls were lined with over 540 mirrors. After all, what's the point in whimsical luxury if you can't see yourself enjoying it?

The birch house at Gatchina has a similar punch line. Some garden historians have written that the architect is unknown, but an information board in the park says that it was built as a joke for Catherine the Great in the 1780s by Swiss court architect François Viollier. The external walls are clad in a bizarre fashion that alternates a horizontally lain birch trunk, its bark white or pale grey, with a row of shorter sections whose cut ends form a line of circles facing outwards. These are weather-darkened for the most part and the result is altogether stripy: the white of the trunk bark, then the dark of the cut circles, white, then dark, and so on. Every so often, one of the sections appears to be more recent – the cut circles still pale golden brown.

Like Tolstoy's bench, the birch logs here must continually be replaced. From the outside, the cabin is quite sizeable, formed of several interlocking rectangles. But most of this is now given over to a ticket office. The windows and doors are flung open to reveal that these logs are just a façade. Plastic guttering pokes out like CCTV cameras. When was that installed? The whole thing is quite ridiculous.

But then that was the idea. The real joke, however, is yet to be revealed. For inside the little house, this rude folk cabin so rural and quaint, a feast of luxury awaits. Once you've paid a tiny sum. There is elaborately patterned parquet flooring and mirrored columns fringed with gilt. All around are mirrored walls, decorated with flowers, painted pink and yellow in a complex lattice pattern. Before you stretches a long turquoise seat draped with pale blue fabric. There are painted cherubs, a *trompe l'oeil* cupola and dainty, lion-footed corner tables. I say 'a feast of luxury', but actually I think most of these things are recent reproductions. The floor is covered in clear plastic. Pre-recorded information plays fizzily in Russian. The obliga-tory old woman stands there in silence.

The idealisation of peasant life was a European import. Writers such as Jean-Jacques Rousseau championed the 'noble savage' as a pure state of nature that preceded the trappings of civilisation. The ideas of Rousseau, who was deeply inspired by his visit to the great English garden at Stowe in 1761, in turn influenced garden designers across Europe. Ironically, Rousseau's influence would later also be felt in the thoughts of those Russian thinkers who specifically sought to reject the European philosophical and aesthetic traditions. It is said that Catherine tried to lure Rousseau to visit Gatchina with offers of girls and hunting. He declined.

In his analysis of structures such as the Gatchina birch house, Hayden cites Jacques Delille's 1782 *Les Jardins*, a series of poems published under the subtitle 'the art of beautifying the countryside', which was translated three times into Russian in the early nineteenth century. In it, Delille – a poet who rose to fame on the back of his translation of Virgil's rural *Georgics* – argues that, unlike the neoclassical temples and statues, the new wave of garden structures ought to appear functional: 'But each delight should wear an useful mien'. Delille's phrasing is precise: these structures were not in the slightest bit useful, at least not in the ways that they pretended to be; but they wore a useful expression. Like the dials on a deep-sea diving watch that has never even been in the bath, these expensive follies appeared at first sight as if they had a purpose. And appearances, after all, were the thing.

But tastes change. Paul I, Catherine's illegitimate son, did not appreciate his mother's little joke. Their relationship was not a loving one. Catherine's two great passions in life were English gardens and her grandson Alexander, Paul's eldest son and the future Tsar Alexander I. Catherine even removed Alexander from the hands of his parents in order to take personal charge of his upbringing. Between Tsarskoe Selo and Pavlovsk was the Alexandrova dacha, a small estate that Catherine built specifically for the education of the young Alexander. There, she ordered the construction of an English-style garden to provide the perfect setting for a series of fairy tales that she herself had written for him.

Paul's feelings about his mother's behaviour towards his son may perhaps be read through his response to Catherine's birch house. When she died, instead of knocking it down, he tried to conceal it with a great triumphal arch. Today, this stone arch stands in front of the little birch house, simultaneously dwarfing it and at the same time – because of the drama of this moment of discord within a landscape of painstaking harmony and balance – actually drawing attention to it. It is such a strange combination: Catherine's aristocratic whimsy butting right up against Paul's severe militarism. I read somewhere that the birch house was ordered as a gift from Catherine to Paul, but if she had known him at all, she'd have known he'd hate it. Maybe that was the point. Paul's arch reads like a surly riposte to his deceased mother.

In trying to decide which of the many great Russian gardens to visit, it was this strange birch house that convinced me that Gatchina would be a place of national significance. I had thought it would tell me something important about Russia, about the tentative emergence of national identity in the eighteenth century and about the relationship between that emergence and the birch tree, as an increasingly important element in the history of Russian landscape design. What I had not expected was that Gatchina would speak instead of the passions and personalities of such a narrow group of people. I was beginning to think that maybe Gatchina had been a dead end. What kind of conclusions could I really draw from one park, designed to please just a few members of the Russian elite? Only later did it occur to me that, in such a hierarchical society as feudal Russia, it was precisely the whims of the elite few that shaped the national narrative.

In *Black Wind, White Snow*, his 2016 analysis of the re-emergence of Russian nationalism under Putin, Charles Clover, former Moscow bureau chief for the *Financial Times*, writes:

> Nations are, as a rule, the creation of writers and poets, not of leaders and generals. Nations existed in books and poems long before politicians began to exploit nationalism to kill kings, tear down empires and build new ones.

I'm not so sure. Many of the poets and artists who would come to define Russia in the nineteenth century would do so, to a large extent, along lines already loosely demarcated by the Russian ruling classes and articulated, albeit tentatively, through the works of their architects and landscape designers. A number of these artists and writers would come to rebel against the narrow limits of the picturesque landscape, but the terms of the debate had already been set.

It was the eighteenth-century landscaped parks such as Gatchina and Pavlovsk that would go on to form the model for artist colonies like Abramtsevo, to the north of Moscow, which I shall visit soon. This is where the great writers and landscape painters of the 1800s would gather to write and paint, argue and build. 'Russian poetry, drama, literature were born of the country estate,' wrote Soviet architects Alexander Kudriavtsev and Alexander Krivov in 1987. The Tolstoy estate at Yasnaya Polyana, Turgenev's estate at Spasskoye-Lutovinovo, Pushkin's estate at Mikhailovskoe, Chekhov's at Melikhovo: each tells its own histories of over-lapping, competing approaches to the significance of the land, and, by extension, the meaning of Russia. And in each instance, it was the reshaping of the land by architects and designers, under instruction from their aristocratic employers, that would mould the art and literature to come.

For me then, it is imperative to probe the values upon which these landscapes were designed. From the beginning, the aesthetics of the picturesque were structured upon the system-atic exclusion of the labour of the peasantry. Ploughed fields, agricultural workers, unsightly peasant huts: these were all considered distasteful. In England, such sights were not only omitted from picturesque landscape painting, but the landscap-ing of estates often entailed the forced eviction of such people from their homes in order to replace them with sheep. Peasants were then crammed into so-called model villages that would look much more neat and tidy on the edges of the estate.

In Russia, the social structures of the eighteenth and nineteenth centuries were even more lopsided than in England. A
few aristocratic families wielded vast power over the land and
the people. The wealthy and influential Sheremetev family,
for example, owned 210,000 serfs. Russia remained largely
feudal until the revolutions of 1917. In this context, anything as
unsightly as real peasant huts – which might draw attention to
the exploitative lived reality upon which the immense wealth
of the aristocracy rested – were mostly kept well away from
the châteaux and gardens of the mighty. Little birch follies like
Catherine's at Gatchina were much more entertaining.

Gardens are exercises in both power and personality. When
it came to the Romanovs, the two rarely combined well. With
Catherine finally out of the way, the militarily obsessed Paul
made several further changes to Gatchina. In particular, he
sought to convert the gardens from a place of leisure into a site
where he could indulge his love of playing soldiers. It was Paul
who ordered those armour-topped pillars I walked past in the
town. He hired Irish gardener James Hackett and tasked him
to take a more formal approach to areas of the garden. Most
notable was the construction of a whole working harbour and
shipyard on the lake. In 1797, it was home to two great yachts,
the *Mirolyubye* with eight cannons and the *Emprenabl* with
sixteen. At its height, Paul's lake-bound flotilla consisted of
no fewer than twenty-four vessels. With his mother Catherine
waging numerous wars abroad, Paul consoled himself with his
toy navy. He even had plans drawn up for a barracks, but they
were never realised. Surprisingly, when he finally did become
Tsar he recalled all his troops from outside Russian borders.

Paul also converted the meadow in front of Gatchina palace
into a parade ground. Hanging in the house today is an 1851
painting by an unknown artist that shows the parade ground
adorned with massed ranks of cavalry and infantry. In the

foreground, officers and society ladies smile decorously to one another. As I trudge across the gravel I curse Paul's taste. A wildflower meadow here would be far lovelier.

I sit on a bench by the lake and eat makeshift sandwiches of bland white cheese with cucumber and dill. Opposite me in the lake is a little island, hardly more than a grassy tuft. Sprouting from its sides, like handsome antlers, is a pair of birch trees. Still quite slim, they can't be much more than twenty years old. I wonder if they were planted like this, around the time Putin came to power, or whether they self-seeded from the birch grove behind me and the gardeners allowed them to remain. The one on the left is completely leafless, while the right-hand one is still fully green. Is this the exact border between the seasons? Winter to the left of me; summer to the right. Maybe one of them is just dead. It leans apart at a dramatic angle, curving down towards the water. Beyond, on the far shore, an arched stone bridge stands between them.

Something spooks the gulls and gradually they rise, all of them, with a high-pitched scratchy jabbering. The air is full of gulls, white against the tree line, dark against a white sky. They swirl for a time and gradually settle back to the water. I spill some cheese down my front and everyone who walks past gives me strange looks.

What is perhaps most intriguing about Gatchina is that it still exists. I had not known about the significant sums of money spent by the Soviet authorities on restoring the great palaces and estates of the Tsarist era. But perhaps I should not have been surprised. The damage had been inflicted by the invading German army during World War II. For the Soviet authorities to begin the repair of places like Gatchina was therefore not so much a betrayal of the proletariat in favour of Tsarist decadence as it was an attempt to heal Russia from wounds inflicted by an external enemy.

In *Leningrad Diary*, her account of the city under siege during World War II, Soviet poet Vera Inber gives a detailed description of the damage wrought upon Gatchina and the surrounding estates by the occupying German forces. Following the city's liberation, she was among the first Russians to survey the destruction. 'Went yesterday to Duderhof, Gatchina, Pavlovsk and Pushkin, in a party consisting of painters and museum officials,' reads her entry on 1 February 1944. While the shell of Gatchina palace survived more or less intact, the interior was a different story: 'Inside, chaos reigned. Ruins, collapsed ceilings ... a fireplace ... dangling in the air'.

There is one especially memorable moment in Inber's account:

As we were entering Pushkin Park, Evegeniya Leonidovna, the former local guide, shouted in rapture: 'The ruins are intact!' And true enough the artificial romantic ruins of Catherine the Great's time remained in a perfect state of preservation.

The ruin is not ruined! What dizzying circles does this cast us into? I keep trying to get my head around this idea of the unruined ruin. I try to imagine if it had been ruined. What if you were the restorer tasked with repairing this ruined ruin? Where to begin? When to stop? Perhaps the guide's rapture is in fact relief at dodging such baffling questions.

The ruin may have remained unruined, but the Germans had left vast areas of these estates almost completely destroyed. In the case of Gatchina, as with several others, the work continues. It will probably never end. The inside of Gatchina palace is today lavishly pristine. It is only on the outside, where bullet holes still pockmark the window frames, that the troubled marks of history may be traced.

Behind me as I look is a solitary oak, ringed around with green fencing, its splitting trunk protected by wire mesh, held together by various supports, a crutch propping up one long, low, horizontal branch about five feet off the ground. It is hard to look at this tree as a real tree now and not simply as an old, exhausted metaphor.

There is, I had forgotten, another palace at Gatchina, arguably more significant than Catherine's château. It is certainly more self-consciously 'Russian'. As I walk along the road, I notice to my left an incomplete avenue of birch trees leading from nowhere to nowhere else. I veer off to investigate, and spot a man standing on a large concrete cylinder with his fishing rod in the lake. This is the Black Lake, and at the far end stands Nikolai Lvov's Priory Palace. It was Lvov, a polymath artist, architect and ethnographer, who, following the shift from the French style of formal gardens to the English landscaped park, called for something new: 'distinctively Russian gardens'. Lvov was obsessed with the myths and folklore of pre-Petrine Russia. His own poetry included elevated, literary approaches to traditional lyrical structures and subjects. He also compiled the first major collection of Russian folk songs. This included 'A Birch Tree Rustled in the Field', made famous in the late 1870s when incorporated by Tchaikovsky into the finale of his Symphony No. 4.

Priory Palace was commissioned by Paul in 1799, when he was Grand Master of the Knights Hospitaller of the Order of Saint John. It was designed to be a residence for the French Prince of Condé, who lived in Russia for a short time following the French Revolution and who was also Prior of the Order of Saint John. Priory Palace is Lvov's vision of medieval Russia: a white-walled conglomeration of rectangular forms topped with red roofs and a dinky tower built of local limestone. The foundations, lifting the whole structure out of the surrounding swamp, are limestone too. The rest is made of moulded earth bricks and compressed earth, beaten down between two panels, then removed, with a solution of lime added every two or three inches. This little medieval fantasy would become symptomatic of the path that nationalism would take: ever harking back to a lost history that never happened. And how typical that this exemplar of an invented Russian tradition should have been built to house a Frenchman. Nationalism has always spoken an international language. The palace was predicted to last just twenty-five years. Over two hundred years later, it still stands.

If Priory Palace demonstrates one way in which nationalism speaks through direct reference to the non-national other, nearby I come across a very different, very recent example. If Priory Palace makes Russia a promise, this is a series of threats. In the waiting room of Gatchina train station is a large poster. Under a big red header, 'Terrorism Warning', this is a classic piece of state propaganda, one that stirs up fear while professing to assuage it. Once upon a time, nationalism might have served to critique those in power; now it is another tool in the imposition of power. The detail of the poster is taken up with exhortations of advice (keep calm, don't panic) and a multiplicity of small images and captions: fire trucks and sniffer dogs, forensics units and chemical specialists. Together, they detail the work that all those arms of the Russian state are carrying out to protect you, dear fragile Russian citizen. Do not be afraid.

But the main message is really across the top: be afraid. Underlined in red are images of men with rifles and balaclavas, a man in military fatigues. There is a Black man in white robes and a kofia hat, a gunman by each side; a man with his face concealed by a keffiyeh; a pair of men holding rifles and wearing ankle-length Arabic tunics. Since Putin came to power, official policy has become increasingly xenophobic. Fear and intolerance of those deemed different has been harnessed and cultivated by the state. This is an especially strange phenomenon in a land where ethnicity has always been diverse, where borders have always shifted.

Posters such as this one at Gatchina station are designed to foster anxiety, to create widespread fear around a particular 'problem' to which the state then presents itself as the 'solution'. Russia has long been a paranoid country and I am an anxious person, especially when travelling. It is not a good combination, and over the course of my journeys it will only get worse. The Russian state, predictably enough, will not be a solution but a cause.

III.

PROTEST (ART)

'On my way to defend the forest
I thought about powerlessness.'

Kirill Medvedev, from 'Attack on City Hall', 2011–12

'I'm ... making ... fields.

'When somebody asks, "What are you doing in art?" that's
what I answer: "I'm making fields."' Sergey, who is telling me
this, is a very big man. He has long wavy hair and wears a dark
blue shirt with a pattern of pale leaves. He leans in close, looks
me in the eye, and speaks as though each and every word were
momentous.

I was introduced to Sergey the night before. 'You must meet
this man,' I was told by a curator when they heard about my
research into Russian art and landscape. Sergey Kishchenko is
perhaps best known for his ongoing work, *Observation Journal*, a
project that recreates a series of crop fields planted by the Nazis
from seeds they had stolen from Soviet geneticists working in
occupied Eastern Europe. It is a powerful way to start thinking
about the relationship between land, agriculture and totalitarian politics.

The first thing you learn when you meet Sergey is that he speaks, in English at least, very slowly. Each word is like a sentence of its own. I've forgotten my Dictaphone for our meeting inside a contemporary art fair in Moscow, so must write down everything he says in my little notebook, word by word. 'I'm.' *I'm.* 'Making.' *Making.* 'Fields.' *Fields.*

I have a stupendous hangover. Sergey's way of speaking is perfectly suited to my tender emotional state. In the long pauses between words my mind wanders backwards, trying to figure out how on earth I could feel this terrible. And then each sonorous syllable brings me right back to the present. Sergey, I quickly discover, is not really interested in birch trees. He wants to talk about fields. As far as my research goes this is already looking like a dead end. But that's OK: everything Sergey says seems so intensely profound.

'A field,' says Sergey. *A field*, I write, 'is a typical landscape from the sixteenth century onwards.'

There had been a gallery opening. Everybody was very beautiful and the cocktails, it turns out, were very strong. With an English art critic, I talked about cricket; to my Russian hosts, about my imminent trip on the Trans-Siberian. Every foreigner I mentioned the trip to was dreadfully jealous. Every Russian – or rather, every Muscovite – simply horrified. 'Why would you do such a thing?' gasped one. 'There is no civilisation in the north,' said another. 'Moscow is not Russia,' warned a third. I don't think any of them had been east of the Urals. Mostly they just wished that they lived in Europe or that Moscow was more like Europe. As the Russian-American narrator of Keith Gessen's novel *A Terrible Country* summarises, 'To be Russian was in some way constantly to have to choose ... between the Russian and Western – in what you ate, what you listened to, what you thought.' Same old story.

And then Sergey speaks again, right up close, and his words vibrate through the entirety of my being. 'Landscape is a point of links.' *A point of links.* God, Sergey, you're so right. I know precisely what he means because this is exactly my interest in writing about landscape. Landscape, like the narrative 'I' that often wanders through it, is a field in which so much intertwines: ideas and histories, people and animals, ethics and aesthetics, industry, agriculture, geology, topography ... and this intermingling does not have to be smooth and rational. It can be rough, accidental, violent, nonsensical, unconscious. Like art, landscape is at once constructed and real: both a framing of the world and a vital part of the world itself. Sergey, this visionary, knows my every thought. If Sergey were the leader of a cult, I would join it immediately. I would write down his every word in elaborate calligraphic script. My notes, when I look at them later, are mostly nonsense.

We're in the cordoned-off VIP section of the art fair. In addition to my birch research, I'm writing a magazine story about the fair and its impact on the city's artists and galleries. The Qataris are on a soft power offensive and seem to have sponsored the whole thing. Qatar Airways and Beluga vodka. The walls are all silver. So too the furniture. We sit side by side on a small dainty sofa in the corner while people around us conduct meetings, make sales. I'm looking quite smart in a navy blazer; Sergey is a little wild. He drinks the free cocktails. I could do with a pint and a toasted cheese sandwich. I have no idea what time it is. Periodically a liveried flunky offers us chocolate truffles on a silver tray. 'I work with seeds,' says Sergey, a little smudge of truffle across one tooth.

The night before my meeting with Sergey, I had somehow found myself having dinner with Pussy Riot. After the gallery opening, some of the people involved in the art fair had taken our little group of journalists to a Ukrainian restaurant.

It was never quite clear whether Pussy Riot had tagged along with us or we with them. The other British writer in our group was gushing in his admiration and kept shaking the hand of Pyotr Verzilov, one of the Pussy Riot members who famously invaded the pitch during the 2018 World Cup final in Moscow. Next to him and opposite me was fellow Pussy Riot member and football pitch invader Veronika Nikulshina, her body angled diagonally away as if I were disgusting to look at. Neither of them spoke to me, nor I to them. Maybe I wasn't gushing enough.

We gorged on Ukrainian food in painfully 'traditional' surroundings of carved wood and acres of white lace. We ate tongue, *kasha*, veal in aspic (my vegetarianism goes out the window in situations like this) and the classic Shuba salad – herring lashed with layers of grated vegetables and mayonnaise. (This is not a salad for summer or for the weak-hearted: Shuba means 'fur coat'.) There were vile flavoured vodkas to numb the senses. I also remember buying a jug of vodka; the Pussy Riot entourage drank all of it without saying thank you. Was that before or after the restaurant? I have no idea.

'DNA is the best library in the world,' says Sergey. My mind takes a bit of time to come back into focus. I mumble something about archives as places that are less about conserving the past than about imagining the future. 'Yes!' Sergey nods vigorously and takes another chocolate truffle.

On the way to another bar, Pussy Riot's Pyotr and Veronika insisted on stopping every hundred yards or so, on the pavement, in a courtyard, and lying on the ground while one of the group took photographs from above. I had no idea what they were doing. Is this how the revolution begins?

The Western media love a Pussy Riot story. Glamorous Russian girls doing outlandish things and getting imprisoned by Putin. The art world goes equally gaga over stories of art-activism against repressive regimes. Witness the ubiquity of Ai Weiwei. As if somehow a bit of that political radicalism and bodily bravery will rub off on the curator-bureaucrats of London or New York. I don't recall the UK's art or architecture institutions doing much for Trenton Oldfield when he was sentenced to six months for interrupting the Oxford–Cambridge boat race or when the Home Office, under Theresa May, tried to deport him (Pussy Riot were given two years for their performance inside Moscow's Cathedral of Christ the Saviour). Compared to Pussy Riot, I find myself far more drawn to the work of, say, Alexander Brener (who I once witnessed take a shit into his own hand in protest at a panel discussion about 'extreme curating' at London's ICA). But then what the hell do I know? Again, Gessen's *A Terrible Country* springs to mind. The novel's narrator is similarly critical of an anti-Putin protest stunt. Like me, he is a non-Russian outsider, who is never quite as invested in the political situation as those he criticises. Like me, he can always escape. He is sharply reprimanded for his comments: 'It's indecent to criticise someone whose position you'll never have to occupy.'

But among their Russian peers, Pussy Riot are not unequivocally celebrated either. In the 2018 issue of *Kajet*, an Anglophone cultural magazine based in Romania, Anya Smirnova wrote a profile of art-activist collective Chto Delat. The name of the group, meaning 'What is to be done?', comes from the title of an 1863 novel by Nikolai Chernyshevsky. Lenin, a great admirer of Chernyshevsky, used the same phrase as the title of a pamphlet he published in 1902. In the *Kajet* profile, one member of the group, Dmitry Vilensky, is quoted in conversation with theorist Gerald Raunig, comparing Chto Delat's own form of 'long durée activism' to the bodily shock tactics of Pussy Riot or Pyotr Pavlensky (most famous for nailing his own scrotum to the stone pavement of Moscow's Red Square in 2013):

'Gerald,' says Vilensky, 'it's fucking winter outside. If you ran outside naked, full of joy with the red flag, you'd be frozen in five minutes.'

A vague link begins to form in my head between what Sergey has been saying and what Pussy Riot and others are agitating against. To control a society you must control production: not only of food and land as in feudalism or of surplus value as in capitalism, but also, above all, of people. To really control production you must control reproduction: of the population, of the labour force. It is a power that must be seized, over and over again, from women by the state. In the Soviet era, marriage was first denounced as a bourgeois institution and then praised to encourage procreation. In 2007, with concern growing over Russia's shrinking population, Putin introduced a pay-out for families who have a second child. At the same time, anti-homosexual rhetoric has been ramped up, with predictably violent results. To be gay is somehow not to be properly Russian.

'Seeds. Wheat. Bread. It's a very dangerous area,' says Sergey. 'These are the oldest symbols of human civilisation, going through thousands of years of human history, art and religion. The field of wheat in Soviet propaganda. With women and children. It is a symbol of the future of the country.'

There are still no birch trees here, though – not yet. Birches are not a crop; so despite what they may be able to tell us about relationships between nature and nation, they are of little interest to Sergey. With our meeting over, I wander around the art fair, half thinking of the review I have to write, half scanning for birches.

One of the galleries, I discover with delight, is showing a series of seven-foot-high vertical cylinders, which, lit by a series of internal lights, glow through a semi-transparent veneer in the unmistakable pattern of birch bark. They are truly hideous. At first, the works look like the kind of tasteless interior design tat that wealthy Russians were sneered at for buying in the 1990s. But this is an art fair in 2018 and this tat is ironic. It is the work of Russian artist Nikola Ovchinnikov, who has long explored the cultural reception of artistic symbolism. And this is not Ovchinnikov's only engagement with the birch as material or symbol: in 1997, he produced his first design for a 'Moscow Parthenon'. Initially a speculative design – incorporating a pediment in the style of ancient Greek architecture placed atop pillars made from birch trunks – the structure has subsequently undergone various iterations, with real, albeit temporary, versions realised in Baden-Baden, Germany, and Toyama, Japan.

In 2010, Ovchinnikov dedicated an entire exhibition to birch trees. Happily bolstering my speculative thesis that every great Russian journey is a return, Ovchinnikov titled the exhibition *They Come Back*. Taking place at Aidan Gallery in Moscow, it stemmed from the artist's own frequently returning fascination with the symbolism of the birch. A text on a Russian art website describes how Ovchinnikov returned repeatedly to the idea of the birch-pillared Parthenon. For Ovchinnikov, the return stems not, I don't think, from a conservative wish to wind back the clock to simpler times; rather, it serves a postmodern strategy of citation or pastiche. His return to a worn-out symbol of Russianness is first and foremost ironic. The exhibition title is also a specific reference to a very famous Russian painting: the celebrated birches in Alexei Savrasov's *The Rooks Have Returned* (1871). This is a painting I will soon need to take a long, close look at, but not until I make my own return to Moscow.

Around the corner from Ovchinnikov's cylinders, I find another gallery in the fair also showing a birch: this time, a sculptural assemblage by Irina Korina. Korina has spoken rather beautifully of her role as an artist: 'If we imagine society as some kind of building, then I give myself the role of balcony.' A balcony, she explains, has multiple uses: it may provide a break from daily routine; it may simply be a place to smoke; but it may also be a place from which to see things differently. Korina's ironic use of the birch does exactly that: it provides a break, a way to see things differently. The work – *Eiffel Tower* (2014) – consists of a gaudily lit, gold-covered model of the Eiffel Tower, hung with crimson tassels, perched atop a slim birch branch and leant against one of the white temporary walls of the fair. Korina has also used birch trees in a number of other works, most notably in a large-scale installation at Helmut List Halle in Graz, Austria. Entitled *Yesterday's Snow* (2018), the work consisted of a series of inflatable objects, some lying across the gallery floor, others tall, upright and waving, like trees, or those large, inflatable figures you see flapping in the wind by the sides of motorways advertising fast food or car washes. Korina's versions are printed with forest scenes or black and white birch-bark patterns.

These works – by both Ovchinnikov and Korina – can certainly be understood as warmly ironic comments on capitalism's deft ability to convert anything, even – or especially – emotionally charged symbols of national identity, into commodities to be bought and sold. This phenomenon is beautifully encapsulated by the website Made in Russia, which promotes Russian brands and businesses. The website's logo is a perfect blurring of capitalism and nationalism: parallel lines of black and white birch trunks placed together to form a barcode, the very icon of modern consumer culture. Such images, seen now through the lens of Ovchinnikov and Korina, show me that, in Russia, the complex relationship between art and commodity can be played out through the birch, a tree that is maybe always in quotation marks. Incidentally, both Korina and Ovchinnikov – like the

Italian Pietro Gonzaga who did so much to create the 'authentic' Russian feel of the gardens at Pavlovsk – trained as set designers. In a further twist, their ironic comments on commodification are themselves commodified. This is an art fair after all, and everything is for sale.

A few days after the art fair, I'm on the Trans-Siberian railway and I've forgotten all about that boozy Moscow evening. But Pussy Riot are in the news again. Pyotr, whom I sat opposite at dinner, who so embarrassed the Russian security services with his World Cup stunt, is in hospital in Germany. All this stuff about birches suddenly seems rather trivial and academic. Pyotr has been poisoned by an unknown 'anticholinergic agent', that many suspect as being on the orders of the Russian state. I am gripped by a dark feeling of dread. Pyotr is lucky to be alive.

In 1949, amid deteriorating post-war relations between the Allied powers and Russia's rapid expansion of the Eastern Bloc (Romania and the Czech Republic in 1948; Hungary and East Germany in 1949), 300,000 copies were released of a new Soviet propaganda poster. Designed by Pyotr Golub, the image shows Stalin, resplendent in a pristine white military jacket, standing before an endless landscape of neatly demarcated fields, each exactly the same size and shape. One field at the edge of the image is as golden as the sunny streaks in the sky above. The others are healthy and green. Russia, struggling to rebuild after the war with Germany, is shown here fully recovered, a land of productivity and plenty.

Before it all, dominating the composition, stands Stalin, facing a little away from us, towards the sunlit future. By his side are two powerful symbols: to Stalin's left a young boy, innocent but serious, the next generation. He wears the red

Petr Golub, Long Life and Prosperity to Our Motherland. Image courtesy of Universal History Archive/UIG/Bridgeman Images

scarf of the Young Pioneers, the Soviet youth organisation founded in 1922, and carries a little posy of white flowers. To Stalin's right is, unusually, a birch tree. The birch was not common in such propaganda images, which favoured productive Soviet landscapes of industry and agriculture.

But wars and patriotism go hand in hand. And during this period, the Soviet regime increasingly harked back to the nineteenth century for its landscape aesthetics. Dr Anita Pisch, author of *The Personality Cult of Stalin in Soviet Posters 1929–1953*, compares the image to a painting from the year before: Fyodor Shurpin's *The Morning of Our Motherland* (1948) in which Stalin looms like a white-clad monument before a wide flat landscape. Pylons and factories signal the productivity of the land under communism. But paying closer attention to the birch, I would trace the art-historical reference back a little further: in particular to Mikhail Nesterov's 1905 painting *By the Volga*. The composition is very similar: a birch tree at the left edge of the painting, a man gazing, statue-like, into the distance. To his left, instead of the boy, a woman sits, holding flowers and wearing traditional costume. As professor of Russian literature, Ellen Rutten has pointed out how Nesterov's paintings sought again and again to feminise the Russian landscape, especially in a series of very similar paintings of the Volga region. 'The connection between the landscape and the figure, so to say, *a single thought* in one and the other, helps to create a unity of mood.' A year later in 1906, he painted a second work, also called *By the Volga*, nearly identical to its predecessor but with the man and the birch removed, leaving the woman alone with her flowers and the Volga. Nesterov had created an emotional and compositional gap in his own painting – a hole that, in time, would be filled by Stalin.

By the Volga, 1905 by Mikhail Nesterov © Astrakhan Museum

By 1949, the birch became once again an important motif of Russia. Stalin, who, according to Pisch, was never shown alongside a female partner, here forms the head of an idyllic little family, all in white. Even though the imagery is the same, Stalin's birch bride is very different to those serenaded by Yevgeniy Ross in 'Birch Trees of Russia'. The Soviet era was famously chaste.

By this time, the equation of the Russian landscape with femininity had been long established, thanks in part to Nesterov. The birch, by the twentieth century such a familiar symbol in Russian landscape painting, marries Stalin to a timeless Russian history, and the boy, like Stalin, looks forward to Russia's bright future. The three figures overlap, even begin to merge within a single visual grammar. Stalin *is* the boy (the future of Russian culture). Stalin *is* the birch (the land, the past). There is no alternative.

Trawling the internet at home, I stumble across an unexpected coda to this pair of images, the Nesterov painting and Pyotr Golub's propaganda poster. In 2017, Moscow womenswear designer Lesia Paramonova commissioned London-based photographer Emmie America to shoot the new collection. Paramonova's label, LES', is an abbreviation of her first name, and is also Russian for 'forest'. Her style is whimsical and dream-like, with an expensive smidge of grit. She draws upon myths and history, loves lush embroidered fabrics. Paramonova's Autumn/Winter 2017–18 collection was entitled *Gobelin*, a reference to the pre-eminent Parisian tapestry makers from the fifteenth century onwards. In the accompanying lookbook one image stands out: a young girl in a forest clearing. She has boyishly cropped hair and eye shadow like heavy bruising. She wears white trainers and a sporty-cut dress made from fabric richly patterned like tapestry with deer and mythical winged creatures and the Latin phrase *Credere in Miracula* (To Believe in Miracles). To the right as you look, the model holds a deer on a leash (the tapestry is becoming real); to the left is, as you might have guessed, a tall white birch tree.

Gobelin Skirt © Emmie America

The composition is therefore exactly the same as both the Nesterov painting and Golub's propaganda poster. But where Nesterov centres the (anonymous Russian) man, and Golub centres Stalin, for Emmie America and Lesia Paramonova, it is the young girl at the heart of the narrative. She is active, modern, but in tune with timeless Russian myths. Nature responds to her. But this is also, I think, an ironic image. Nesterov and Golub's images both flatten differences in an attempt to fix a permanent present. Paramonova's is a postmodern present that deliberately juxtaposes the old (baroque tapestry, birch trees, nature) against the new (trainers, sports socks) and the urban against the rural. Both Stalin and Nesterov's anonymous men have their arms down by their sides. But in America's photograph, the girl's right hand is raised to her forehead. She does not gaze powerfully into the distance. Her eyes are closed. Is she shielding her face from the sun or refusing to confront the future? To me, she looks exhausted or maybe a little bored: tired out, I like to think, by the sheer weight of all this symbolism.

In the Russian Forest Museum in the south of central Moscow, the director is keen to give me the full guided tour. I think everyone there is simply delighted to receive a visitor. They unlock the front door for me. They turn the lights on. Judging by the expressions of surprise on the faces of the staff, I'm probably the first foreign visitor they've had in years.

Founded in 1998 to mark the two hundredth anniversary of the creation of Russia's state forestry department, the museum is housed in what appears to be a typical nineteenth-century residential building, but was in fact purpose-built. With a collection comprising several thousand documents and artefacts, it aims to educate visitors on the role played by the state in the economic and ecological management of Russia's forests. It is not a place likely to pull in the crowds.

'*Ya zhurnalist*,' I mumble as I enter, paying the minuscule entry fee anyway. Not for the first time, the complete lack of shared language does not stop a Russian from taking considerable time to explain things in great detail to me – in Russian. After the initial period of awkwardness in which I nod and say '*da*' from time to time, I gradually find the whole charade strangely charming. The director is fearsomely glamorous, her blonde hair coiffed and sprayed into a sturdy meringue.

In all honesty, I'm doing myself a disservice. I do speak *some* Russian. '*Berezka*,' I say, pointing at the painted birch backdrops to the museum exhibits. The director nods. It is her turn to say '*da*'. And then my real linguistic triumph. Among the artfully arranged tree stumps and information signs are numerous stuffed animals, including, I spy with delight, a hedgehog. *'Yezhik,'* I grin, unfeasibly pleased with myself. *'Da,'* says the director.

The history of Russian forestry is more interesting than it sounds.

A key book on the subject is Stephen Brain's *Song of the Forest.* Brain's remit is the period from 1905 to 1953 with a particular focus on environmentalism under Stalin, but his conceptual and historical reach is much wider. In order to explain how Russia treated its forests under communism, Brain delves right back to the depths of feudalism (although, in Russia, that's not really so far back). In particular, what interests me about Brain's narrative is the relationship between forestry policy and the ideological discussions whirling through Russia during these periods. I was surprised to read that the debates shaping forestry policy under the Soviets in the twentieth century were so similar to those taking place under the Tsars in the nineteenth.

Partly, this might be explained by the age of the Soviet regime's senior scientists. In 1944, scientist Eric Ashby spent a year in the USSR on the initiative of the Australian government. 'By and large science is in the hands of old men,' he wrote, noting that there was no age limit for retirement. These scientists lived a privileged existence: special shops, summer houses and generous allowances. There was no incentive to relinquish one's position. Only six scientists born in the twentieth century had by 1944 been elected to the Soviet Academy. The mean age of the 139 Academicians was, according to Ashby, about sixty-five.

But there is also a link to be made here, I think, between the Soviet attitude towards Russia's architectural heritage (as exemplified by the careful restoration of war-damaged palaces such as Gatchina) and the regime's approach to environmental policy. There is, at the heart of both, a conflict between, on the one hand, communism's prioritisation of an international community of workers that transcends national boundaries and, on the other, Russia's repeated attempts to define itself as a nation with an identity that is not the same as the nations of Europe. Sometimes these twin imperatives could be forced to align; at other moments in history they would splinter dramatically.

By the late nineteenth and early twentieth centuries, fears were growing that Russia, extraordinary as it may seem, was running out of woods. There was some truth to these fears. In 1696, Russian forest cover stood at 56 per cent of its total land area. This had fallen to 36 per cent by 1888 and then again to just 30 per cent by 1914. Not only was the forest retreating, but it was changing too: as valuable 'ruddy-barked' pine and spruce were cut down, 'pale-skinned' aspen, alder and birch filled the gaps. As Brain puts it, 'the mighty red Russian forest was turning white'.

This is significant. For, while the Russian peasantry had long made extensive material use of birches – for furniture and ornaments, woven baskets and traditional slippers known as *lapty* – the state-run forestry industry was much more selective. This was to become a substantial point of contention between the city-based central government and the rural peasantry.

Fears that Russia might be exhausting its woods have never gone away. Forest area was reported at just under 50 per cent in 2015. And yet, just the year before, an article in the *Moscow Times* was published under the alarmist headline 'Russia Is Running Out of Forest'. What this actually meant was that the country is running out of easily exploitable 'commercially usable forests'. This is a very different scenario.

The article cites the glory years of the post-war Russian forestry industry:

Some forests cleared between 1940 and 1970 have actually regrown enough to be cleared again, said WWF's Kobyakov.

But those offer mostly aspen or birch – which, despite being considered the archetypal national tree in Russia, is subpar timber compared with many conifers.

This was in 2014. It could have been 1914. I find it fascinating that these apparently quite niche debates were, and still are, influenced by wider ideological questions about the importance of national identity and about the relationship between urban decision-makers and the rural peasantry. People are not the only ones affected by questions about what it means to be Russian or by the transition from communism to capitalism; forests are also altered by human ideologies. At the same time, the reverse is true too. Debates over how to live in and work with Russia's forests have had a tangible impact upon the way people understand the places they inhabit, their relationship to Europe, to the land, and to the future itself. We shape the forest and the forest in turn shapes us.

Once again my pre-existing ideas about Soviet environmental policies were so very simplistic. In school, all we learned was how the communists had turned the Aral Sea, once the fourth largest lake in the world, into a desert by diverting the surrounding rivers for irrigation. Communism, we were told, understood nature as something that must be dominated and exploited. Oxana Timofeeva, philosopher and another member of art protest group Chto Delat, summarises the usual picture:

Bolsheviks dreamed of revolutionizing not just society, but nature itself, for nature was considered a realm of unfreedom, inequality, injustice, need, exploitation, and death. Turning rivers, blasting mountains, making animals speak; the idea was to transform the Earth by means of technology in order to make it, as [Soviet writer] Andrey Platonov says, more 'kind to us'.

Obsessed with technological and industrial progress, communism was underpinned by Promethean ideas of man's supremacy over nature: ideas expounded in, for example, Stalin's *Great Plan for the Transformation of Nature* of 1948, in which the canals that would empty the Aral Sea were first outlined. The plan also included the first state programme to reverse human-induced climate change: a vast scheme to plant over 14 million acres of forest in the southern Russian steppe. In *Song of the Forest*, Brain describes this as 'an exceedingly old Russian dream: to make the southern steppe more like old Muscovy'. It did not go well.

But the assumption that the Soviet's were solely interested in productivity is, at best, a simplification. It is certainly true that the Soviet era was guilty of reductive readings of Marx in support of a certain Promethean hubris. But there were other, more intriguing factors shaping official environmental policy: not only the shifting ideological debates of the period but also the frequent restructuring of the state bureaucracy. The communist state is often viewed as a monolithic entity, but the debates over forestry that raged across the twentieth century suggest that it was anything but.

In the 1920s, for example, with Russian policy-makers concerned about the economic damage that would result from the loss of the country's forests, conservationism was a surprisingly significant influence. Narkomzem, the ministry of agriculture, initiated a travelling forest museum in order to educate the population on the importance of conservation. Suggested topics for events included 'The Forest as a Symbol of the Collective' or 'The Nature of the Forest and Its Imprint on the Life Patterns of the Russian People'. How I would love to attend events with names like that today!

But following a period of careful manoeuvring against Narkomzem by the state institution for the management of the economy (VSNKh), the conservationist legislation of the 1920s was repealed. This ushered in a period of unchecked forest exploitation. In 1930, during the first of Stalin's Five Year Plans, over-logging was widespread: targets were exceeded by 47 per cent in Leningrad province, 125 per cent in Western province and 129 per cent in Moscow province. This is precisely the image of communist forestry policy that one might expect: exploitative, short-sighted and utterly irresponsible. And to me it sounds rather a lot like capitalism.

In the 1930s, ideas began to shift once more. The link between tree-felling and increased flood risk began to be understood, and logging was eventually forbidden along rivers. In 1936, a new forest protection agency, Glavlesookhrana (GLO), was established, whose remit covered one third of the forests of European Russia, mostly along major rivers. As GLO's power, budget and territories increased in the second half of the 1930s, the organisation was gripped by what Brain describes as a 'strange institutional schizophrenia'. Internal debate centred on exactly what constituted a healthy forest, and what role humans ought to play in ensuring that health. On the one hand were the *preservationist* ecologists who sought to leave utterly untouched the wide-ranging network of national parks (known as *zapovednik*) that had been conceived under the Tsars and had expanded and contracted like a concertina in the Soviet period. On the other hand were *conservationist* foresters who believed that a healthy forest was one managed to be economically pro-ductive and, to a lesser degree, sustainable.

Stalin's response was not to crush one side in favour of the other but to maintain these divisions. Brain describes this as 'a dictator's solution to the problem of conflicting interests: rather than blend priorities, Stalin created separate spheres where smaller dictators could rule'. The result was a proliferation of departments, agencies and committees, often with their own

remits, responsibilities, personalities and approaches to inter-
preting orders from the centre. Power struggles between them
were unavoidable.

In any discussion of Soviet agricultural or environmental
policy, Trofim Lysenko is inevitably a central figure. He is
frequently derided as a prime example of what happens when
politics interferes in science (as if science could ever really be
free from politics). It was through experimental research into
crop yields that Lysenko emerged as a significant figure in
Soviet science. Lysenko rejected the genetic theories of Gregor
Mendel as bourgeois determinism; instead, he argued that
crops and other organisms could pass on characteristics that
they had acquired during their lifetime to their offspring. Much
of the research published by Lysenko and his followers was
fabricated.

Lysenko's ideas fitted with the regime's needs of the era. As
Sergey explained to me in the art fair in Moscow, the field of
wheat is not only a symbol of national productivity; it is also
vital to the running of the country. There can be no industri-
alisation if you cannot feed the workers. Lysenko promised
that he could increase the year-round wheat yield, that he
could induce winter peas to grow in Azerbaijan. Several of
the 'pioneering' theories he claimed as his own had been in
use by farmers since 1800. Some of his other theories were
simply false.

Nonetheless, Lysenko became a great favourite of Stalin, who
promoted him to director of the Institute of Genetics in 1940.
From this new position of authority, Lysenko ruthlessly dismissed all those who opposed him. Hundreds of scientists who
refused to fall in line were sacked from their posts, imprisoned
or executed. But debate was never entirely stifled. Lysenko was
frequently contradicted by forestry experts. 'The state,' writes
Brain, 'was speaking with two voices'.

One of Lysenko's best-known undertakings was the doomed quest in the 1950s to turn Russia's southern steppes into thick forest. He believed that acorns should be planted in plus-shaped 'nests' of five so that each oak sapling would help defend the others from weeds. He also advocated simultaneous planting with agriculturally useful crops such as wheat, oats, barley and potatoes to be sown among the acorns in order to provide another line of 'defence' against the weeds. Brain describes Lysenko's theories of plant battles and co-operation as attempts to 'reimagine the entire landscape in terms of ... Cold War rhetoric'. Thousands worked on replanting the steppes. Within a few years, all the trees had died.

The death of Stalin in 1953 signalled another series of rapid about-turns. Lysenko remained in his post but was increasingly sidelined from decision-making. Soviet forestry policy shifted away from conservation and back to full-speed-ahead industrialism. An aerial photograph in the Russian Forest Museum shows the results: a rigidly divided landscape, all straight lines and gridded boundaries. Below, the caption proudly proclaims the new era: 'By 1957, for the first time in Russian forest economy, all forests of Russia were explored and forest management plans in every forest range were developed.'

'Science is how capitalism knows the world,' wrote Rebecca Solnit in *A Field Guide to Getting Lost* (2005). And communism too, I'd be tempted to add. Both, after all, are discourses of domination.

Forests remain so important that some Russians are still prepared to die for them. In December 2011, 100,000 people took to the streets of Moscow to protest against the Putin government. Or rather, to protest against one policy in particular: the construction of a second motorway between the capital and Saint Petersburg.

'It is a very tangible affair,' wrote researcher Tena Prelec in a 2012 blog post, 'involving birches, bears, squirrels, cement, women, men and blood: the destruction and defence of Khimki Forest.'

Khimki Forest Protest © Daniel Beilinson

The Khimki Forest is part of Moscow's 'green belt', which was established in 1935 during one of those periods when the Soviets embraced forest conservation. But it has been gradually eroded by industrial and residential developments and transport infrastructure. Since the end of the USSR this has only accelerated: during the 1990s, when the city handed control of the green belt over to the federal authorities, as much as half of the forested area was destroyed – mostly by the forestry industry or by developers building swathes of gated suburban communities.

The instinct to protect what remains is therefore well justified. It rests on arguments of public health and a love of nonhuman nature that is at once instinctive and historically conditioned. Contracts for the project were also thought to be mired in corruption. In the forest itself, protesters gathered over many months: a mix of local residents, environmental and political activists, lawyers and politicians – Russian and non-Russian alike. The story garnered international attention, in part due to the involvement of French construction conglomerate Vinci, which has also been involved in controversial projects such as HS2 – the high-speed trainline in the UK – and the Aéroport du Grand Ouest in Notre-Dame-des-Landes near Nantes, France. In 2016, a group of NGOs filed a complaint against Vinci for alleged corruption of Russian public officials, but they were unable to put forward enough evidence to win the case.

Eyewitness accounts from the Khimki Forest reported continual surveillance of protesters by the FSB (the Russian security service, formerly the KGB), violence at the hands of unidentified men, and indifference or impotence from the local police. Large areas of woodland were cut down, apparently illegally, despite brave resistance. Online accounts document haphazard violence and brutality. RT, one of Russia's state-run news channels, blamed 'migrant workers' for cutting down '120 ancient birch trees'. Most of the protesters believed the felling to have been in preparation for the motorway.

On photo-sharing website Flickr is a photograph that shows the forest not as a site of peace or escape but as violently contested territory. A line of riot police dominate the image while to the right a man in pale blue jeans stands upon a tree stump, filming something beyond the edge of the frame. Lines of felled and broken white birches lead the eye towards the centre of the composition where a little white Soviet-era car (a Lada, I think) stands just in front of the assembled police. The contents of the scene may date precisely to May 2011 but the style in which the image has been composed is much older. In particular, the photograph reminds me of the Russian landscape painters of the nineteenth century – especially Ivan Shishkin in its airless, near-skyless, claustrophobic intensity. Below the photograph is a detailed account of the experience of resistance.

Today we came to the Khimki forest.

The deputy Gudkov of the State Duma came with us.

We observed freshly cut down trees – birches with leaves and a huge harvester . . .

We demanded the documents. They said 'none'.

Greenpeace lawyer Blatova, Save Khimki Forest movement lawyer Kozlov both agreed that the required by law documents are absent.

We called the Khimki police.

The activists called the investigating department and started to wait.

They didn't come . . .

That's why we decided to make a camp in the forest and to stand to protect ourselves the trees.

During the presence on the first clearing, a call from the witness came that near Starbeevo, near the old pioneer camp, workers with chain-saws cut down trees . . .

When came to the spot, activists saw many trees fallen.

Big birches with the new fresh green leaves. Especially sad looked the oaks very wide, of a few hundred years old which lay down on earth split into a few chunks . . .

Suddenly an activist cried out: 'Look! He hit him!'

We rushed to him.

A guard came to him, hit his mobile out of his hands and wanted to make him more harm.

We ran closer. The guy went on me, I managed to make a photo of him from a close distance, he couldn't touch me though. Instead he severely hit Alesha Belikh in face. Immediately blood flew out of his nose, that was broken.

The guy ran away into the forest. The securities just laughed at us, and the FSB which constantly spies at us just stood with the securities.

The bravery, ingenuity and sheer tenacity of these protesters eventually resulted in a surprising victory. Construction on the project was paused by President Dmitri Medvedev, but not for long: the motorway was eventually completed in 2019. Even this brief delay came at a severe cost: in the ensuing years Russia has become even more repressive. Protesters have been threatened in their homes, journalists brutally beaten. Leading Khimki Forest activist Yevgeniya Chirikova now lives in Estonia. Mikhail Beketov, fifty-five, the founder of local newspaper *Khimki Pravda*, had his car set on fire and his dog killed before he was left brain-damaged following an attack in 2008. He died of his injuries in 2013.

Today in Russia, the state is not ignorant of the popular power of the birch tree. I will soon visit the recently constructed Zaryadye public park in Moscow to explore how this power can be wielded from the top down. But the popular love of the natural environment must never be allowed to stand in the way of power or profit. Nature has always been an ideological battleground. Sometimes that battle is a literal one too, and losses are not only symbolic but bloody and real.

IV.

MYTHS AND MATERIALS

'Landscapes with birch trees placed into kitschy, heavy gold-plated frames only attract a few tourists and the provincial nouveau riche.'

Ekaterina Drobinina, 'The Russian Online Art Market',
Arterritory.com, 2015

The domes of Saint Sophia Cathedral glint gold and silver against cloudless turquoise skies. The foreground is a strip of white, the earth concealed, rendered clean and pure by a covering of pristine snow. 'Once upon a time . . . ' the painting seems to say. It points backwards to a dream-like past that remains miraculously unchanged today. Unlike many cathedrals in the UK, which so often seem like multilayered collages of their own histories, patchworks of different architectural approaches, this particular style of Russian church architecture appears to have fallen, faultless, from the skies.

Saint Sophia Cathedral in Novgorod was built in the eleventh century, but in this little painting it is difficult to get any sense of the building's long history. It tells us nothing about the people who built it under orders from Prince Vladimir, the people who cared for it over the subsequent centuries, the people who looted it or defiled it – from Ivan the Terrible's *oprichnina* (a kind of sixteenth-century state of exception) to the Nazis in World War II – or the people who subsequently restored it. White in a white landscape, the cathedral masks the traces of its history. It looks as if it landed yesterday or as if it has simply always been there. Even its name refers not to an individual saint who might be associated with a particular era or location, but, like Hagia Sophia in Istanbul, to *sophia* – the wisdom of God. Once upon a time this style, directing the eye upwards, was new. Saint Sophia asks us to look not towards other men but towards God and, perhaps in time, towards a Russia that transcends time. It has been here forever, it has only just arrived.

Dividing the composition is a single birch. It stretches the height of the painting, its leaves clipped by the frame at the top, its roots cropped at the bottom. If visible brushmarks are understood as evidence of the hand of the artist – and therefore of the time of the making and the individuality of the maker – then here the artist has taken their lead from the subject matter. The painting is flat and smooth, the paint carefully blended using small, soft brushes. Some might call it timeless; others bland. But not all of it: the handling of the birch trunk is quite different. It juts up and out from the pristine polish of the rest of the painting – a pile-up of impasto and bursting crusts of black and white paint. Unlike Sophia, this is a living thing, a tree trunk whose very form is a product of its living history.

And there's more: this is not a painting on canvas or paper but on birch bark. The little horizontal lines known as lenticels that are so characteristic of birch bark are just visible through the white of the snow and the sky. The scene's apparent purity is not quite as absolute as it first appears. A thought begins to emerge from the etymology of this dulcet word 'lenticel', which comes, via the French *lenticelle*, from the Latin *lens*: a lentil bean. It was only much later, during the medieval period, that it came to be associated with lenses and vision. It is an etymology not of signification but of formal similarity: both lenses and lenticels are, roughly, bean-shaped.

If I were in art criticism mode, I would draw this thought out a little further. I would perhaps make the point that the etymology of 'lens' is an appropriately visual one for this aid to human vision. I might mention that in some cultures the birch is known as the 'watchful tree' on account of these eye-like lenticels. I would try to find out whether the artist wears glasses.

If I were in art criticism mode, I would also note that the work is pointing to its own materiality, that in painting birch on birch in such a self-consciously painterly way the artist is explicitly nodding towards the diverse ways in which birch trees have appeared in Russian art history. In so doing, the work reframes an entire history of Russian landscape art and draws our attention to the complex relationship between materiality and representation, between signifier and signified. I would observe perhaps how the work points to the constructed nature of our relationship with nature, indeed of the very concept of nature. A depiction of birch on birch: the cracked bark here coming to function not only as itself but also as a depiction of itself. Birch *presents* itself bodily at the same time that it *represents* itself as type (species, symbol); birch as subject and object, surface and substrate ...

And then I would cut it all down to fit in a 500-word magazine review.

Alas, I am not in an art gallery. I'm at one of the many souvenir stalls in Novgorod (or Veliky Novgorod, as it's also known), a few hours' train ride south of Saint Petersburg. These kinds of paintings are towards the more expensive end of the souvenir spectrum but that does not make them art – does it? There are dozens of them on display across the various stalls, many almost indistinguishable from one another. I consider trying to ask one of the stall-holders for some more information. But my Russian isn't good enough and, besides, I'm not entirely sure I trust these 'gallerists'. I've already made one purchase and been ever so mildly fleeced. I spotted a knee-high pair of woollen socks woven with pictures of swans and decided to buy them for my wife, Crystal. I ask the price; 450 roubles, the woman tells me, gesticulating with her hands. '*Da*,' I nod in agreement. She takes the socks and disappears around the side of her stall for several moments. She then re-emerges, pointing to a sticker that was definitely not on the socks before; 550 roubles, it reads. A 22 per cent price increase. She shrugs, as if some unknown authority far away had made a decision and there's really nothing she can do about it if that's what the sticker says. I laugh: I know your game, lady. I split the difference, pay her 500, and we both part happy.

Apart from these socks, many of the tourist offerings are made from or decorated with strips of birch bark: combs, chopping boards, cigarette lighters, fridge magnets ... You can buy these kinds of things all over Russia, but in Novgorod they have a particular significance. And it's that significance that has brought me here: the city's famous collection of birch-bark manuscripts.

Up to now, my thinking around the birch has been predominantly symbolic. Yes, I've been looking at real birches planted in the soil, but for the most part this has been an aesthetic engagement: what do they look like? Why have they been planted like this? In order to expand my understanding of the role that the birch has played, and continues to play, in Russia, I need to start thinking about the birch as a material.

What I need to try to understand is, on the one hand, how these material uses might colour in some of the meanings that I have begun to sketch. And, on the other hand, how such uses might actually contradict or overwrite those meanings. Put another way, do the multiple ways in which Russians make use of the birch correspond closely with the significance that they also attach to it? Or does the everyday reality of material usage somehow challenge, or even negate, the abstract ideas such as nation or purity attributed to the birch by so many different people across Russia? How closely does the image of the birch map onto the reality?

The birch is a versatile tree, used by resourceful peoples in myriad forms. Outer bark, inner bark, wood, sap, leaves, branches, roots: all have been used for a wide range of purposes by different cultures in different times and places – right across the northern hemisphere.

During the course of my research, I have been sent a wealth of birch-related links and stories and photographs. Artist Taus Makhacheva, for example, emailed photographs of an aquarium in a Moscow restaurant papered around with imitation birch bark. Garden photographer and translator of Russian Sheila Sim sent me a link to a series of tweets about a full-length Soviet-era portrait of a woman made entirely from collaged pieces of birch bark. Artist Olga Koroleva, with whom I visited Tolstoy's estate at Yasnaya Polyana, emailed photographs of a bird box made from birch wood in a public park in the city of Tula. She sent images of birch-bark souvenirs too: combs and cups and little bowls and boxes. To me, they feel charged with meaning. My favourite image is of a rectangular birch-bark object decorated with floral motifs and the double-headed Russian Imperial eagle. *Rossiya pasport*, it reads, in old-fashioned script: it is a Russian passport holder. This unnecessary object enables the bearer to carry legal confirmation of their Russianness within a clichéd declaration of that Russianness: bureaucracy and over-determined cultural baggage speaking together in perfect harmony. It's just a photograph of a piece of tat – but it speaks to me.

I have also been searching the internet. Among all the familiar souvenirs and dreadful paintings, I stumbled across young Russian designer Anastasiya Koshcheeva, making sleek modern furniture and objects from strips of Siberian birch bark. Koshcheeva is based in Berlin but her company, Moya (meaning 'mine' in Russian), draws heavily on her Russian heritage: 'We source our birch bark from the endless Siberian taiga,' reads the website, 'and let its natural beauty unravel to the fullest with the help of clear shapes, contrasting details, and playful colours.' Anastasiya and I tried and failed to arrange to speak via Skype. I purchased a selection of little birch-bark Christmas decorations instead.

Via online magazine *The Calvert Journal*, I came across a 2013 public performance by Irish artist Gareth Kennedy. The work told the story of Alexandra Nydskova, who refused to move out of her home – the last wooden house in Kupchino, formerly a rural village gradually swallowed up as Saint Petersburg expanded. An eighty-year-old woman, she sat in the house for five years, as the water and electricity were cut off and all her furniture taken away. On 6 March 1976 she was dragged out by the authorities and her home destroyed. Kennedy's participatory performance brought together family members of Alexandra Nydskova and many local people, clad in birch-bark masks. They paraded through the city streets, erected a house-shaped frame of birch logs, drank birch juice, and retold the story of Alexandra Nydskova's brave and heart-breaking protest.

And then I discovered an egg. It is said to be the very last egg completed by that magic name in the history of Russian jewellery – Peter Carl Fabergé. This particular egg, made from Karelian birch, was one of two Easter eggs that Fabergé designed in 1917 for the last Tsar, Nicholas II. The other, made from blue glass and known as *Constellation*, was never completed. Both eggs were commissioned by the Tsar for his wife, Empress Maria Feodorovna. Following the October revolution and Nicholas's execution, the egg was acquired by the Rumyantsevsky Museum (later the Lenin Library, now the Russian State Library) in Moscow. During the 1920s, the cash-strapped Soviet government sought to raise money by selling off the Romanov collections to foreign buyers. In January 1927, the Rumyantsevsky Museum was closed and some 450 items from the collection – including, it is thought, the Karelian birch egg – left the country. There was no further trace of it for the rest of the twentieth century.

It was not until 2001, a decade after the end of communism, that the egg reappeared at a London auction house when it was sold – apparently by the descendant of Russian émigrés – to businessman and collector Alexander Ivanov. The exact price that Ivanov paid is unknown but it is thought to have been several million dollars. If online images are anything to go by, the egg is a handsome thing: curved panels of swirling, burr-patterned Karelian birch set into a frame of gold. In comparison with some of the more outlandish Fabergé designs, dripping with precious jewels, the birch egg is comparatively restrained: a luxury product of war-time austerity. The egg is now in the Fabergé Museum, owned by Ivanov, in Baden-Baden, Germany.

I discovered something else too, which brought an old and trivial memory suddenly back to life. Once upon a time, upstairs in a gentlemen's outfitter on Jermyn Street in Mayfair, I picked up a pair of leather shoes. It was clear straight away that there was something special about them: not just the calibre of the workmanship but a quality of the leather. It was not simply the colour: dark and chocolatey at heel and toe cap, fading russet in the light. It was not the pattern of the grain, although that too was beautiful. Was it some glow emanating from within? Or an aura, pulsating around the outside?

It was only recently that I discovered what made those shoes so special. The leather out of which they had been made was over two hundred years old and had the most extraordinary backstory. In 1973, the wreck of a two-masted sailing ship was found, quite by accident, at the bottom of the sea in Plymouth Sound. The ship, the *Metta Catharina*, had set sail from Saint Petersburg in 1786 but ran aground on Drake's Island. Its cargo – reams of carefully rolled leather – was found to be in surprisingly good condition. You can still buy shoes and luggage and other accessories made out of this leather today. In contrast to the cheap touristy passport holder photographed by Olga Koroleva, a passport holder made from this 1786 Russian leather costs £495 from George Cleverley in Mayfair's Royal Arcade.

What I had not known was the ingredient that made Russian leather so highly valued. That ingredient was birch oil. Used as part of the tanning process in Russia, birch oil helps to keep the leather supple, it lends it a rich hue (and smell), and it helps preserve it too. So strongly associated with Russia was leather treated with birch oil, its appearance and above all its distinctive fragrance, that when fashion designer Coco Chanel released a perfume containing birch tar in 1924, she named it – what else? – *Cuir de Russie*.

It was while reading Anna Lewington's book *Birch* that I discovered this information about the birch oil used in Russian leather and the Chanel perfume. The book is full of many such fascinating nuggets, from Russia and all over the world, stretching right back to earliest human history. Lewington, an

ethnobotanist, begins with a 'lump of birch-tar': 'thought to
have been formed by our Neanderthal ancestors over 250,000
years ago' and used to glue an axe head to a handle. According
to Lewington, this lump of birch-tar, or others like it, 'may be
the first synthetic product ever made'.

As I seek to expand my understanding of the meanings and
uses of the birch in Russia, Lewington's book proves invaluable. It is through Lewington that I learn of many other uses
to which birch has been put. Birch tar, for example, has been
used to protect wooden houses, fences, boats, cart wheel axles
and livestock enclosures; it has been applied to horses' hooves
to protect them against disease; it has been diluted with water
and sprayed on plants and fruit trees. The Yakut people of
Siberia have used heated strips of birch bark to make bandages. During World War II and inside the Soviet gulag such
uses returned.

But the birch is not only a product; it is also a powerful agent
of change. Each tree creates a network of roots that take up
minerals from deeper in the soil than plants such as heather.
Lewington writes:

> These minerals are effectively recycled as they are released
> back to the surface when leaves shed by the tree, which are
> slightly alkaline, rot down. The white-barked birches are
> known to improve the soil in this way, increasing its fertility,
> especially on acid heath land or in areas of former conifer
> forest, preparing it for other species which, given the oppor-
> tunity, may replace them.

Birches 'improve' the soil, 'preparing' it for other species and,
Lewington continues, they 'work' in symbiotic relationships
with particular kinds of fungi. These active verbs show quite
clearly that birches, like humans, are living beings with agency.

As artist Fiona MacDonald has written, 'The ants, soil, deer and trees in the forest coproduce the forest. Indeed, in living systems, the difference between a place and its inhabitants is one of focus, rather than of kind.' But while all living beings (and non-living beings too) contribute actively to the places they inhabit, not all plants are like birches in enabling others to thrive. *Rhododendron x superponticum*, for example, now so common across the UK, blocks out light and prevents anything from growing under it. All trees change the world; birches, it could be said, do so for the better.

The 'birthplace of Russia' is how Novgorod likes to describe itself, in texts aimed squarely at tourists. 'Over here people used to wear leather boots instead of bast shoes,' proclaims the website of Visit Novgorod. Bast shoes – or *lapty* – were the distinctive footwear worn by peasants in Russia, Eastern Europe and Scandinavia from the medieval period right up until the decline of feudalism. Made from woven strips of birch or linden fibre, the shoes take the form of a kind of basket. Easy to make, they required regular maintenance. A 'birch-bark mile' is the distance one could walk in a pair of *lapty* before they needed repair: apparently around ten miles.

But the Visit Novgorod website is proud of the city inhabitants' distinctive, and more apparently advanced, choice of leather footwear to protect against the wet ground, as opposed to the flimsier *lapty*. This is just one sign of Novgorod's culture during the medieval period. The website further emphasises the city's characteristic built environment and the literacy of its inhabitants: 'the streets were cobbled from ancient times,' it says with pride, 'the commoners were in correspondence with each other, and all the rulers were welcomed and banished whenever the Novgorodians wanted.'

Novgorod, we're encouraged to believe, was a bastion of literacy, democratic good governance and sturdy footwear, long before the rest of Russia, even the rest of the world. This summary of the city's history is not exactly untrue, but, as with many tourist-focused descriptions, it is not entirely accurate either. It all sounds so simple, but then you start to ask what is really meant by words like 'birthplace' or 'birth' or even 'Russia'.

These are not merely idle or academic questions. When it comes to the origins of Russia, the stakes are high and nuance in short supply. But then that is true of many questions of identity: the fewer clear facts available, the more entrenched become opposing interpretations.

Long before Russia came the people known as the Rus'. From the 750s onwards the Rus' increasingly came to occupy areas of land along the Dnieper River that flows from the Valdai Hills near the city of Smolensk in Russia, through Belarus and Ukraine and down to the Black Sea. But who were the Rus'? And where had they come from? And will answering the second question help us to answer the first?

Before I get to those questions, it is worth saying that even to frame this early history as 'Russian history' is to suggest that people and events from over a thousand years ago are in some way properly Russian, rather than, say, properly Ukrainian, or properly neither. If the Rus' really formed around Kyiv, which is now part of Ukraine, then should this not be Ukrainian history? In *Russian Nationalism from an Interdisciplinary Perspective*, Daniel Rancour-Laferriere notes that it was only in the seventeenth century that Russians tried to reclaim the history of Kyivan Rus' as Russian history. 'Kievan Rus' and later Muscovy were not nations in any meaningful sense of the word,' he writes, and the purpose of such retrospective reclamations was arguably to present the contingencies of history as the inexorability of destiny: 'to deny legitimacy to any potential heirs besides Russia'.

One important debate centres on what has become known as the Normanist controversy. The controversy is a question of origins. The Normanists argue that the Rus' were to a large degree Scandinavians (Norman here is derived from North men or Norse men). From the eighth to the eleventh centuries, Scandinavian peoples travelled the rivers from the Baltic to the Black Sea, trading goods, raiding local settlements and gradually settling along the route. It is argued by the Normanists that these settlers are the Rus', or that in time they became the Rus'. This theory began to gain prominence in the eighteenth century and is now more or less the established consensus – among Western historians at least.

The anti-Normanists, whose early proponents were also in the eighteenth century, believe that the origins of the Rus' are properly Slavic rather than Scandinavian. They cite the migrations of the Slavs from Hungary and Eastern Europe between the fifth and seventh centuries. Some went north; some went south to the Balkans; and some east to Russia, Ukraine and Belarus. This position had broadly fallen from favour by the dawn of the twentieth century, but then returned with a vengeance, especially around World War II. A prominent figure here is Boris Rybakov, who published papers on the economic superiority of medieval Rus' over Western Europe and later argued that the Rus' were descended from the Scythians, nomadic peoples who were especially powerful across Eastern Europe and Asia from the seventh century BC to the third century AD.

I don't wish to scald my fingers upon such heated debates except to note two things. The first is that in both theories there is a process of change from one thing to another, a becoming-Rus' of people who were previously something else – either Slavic or Scandinavian. To me, this suggests that to ask where a people came from is a question that, in fact, can never be answered; it is always to shift the origin elsewhere.

The second is the extreme ideologies that have repeatedly co-opted such apparently niche debates. History matters not only for the truths it tells but for the ends to which those truths are put. And at various times both of these conflicting theories – Normanism and anti-Normanism – have been embraced by the far-right. The Nazis, for example, argued that Russians were an inferior race who could only be civilised by a Germanic ruling elite. In response, it is hardly surprising that Stalinist historians such as Rybakov sought to mobilise alternative narratives. Conversely, Russian historians who lump all Slavic groups together often end up by arguing, implicitly at least, that Russia ought to rule them all. This, as I shall soon discover in more detail, is conveniently in line with certain tendencies in Russian foreign policy today. It is no coincidence therefore that under Putin anti-Normanism has returned once more.

'Caution is never a vice when dealing with the early history of Rus'', write historians Simon Franklin and Jonathan Shepard in their admirably patient and level-headed history, *The Emergence of Rus 750–1200*. The book is dry and slow. But as I sit in the domed reading room of Edinburgh Central Library, I take unexpected pleasure in the way that these two wry historians carefully tip-toe their way through fragments of evidence, disputed sources and over-excitable, ideologically motivated interpretations. And, after just a dozen pages or so, I find exactly what I'm looking for.

The story begins, appropriately enough, in the woods: in a forest referred to in the Primary Chronicle as the Okovskii forest. The Primary Chronicle is the key text for historians of the early Rus' – a history compiled by monks in Kyiv in the early twelfth century. The narrative may be more concerned with Christian genealogies than with historical accuracy, but it is one of the few sources available. And a forest is certainly a likely starting point: the entire region would have been wooded, except for the banks of rivers and those hard-won tracts of land, claimed from the trees for humans.

This was long before any idea of Russia, of the motherland, even of a fixed place to call 'home'. '"Home",' write Franklin and Shepard, 'was itself a movable and uncertain affair for the inhabitants of the river valleys and the depths of the forests alike – part hunter-gatherers, part fishermen and part agriculturalists.' During this and later periods, these lands were also occupied by a diverse range of other peoples. Much of the countryside was populated by Finno-Ugric peoples. There were the nomadic Khazars in the steppes north of Darban and the lower Volga from about the 730s; Muslim Bulgars around the Volga River from the ninth and tenth centuries; Vikings (or Varangians), Chuds, Slavs, Oghuz Turks, Pechenegs and more.

It was not until much, much later that we could start to speak of Russia or Ukraine or Belarus. It is in the mid-ninth century that the first written evidence appears of a people called the Rus': *Rūs* was used in Arabic, *Rhōs* in Greek and Latin. In Finnish *Ruotsi* means 'Swedes'; in Estonian it is *Root'si*. These words are often cited as evidence that the Rus' were indeed of Scandinavian origin, but this is not conclusive. Certainly, the Rus' were beginning to be considered as a people worth naming, even if that name was not always used to refer to the same people.

For Normanist historians, a very early settlement called Staraia Ladoga is of significant interest. There, on the Volkhov River, near Lake Ladoga, eighty miles east of present-day Saint Petersburg, was a small trading post. Glass, ivory, silver and amber have all been found there, as well as significant quantities of silver dirhams – evidence of exchange between Persia and Scandinavia.

For me, this is a potential lead, because it is thought that at least some of those who lived in Staraia Ladoga came from a place near Stockholm called Birka. Often considered to be Sweden's oldest town, Birka is thought to have been founded around AD 750 on the island of Björkö. It flourished for more than two hundred years, with a population during the Viking era of between five hundred and a thousand people. Today it is a Unesco World Heritage Site. Archaeologists have discovered rock crystal and cornelian beads there very similar in form to those at Staraia Ladoga and further south in Dagestan on the Caspian Sea. Together, these findings suggest at the very least that these places were linked through a network of trade or exchange. The place name 'Birka' (and this is the reason I'm so interested) stems from the Swedish *björk* and the Old Norse *bjǫrk*. Yes, 'Birka' means birch.

Perhaps, oh so tantalisingly, perhaps, Birka is my first birch tree. It's not *the* first birch: birches pre-date humanity by millions of years. But it may be *my* first birch. In my mind stands one solitary tree, grey-white and leafless in early winter, slender on a flat grey land surrounded by a flat grey sea. The mist rises and gusts. And the camera pulls slowly away.

Enough. It is time to set aside this speculation and focus on what I can see with my own eyes, touch with my own hands. Physical reality is more reliable – surely? – than the abstractions of long-lost origin stories. It is time to take a look at the famous birch-bark manuscripts of Novgorod. That is why I am here in this beautiful old city.

'Manuscripts' is perhaps the wrong word. Known in Russian as *beresty* (birch bark) or *beresty gramoty* (birch-bark

letters), these are not lavishly produced documents intended
to convey the wonders of God or the unquestionable authority
of an earthly ruler. They were not painstakingly copied out by
trained scribes or exquisitely illuminated by dedicated monks.
There is – bar one or two notable exceptions to which I shall
return – no ornamentation. In some ways, they don't signify
anything at all, and that is why they are so fascinating and so
significant.

I've arranged to meet one of the team at the Novgorod State
Museum, a long yellow building with a pair of large bronze
lions guarding the entrance. Dmitry and I shake hands in the
foyer and begin the tour. In jeans and a hoodie, Dmitry moves
fast, speaks in rapidly unfurled reams of information. No time
for idle chatter. It's not that he's in a hurry to be rid of me; he
just has so much knowledge and feels a sense of urgency in
conveying it to this ignorant visitor. I must learn what Dmitry
knows, and fast.

We begin at the beginning. Novgorod, Dmitry tells me, has
been inhabited for over six thousand years – since the last Stone
Age. Around 1000 BC there was a gradual shift from a nomadic
way of life towards agriculture. Farmers began to gather in the
plains where the soil was more fertile. But Dmitry's history is
a little different to the version that I'd read: it is the arrival of
Eastern Slavic settlers that he chooses to draw my attention to.
Dmitry conspicuously makes no mention of Scandinavians.
Anti-Normanism really is back.

The museum is a wealth of objects and stories. But I have
eyes only for *beresty*. It was long suspected that the earth below
the city might hide a wealth of stories, but it was not until the
1930s that archaeological research commenced in earnest.
Then came Hitler and the war. After the Allied victory and
the expulsion of the German army, excavations resumed.
On 26 July 1951, the first *beresta* was discovered, rolled up,

says Dmitri, 'like a cucumber'. These *beresty* have been found in a number of places in Russia, Ukraine and Belarus, but Novgorod has by far the most: some 95 per cent of all those found in Russia have been found here. At the last count, that's no fewer than 1,113 letters, including one discovered just a couple of weeks before my visit.

The *beresty* are medieval notes: most dating from before the fifteenth century, some as far back as the ninth. Spanning a range of languages, they reflect the diversity of the population: Old Slavic, Old Russian, German, Latin, Finnish, Karelian (a language that Dmitry describes as akin to Finnish but in Cyrillic script). Each scrap of bark bears a message: they would have been passed from one person to another and then instantly discarded. In Novgorod, children were often employed to run messages. Aristocrats used riders to take letters from their country properties to town and back again. One of the notes is a spell to protect against 'God's arrow' – thunder perhaps, or lightning. Many of them are about money. One is a note from a merchant about the price he received for four beavers (ten *hyrvnia*); another notes the high price of salt; another is about a bucket of fish. A particular favourite is a reminder of an unpaid debt: four and a half *hyrvnia* for a wooden cross some time in the eleventh century – unpaid for nine years. One thousand years of freelance life and I fear that very little has changed.

But what I really love about these *beresty* is the materiality. Each is made from the easily peeled outer bark of the birch trees that grow so commonly here. There is something exhilarating about getting right up close to them, tracing the movements of a medieval hand as it scratched a stylus made of bone or metal into the soft bark. Mostly these *beresty* are small rectangles a few inches long. They look not dissimilar to paper, a little thicker perhaps, a little more textured. Like scraps of bandage or fragments of skin, they vary in colour from bone white to ash grey, soft yellows and rich, earthy browns. As I look at them up close, I notice the black horizontal lines of the lenticels like traces of some far older language just visible within the fabric of the substrate. The human messages are interesting for historians, but it is the birch itself I am trying to read.

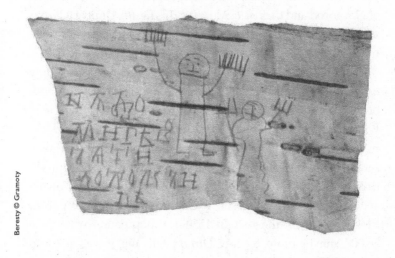

Beresty © Gramoty

History is rarely fun, but among the most famous of the *beresty* are those produced by a boy called Onfim who lived in Novgorod in the thirteenth century. It's hard not to be charmed by them. Seventeen documents thought to be by Onfim have been found. Most are writing exercises: letters, repeated syllables, or psalms. But Onfim's attention quickly wandered and most of these documents are emblazoned with a range of imaginative doodles – battle scenes, animals and mythical monsters. Onfim's figures have multi-pronged, rake-like hands. There is something winningly manic about them. 'I am wild beast,' proclaims a drawing of a four-legged dragon.

The *beresty* in general, and Onfim's writing exercises in particular, point to a highly literate medieval society. The preponderance of examples relating to money is to be expected from a settlement based on trade – at the hub of a network of exchange between Scandinavia and Byzantium. Dmitry tells me that approximately 90 per cent of the medieval population could read and write: not just the privileged aristocracy but 'even children, women, craftsmen, sometimes peasants'. With the decline of Novgorod and the rise of Moscow, this figure, Dmitry tells me, went down dramatically. It was only with the arrival of the communists several centuries later that literacy rates rose once more.

The quantity of *beresty* found in Novgorod is not simply a result of medieval literacy levels; it is also a reflection both of the region's climatic conditions and of historical accident. Poor drainage means wet soil while high clay content and low oxygen levels mean that deposited materials – bone, timber, scraps of birch bark – are very slow to decompose. Novgorod's decline is also an important factor. Towards the end of the sixteenth century, Novgorod was fading as a political power. Moscow was on the rise. In 1550, the population was up to 30,000, maybe more; by 1617, Dmitry tells me, it was down to just 500. This decline meant that there was very little need for new building works and therefore nothing to disturb the manuscripts buried in the earth. Those rolled-up Novgorod cucumbers were pickled perfectly.

After Dmitry and I have said our farewells, I walk upstairs to spend some time with Novgorod's famous icons. I watch a while as a young art student painstakingly copies the saintly image before him. I walk through room after room of icon painting, doing my cultural duty, thinking not of Novgorod's great past but, in all honesty, of lunch.

There is also a temporary exhibition about World War II. It focuses on the damage wrought to the local area by the German army. As in the UK, amid rising nationalism under a decade of Conservative government, the war is constantly evoked as an example of a heroic past when the nation stood against the forces of evil. A generation born after the war so often speak as if they lived through it.

I walk quickly around the exhibition, not intending to spend long, when something white catches my eye: a propaganda poster from 1943 by artists Viktor Ivanov and Olga Burova. The poster – a copy of which, incidentally, is in the Tate collection – shows a blonde woman dressed in red, imprisoned behind a barbed-wire fence. It is the fence posts that have caught my eye for they are made from bright white birch. In the background a Nazi soldier is executing innocents. As is customary in Soviet imagery, the woman gazes ahead into the distance. Fear is written across her face, perhaps with a trace of defiance. The caption in Russian reads: 'All hope is on you, red warrior!'

Here the birch tree symbolises all that must be protected, all that is Russian and worth fighting for – family, land, love. But it has been commandeered by the occupying Germans to form a prison. The white bark in the foreground is encircled by sharp ribbons of spiked wire. The contrast could not be more pronounced between the birch as a symbol of Russian purity and innocence, and its co-option in the service of war by an invading force. 'Look what they've done to our birch tree,' the poster seems to say. 'Look what they've done to Russia.' The birch here is drenched in meaning and its use as a mere material is tantamount to sacrilege.

And yet, what the *beresty* of Novgorod have shown me is that, long before it became a propaganda symbol, long before it was used to urge Russians to fight – and die – for Russia, the birch was already being used as a material. The question therefore is not simply of lofty symbolism against vulgar material usage, but of who is making use of the birch, how, and for what ends.

For symbolism too is a kind of use – especially in the service of political propaganda. Just downstairs are those *beresty*: vastly significant in our understanding of Russian history, but in that context the birch itself hardly means a thing. It is just a material. 'The medium is the message,' wrote theorist Marshall McLuhan in his hugely influential 1964 book *Understanding Media*. But not in medieval Novgorod.

Outside the museum, I wander around the city, admiring the churches: bright and white, just like the depiction on birch bark that I looked at when I arrived here, or pink unrendered stone. I try to cast my mind back, to imagine what it would have been like when these churches were constructed – here in Novgorod and elsewhere across the region. Christianity arrived here in fits and starts, and was variously embraced, imposed and disseminated. As it spread, it sometimes replaced, sometimes merged with existing pagan and folk beliefs. When it comes to trying to analyse the role of the birch tree in all this, it is very difficult, several hundred years later, to disentangle the Christian from the pagan and the authentically medieval from later interpretations and misinterpretations.

During the medieval period, the spread of a single religion – and the customs, culture and construction that accompanied it – was a significant factor in the gradual cohering of people towards a sense of identity and nation. But it took a long time and was not always welcomed. Despite the image of Christian piety retrospectively applied during the nineteenth century, the Rus' were actually comparatively late adopters of monotheistic religion. Mieszko I became the first Christian ruler of Poland when he was baptised in 966. The fabulously named Harald Bluetooth, king of Denmark and Norway, converted around the same time; and Géza, Grand Prince of the Hungarians, was baptised a little later, in the mid-970s.

As each of these rulers converted to Christianity, however, Vladimir the Great remained undecided. It is suggested in the Primary Chronicle that Vladimir sounded out or invited pitches from Islam and Judaism as well as Christianity. But he eventually settled on Greek Christianity, possibly in order to marry Anna Porphyrogenita, daughter of Byzantine Emperor Romanos II, and so link his own authority with that of a more powerful ruler.

Once converted, Vladimir took to Christianity – or at least its external manifestations – with gusto, and he embarked upon a major programme of church-building. At the same time, he also built earthworks and palisades and initiated a process of populating the hinterland around Kyiv. In deeds that prefigure those of the Tsars and Stalin centuries later, Vladimir oversaw, in the words of Franklin and Shepard, the 'compulsory transplant of inhabitants of the northern forests to the region south of Kiev'. These recently transplanted peoples, the historians suggest, would have been 'highly susceptible to the prince's will and the ministrations of his priests' and therefore 'may have gained in security and a sense of identity as Christian folk'. Uproot the people and you can sell them anything: from feudalism to communism and capitalism, it's an age-old story of power. The internet is perhaps just the latest example.

In the legends of the Rus', the story of one prince stands out: Prince Igor of Kyiv. It is not his life that draws my attention but his grisly death in 945. Igor was killed while attempting to collect tribute from the Drevlians, a group of East Slavs. According to an eyewitness account from a Byzantine chronicler known as Leo the Deacon, Igor's death was gruesome: the Drevlians bent two birch trees low to the ground and tied one to each of his legs. When they let go, the flexible trunks of the birches straightened quickly and ripped Igor's body apart.

Igor's unpleasant death is not the only association between the birch and violence. In ancient Rome, one symbol of the power of the magistrate was a bundle of twigs – usually birch twigs – known as *fasces*. This symbol and the word that denoted it were later adopted by Benito Mussolini's National Fascist Party.

Rods made from birch have long been used to administer corporal punishment – usually to the bare buttocks of the victim. It was a punishment both painful and humiliating. In a little museum in the town of Fort William, Scotland, I came across an old wooden table that was used especially for 'birching'. The explanatory text reassures visitors that this violent punishment involved medical and judicial authorities and was therefore somehow acceptable:

> Birching was a punishment handed down by the courts and a doctor had to be present and other officials to see it was delivered correctly. The convicted person was placed face down on the table with his arms through the holes and his wrists tied underneath. The body and legs were strapped so movement was limited.

The last birching in Fort William was carried out, the text tells us, in 1948: 'It was delivered by a young constable to a boy convicted of shop breaking.' But that was not the last birching in the UK: when Westminster abolished corporal punishment in 1948, the Isle of Man did not. Authorities on the island continued to wield the birch rod until 1971 and the so-called birching laws were only finally repealed in 1993.

Russia has also witnessed extensive use of the birch as an instrument of oppressive violence. In his 1911 book, *Solitaria*, controversial writer and philosopher Vasily Rozanov (a rabid antisemite) wrote the following:

> From the foundation of the world there have been two philosophies: the philosophy of the man who for some reason longs to give someone a flogging; and the philosophy of the flogged man. All our Russian philosophy is that of the flogged man.

This note on the 'philosophy of the flogged man' was quoted by twentieth-century British sex writer George Ryley Scott by way of introduction to his 1918 book, *The History of Corporal Punishment*. Throughout the book, Scott makes more than one hundred and fifty references to the birch rod. But it is the Russian knout, like the English cat-o-nine-tails, that draws particular fear and fascination from Scott: 'In no country in the world,' he writes, 'was whipping so widely practised, so savagely and so vindictively inflicted, as in the Russia of the Czars.'

Less fearsome but more widely used than the knout was the birch rod: employed in the Tsarist labour camps and by landlords and their agents to exert control over peasants during the feudal era. This practice continued well after the emancipation of the serfs by Tsar Alexander II in 1861. In fact, it may well have expanded. A birch beating was used as punishment for disobedience, drunkenness, theft, fighting, non-payment of taxes (even if the cause was beyond the victim's control, such as a bad harvest), moving to another settlement without permission, damage to another's property and many other petty infractions against the feudal order.

While the killing of Prince Igor was conceived as an elaborate spectacle, birching by contrast was administered swiftly. It would rarely cause lasting physical damage and therefore would not prevent the peasant from the productive labour required by the authorities administering the punishment. A violence imposed upon the body, rather than a sanction of time or private property, birching was an ideal means by which a system of vast inequalities could inflict punishment upon those who had nothing to lose: no money, no property, no rights. For Russia's peasants, therefore, the birch rod would have been immediately associated with pain, humiliation and a rigidly unchanging social hierarchy. Historian of Russia Stephen P. Frank has described the birch rod as 'the most shameful symbol of serfdom'. I must try not to forget this: for all the subsequent layers of meaning that accrue around the birch, the fear of humiliation will perhaps never quite be erased.

In the medieval period, the visibility of the birch is not in the self-conscious assertions of power by the newly Christianised elites, but in the folk tales and customs of the rural peasantry. But these customs can be difficult to access and understand, especially for an outsider like me. They are often described in generic terms, without reference to politics, economics or history, as if rural peasant customs exist in some fixed, unchanging state outside of history or prior to its arrival in the form of Christianity or modernity or electricity or something. Descriptions rarely refer to dates, while – until the appearance of tractor- and pylon-filled Soviet propaganda landscapes – photographs and paintings tend to depict peasants wearing 'traditional' dress in fields or forests with no visible temporal markers. It is as if nothing has ever changed in the countryside.

In *Heart-Pine Russia* (2013), art historian Jane T. Costlow sketches a geography of belief:

The boundary between the forest and village is one of the fundamental organizing categories in Russian traditional culture. The village is presided over by the spirits of human ancestors and their benign representative, the *domovoi* or house spirit; the forest domain is ruled by the *leshii* – a trickster figure who leads astray those who enter his world without taking appropriate precautions.

As a tree able to grow on disturbed ground, along paths or by the edges of deeper forests, the birch breaches this distinction between forest and village. Both *domovoi* and *leshii* have in various cultures had associations with birches. One Russian website suggests that when moving house you should take your *domovoi* with you, carried in a birch-bark shoe. Another website mentions a practice of writing notes to the *leshii* on pieces of birch bark and then nailing them to the trunk of a living tree. I also found instructions for how to summon a *leshi*: cut down several young birch trees and place them together in a circle. Remove your cross (assuming, as a devout Christian peasant, you are wearing one), stand inside the circle, and call out in a loud voice, '*Dedushka!*' (grandfather). The *leshi* will appear immediately.

Costlow explores a series of narrative sketches published in the *Russian Herald* in December 1871 by the 'now forgotten' N. Boev. She quotes Boev's descriptions of 'impassable forests' in which 'birch and pine slumber peacefully'. This is not an empty landscape but one populated with 'villages and farmyards' and 'the golden domes of Russian monasteries'. What interests me here is that right at the origin of Christianity, or the transition to Christianity, Boev places a birch. Here is Costlow's summary and interpretation:

> Christianization is for Boev bloodless, a matter of persuasion and peaceful surrender rather than violence: when monks come into the northern woods in the late fourteenth century they find a 'peaceful, half-wild population' ... This half-wild

population worships a great birch tree, but when the missionary cuts it down he does not attempt to defend himself from the 'enraged heathen' – and they are immediately and miraculously won over by his act of nonviolent submission. Five centuries later the monastery he founded is a refuge in this 'wild forest place' – 'closely surrounded by its ancient protectors from wind and storm – old birches and pines.' The trees that once were worshipped have become the protectors of this holy place – and, one suspects, are still part of the aura of sanctity that extends beyond the monastery walls out into the surrounding woodland. What is more holy here, the trees or the monastery walls? Boev's rhetoric doesn't force us to make a choice.

What this account says to me is how powerfully the birch signified in both pre-Christian and Christian discourses. In Boev's text and Costlow's analysis, its felling marks a moment of rupture, but its continued presence offers the reassurance of a consensual transition.

In many Slavic cultures, the birch has been especially prominent during *Semik*, or Green Week. Usually taking place in early June, this festival period serves a number of functions including, on the one hand, honouring the dead and, on the other, celebrating fertility and the harvest to come. During these festivities, the birch has played a number of different roles, although there is still some debate over their exact nature. Pioneering Soviet folklorist Vladimir Propp, famous for his 1928 book *Morphology of the Folktale*, understood *Semik* as a series of fertility rites geared towards securing a successful harvest. But Elizabeth A. Warner, author of *Russian Myths* (2002), has suggested that, in fact, many of the rituals enacted during *Semik* aimed to prevent water supplies and the soil from being polluted by the 'unclean dead'.

Either way, the birch played various significant roles. Some birch trees were believed to house the souls of the dead and so they were richly decorated. Other birches were lavished with gifts of beer or eggs by young girls wearing garlands of flowers and greenery. Villagers would also bring freshly cut birch branches into their homes as tokens of growth and life.

But shadows lurk beneath *Semik*. These shadows are the *rusalki*: female water sprites, often depicted like mermaids, and usually associated with death and the unclean. The *rusalki* were believed to be especially troublesome during Green Week, when they would emerge from the waters to swing from the low-hanging branches of birch or willow trees. One common solution was to designate a particular birch as the *rusalka* birch and then submerge it underwater at the end of the week. Many of the festivities that sound so joyous – the eggs, the beer, the beautiful garlands – may in fact have been performed in order to appease the *rusalki*.

An associated Slavic custom is known as *kumlenie*. *Kumlenie* demonstrates the ways in which multiple layers of belief – Christian and pre-Christian – could conflict, co-exist, or merge together. Like the birch-bark manuscripts of Novgorod, where lenticels are visible through the handwritten script, the overwriting of new beliefs and practices does not necessarily obscure the old. Enacted at Pentecost, *kumlenie* was, and sometimes still is, performed mostly by young unmarried women, but also sometimes between men and women or only between men. Again birch branches are of significance: they are made into wreaths, through which participants, in pairs or groups, kiss each other and exchange gifts such as crosses or rings, scarves or clothes, beads, eggs or cakes. *Kumlenie* is also accompanied by an oath: the girls kiss a cross that hangs in the wreath and this forms an important bond with the person they've kissed. These bonds are related to the Slavic custom of *pobratimstvo*, usually glossed as a kind of ritual brotherhood. The assembled groups then hold hands and perform a circular sun dance, known as a *horovod*, often around a birch tree. This ritual usually ends with feasting. A week or so later, the bonds formed during *kumlenie* are undone via a ceremony called *raskumlivanie*, during which the opposite actions are performed: girls step back across the wreaths, return the gifts they've been given, and sing songs to indicate the end of the ties between them.

The Sunday after Pentecost is Trinity Sunday. For Russian Old Believers (people who defied a series of liturgical reforms made by the Russian Orthodox Church in the mid-sixteenth century) the birch played an important role on this Christian holy day. 'Women cut birch fronds to decorate a chapel,' writes Costlow, citing Pavel Melnikov's 1870s novel *In the Forests* (published under the pseudonym Andrey Pechersky), '*not*, one of them insists, aspen or mountain ash, which are too "bitter, not sanctified"'.

The origins of Russian birch tree symbolism are often traced not only to folk traditions but also to fairy tales. I started to read these tales expecting to encounter birches turning into beautiful maidens and back again, to find birches represented as ethereal, sacred, fragile and feminine. But as in many cultures, Russia's folk and magic tales are complex and resistant to reductive interpretation. As I read through many of these tales, I found the significance of the birch tree surprisingly hard to comprehend. Sometimes it is simply there – one feature in the fairy-tale landscape among others. In one of the many tales of the witch Baba Yaga, for example, a young maiden appeases an angry birch tree by tying a little ribbon around its trunk. Another Baba Yaga story sees the old witch displaying her power by grabbing and snapping a young birch. In 'The Fool and the Birch Tree', the youngest of three brothers finds a stash of gold inside the trunk of a birch he has just felled. In 'When the Crayfish Whistled', a later tale written by Nadezhda Alexandrovna Lokhvitskaya (aka Teffi), who became disillusioned with the Bolsheviks and emigrated to Paris, a little boy receives as a Christmas present a rocking horse with a birch-bark tail.

In the fairy tale 'The Brother', three daughters take it in turns to go looking for their lost little brother. Each is given advice by, first, a birch tree, then an apple tree, then a stove. Only the youngest daughter takes their advice, including picking leaves from the birch tree at its behest, and eventually she locates her little brother and is given shelter by the birch who conceals her from a vengeful grey eagle. As so often in Russian folk tales, the moral seems to be: if you're given advice, no matter who (or what) it comes from, take it. The birch tree may be able to speak, give advice, and even lie to the grey eagle, but this is merely the enchanted world of the magic tale. The birch itself, like the apple tree and the stove, seems not to carry any particular weight of symbolism; it is simply a sight of immediate familiarity to the audience of the tale. In Russian landscapes, both real and fanciful, the birch is simply always there.

Some examples are more, as it were, clear-cut. One is 'The Wonderful Birch', collected and first published by Scottish poet Andrew Lang in 1890. Lang was rarely especially clear about his sources, and this particular tale is listed only as 'Russo-Karelian'. In the tale, which has several parallels with 'Cinderella', a loyal peasant daughter plants the bones of her mother (slaughtered through the trickery of a witch) by the edge of a field. The bones grow into a birch tree. The birch speaks to the daughter as she weeps, helps her overcome a series of impossible tasks set by the witch, and gives her fine clothes to wear to the king's feast, where she and the king's son meet and fall in love, before the daughter flees home. When the king's son eventually tracks down and marries the girl, the birch bestows great riches upon the happy couple. Here, as in the *rusalki* traditions, the birch is home to the soul of the deceased. But instead of causing trouble, this birch rewards the loyalty of her daughter.

Over time I do find some examples of birches associated with femininity in ways that I had expected. In 'The Little White Duck' the story ends as the hero, a prince, calls to the titular white duck, actually his princess, transformed into a duck at the beginning of the story. 'Be a silver birch behind me!' he cries. 'Be a fair maiden before me!' And lo, it came to pass: 'A silver birch sprang up behind him and a fair maiden appeared before him.' Here is the kind of equation I had expected – between the beautiful, loyal young woman and the silver birch. But it is not as common as I had been led to believe.

As Lang's example suggests, none of these magic tales come to us freshly excavated from the rich black soil of history, but through the lenses of numerous overlapping, occasionally contradictory, literary, aesthetic, political and ideological imperatives. It was during the nineteenth century that Russia's artistic and intellectual elites became enchanted with these folk traditions because of what they seemed to say about Russian history and identity. And it is the way they were presented and interpreted during this period that shaped subsequent ideas about the birch tree in Russian culture: both in the Soviet Union and today in the Putin era. These stories have been heard and collected and adapted and rewritten; they have been edited and published; some have been censored; some translated; some invented entirely anew. As with so many genres in the history of Russian literature, a beginning of sorts might be traced to Pushkin. He became enthralled listening to traditional Russian folk tales while in exile in Mikhailovskoye, northern Russia, in the 1820s and proceeded to reproduce these tales in a written form that most agree remained faithful to the language of his oral sources. But it was later in the nineteenth century that fascination with folk culture really began to blossom. And to understand this, I'm going to have to return to Moscow.

V.

PAINTING RUSSIA

Over the lake, over the forest backwater –
Elegant green birch . . .
'Oh girls! How cold it is in spring:
I'm all trembling from the wind and frost!'

Ivan Bunin, 'Northern Birch', 1903 or 1906

I'm standing in Moscow's Tretyakov Gallery in front of one of the most famous paintings in Russian art history. Pavel Tretyakov was a businessman and banker who, as an art collector, became an influential figure in the development of Russian art – and landscape painting in particular – during the second half of the nineteenth century. By buying so many works he helped to support an expanding group of artists, and then in 1892, six years before his death, he bequeathed his entire collection to the nation. Today, the Tretyakov Gallery is one of Moscow's most popular attractions: over two million people visited in 2018. The nineteenth century, in which Tretyakov was so influential, was the age of nationalism and it was in this era that the symbolism of the birch tree was refined and condensed. As the foremost collection of Russian landscape painting of the period, it is in the Tretyakov where I will learn more about the importance of the birch tree not only as material resource or folk figure but also as powerful symbol of an emerging national consciousness.

I'm starting with an 1871 painting by Alexei Savrasov entitled *The Rooks Have Returned*. Instantly recognisable to millions of Russians, it has been reproduced on phone cards and cases, t-shirts and cushions. It was issued as a commemorative Soviet stamp in 1956 to mark 100 years since Tretyakov purchased his first work of art (odd, to say the least, for a communist regime to commemorate the consumerism of a wealthy capitalist). In his famous 1935 essay, 'The Work of Art in the Age of Mechanical Reproduction', Walter Benjamin worried that 'that which withers in the age of mechanical reproduction is the aura of the work of art'. Yet, if anything, dissemination of reproductions can increase the desire to stand before the original work, to see the physical object first-hand and retrace in one's mind the movements of the hand of the absent artist. What is really lost is an understanding of the materiality of the work: its size as a physical object, the tactile texture of its surfaces, and the materials and processes employed in its making. It would be tempting to argue not that *The Rooks Have Returned* has been reproduced so many times because it is loved but the exact opposite: that it is loved because it has been reproduced so many times. Every Russian schoolchild, I read somewhere, has to write an essay about it. It's a long way for them all to travel to the Tretyakov: it is from reproductions that they must write.

As its title suggests, this celebrated work of Russian art is little more than a picture of some rooks. A landscape painting in portrait format, the work depicts a flat land of snow and muddy puddles, cut in half horizontally by a low wooden fence and vertically by a small church spire. A band of birch trees in the foreground further divides the painting, providing the eye both with a subject to look at and a frame to look through.

As I stand and scrutinise, a guide bustles over with a group of tourists. 'Some painters only *included* landscape,' she explains in the bite-size snippets of an aspiring television presenter. 'Others painted *nothing but* landscape. Like Savrasov. This is his most famous work. *The Rooks Have Returned*. Can you guess what it symbolises?'

'Spring!' yells a middle-aged American with glee.

'Correct,' says the guide. She stops talking to allow the group time to examine the work. I count to three. One. Two. Three. The number of seconds that they look at the painting. Then they take photographs, each one exactly the same as the others. Then they move on.

With the group already in the next gallery, I lean in as close as I dare to the painting, peering at the nests, smudgy in the birch branches against a dirty white sky. The brushmarks taper from firm to light as the trunk of the birch tree thins to branches, branches to the tiniest twigs. I spot a little rook on the ground to the left, a twig in its beak, building its nest, making a home for the summer. The painting of the rook is, I hate to admit, a little clumsy.

Now a Chinese tour group arrives. I cannot understand what this tour guide is saying, but I stay close to the painting, blocking the cameras of the assembled group, and pretending not to notice them. Sounds of tutting and huffing indicate displeasure. As I grudgingly stand aside, the guide explains something, leaning in right up close to the work and gesticulating with her arm. She is touching the painting! Not accidentally brushing it for a moment but quite deliberately running her fingers over its surface. It's all very well to theorise about the tactile materiality of paint, the work of art as physical object, the hand of the absent artist, but that doesn't mean you simply go up and touch the thing. The Chinese group moves on as quickly as the Americans and I'm left harrumphing to myself. I take consolation from Savrasov: beyond the church is a flat, swampy landscape. The church spire is topped by the tiniest of crosses, no bigger, I notice, than the twig in the rook's beak.

And now the French arrive.

'C'est beau, uh?'

'Oui, c'est comme une photo.'

As a person who writes about art for a living, it can be very depressing to overhear somebody judge the quality of a painting solely according to its similarity to a photograph. Especially when they're just about to take a photograph of it. What would Benjamin have made of it all?

But if the power of *The Rooks Have Returned* is not simply its photographic realism (and it really isn't that photographic if you actually stop to look at it), then just what is it about this painting that has made it so emblematic of the relationship between landscape and identity in Russia?

After visiting the Tretyakov I learned that it is not only Soviet stamp-issuers or makers of souvenirs who have been reproducing *The Rooks* and thereby contributing to its fame. Savrasov himself did, too. Tretyakov bought the original directly from his studio before it had even been exhibited. Shown in Saint Petersburg a few years later, with the addition of an exclamation mark to the title, the painting caught the eye of Empress Maria Alexandrovna, who commissioned Savrasov to make a copy in early 1872. This version of the work was sent to the World Exhibition in Vienna the following year. Strangely, its whereabouts are now unknown.

In addition to the Tretyakov painting and the Empress copy, Savrasov produced at least five variations upon the same composition. These range from quick pencil sketches made in preparation for the Tretyakov painting to later variations on the work in slightly different colour palettes or compositional formats. There is a wispy black and white preparatory sketch; a slightly lumpen version in the collection of the Penza Regional Art Gallery; another taller, slimmer sketch; and a composition now owned by the Russian National Library of Music that includes an extra building. Savrasov produced these different versions of the work from the early 1870s to as late as 1894.

A few days later, I come across yet another version of the completed painting, this time in the State Art Museum in the city of Nizhny Novgorod. Could it be the lost version once owned by Empress Maria Alexandrovna? As I look at it right up close, the cross on the spire appears to be even less prominent than that on the Tretyakov version – it is hardly there at all in fact – and the rook in the bottom left corner of the painting seems even less convincing. But maybe I'm just imagining differences that aren't really there – it's hard to compare two paintings with any great accuracy unless you can see them hanging side by side. Rather oddly, the museum label dates the work to 1871 – the same year as the accepted 'original'. Is the museum claiming that *this* is in fact the first painting? Subsequent internet searches suggest that it is in fact a third version of *The Rooks Have Returned* produced in either 1879 or 1889. Somebody, somewhere, has got something wrong.

For whatever reason – the demands of paying clients perhaps (Savrasov, an alcoholic, eventually died in a hospital for the poor) or simply the artist's own enduring interest – over a period of more than twenty years Savrasov felt repeatedly compelled to revisit this really quite limited subject matter: rooks, church, snow, sky, birch trees. I'm tempted to say that the return of the rooks is not only their depicted return at the start of spring but also their return to Savrasov as subject matter. Perhaps the cyclical relationship to time that the painting evokes is therefore precisely the product of the artist's own pattern of departure and return.

While watching Maria Kapajeva's Russian 'mail-order bride' film and dipping into the novels of Boris Pasternak, I speculated that perhaps every great Russian journey is actually a return journey. This thought itself returns as I'm trying to think through the implications of Savrasov's painting. The titular rooks, black against the sky, point to the imminent arrival of spring. It is a known characteristic that rooks often return to the same nests year after year. Savrasov transforms this habitual behaviour into a humble symbol of hope and a desire to build for the future.

But how? One notable feature of the painting is the lack of humans. This absence of people – which became increasingly common in Russian landscape painting of the period – exemplifies what art historian Christopher Ely has described as 'the depopulation of Russian landscape imagery'. In *This Meager Nature* (2002), Ely traces the development of the genre in the nineteenth century and its celebration of humble, 'meagre' scenes as something specifically Russian. In this period, many in Russia were becoming increasingly conscious of deep divisions within society: on the one hand, a predominantly Westernised cultural elite; on the other, a resolutely traditional rural peasantry. Nationalism, as expressed through landscape painting, offered the possibility of a glue to hold together these disparate elements of Russian society. Of the period's depictions of depopulated landscapes, Ely writes:

These paintings offered urban viewers the opportunity not to look at peasants, but to partake of the peasant perspective, to see what the *narod* [peasant] saw. In this way, images of Russian landscape became a ground of common perception, an imagined locus from which it was possible, for a fleeting moment, to bridge the abyss that still divided Russian society.

After re-reading Ely, I take another look at Savrasov's famous painting at home on my computer screen. I ask myself exactly who is exclaiming, with or without the exclamation mark, that 'the rooks have returned'. Is it Savrasov himself, resigned to his fate painting corvids over and over again? Is it some overheard villager just outside the frame of the painting? Or is it in fact the urban-dwelling, middle-class Russian gallery visitor, imagining themself via Savrasov, just for a moment, into the life of the *narod*? The time of year that Savrasov depicts was traditionally very tough for peasants. With stocks running dry at the end of winter, but the bounty of summer still a long way off, peasants would often resort to tapping birch trees for their sap as a way to fend off hunger. For such people the return of spring is indeed a moment of excitement – they've made it through another Russian winter alive.

It is also worth remembering that Russia is a big place, the paucity of its roads a recurrent topic in literature and public discussion for centuries. To make any journey in Russia has traditionally been a significant undertaking, likely to be long, uncomfortable, and possibly dangerous. To make it home again safely was not always guaranteed. In such circumstances, it is hardly surprising that the idea of the successful return home became such a powerful one. At the centre of this idea, for Savrasov, is the birch tree. By eliminating actual humans and offering instead the rooks as an open-ended allegory, the painting creates a powerful identification between the birch tree and the idea of home. This is a highly appropriate association: thriving on disturbed ground, birches grow easily on the edges of the village, or just there, by the side of a peasant hut.

Time, as conceived in paintings like Savrasov's, is cyclical. The landscape is not fixed, but subject to the cycle of the seasons. The dream of returning home is that nothing will have changed. This is as true for the aristocrat returning in his fur-lined carriage to the country estate as it is for the worker trudging back to the family village after casual labour in the city. It was true for so many of those émigrés who returned to Russia after the arrival of communism in 1917 and true for many of those who returned to Russia after communism's demise in 1991.

The dream evoked by Savrasov is that all will be as it was; that a geographical return is necessarily a historical return too, that to travel back in space is also to travel back in time. For returning émigrés, however, lived reality has rarely mapped accurately onto such images. Many diaspora Russians 'returned home' in the 1990s – some seven hundred thousand in 1994 alone. But, as Rancour-Laferriere has noted: 'many are not always welcomed, in many cases being shunted off to remote rural backwaters, and almost always experiencing worsened economic circumstances and culture shock'. You can never step in the same river twice, as Heraclitus is thought to have said. The 'return home' is therefore no return at all. Hence the power of Savrasov's painting: it offers the possibility of a return that reality itself has proved to be impossible.

And yet there's a problem with my ever-so-slightly self-satisfied interpretation of Savrasov's painting: the title. As Russian landscape painting developed in the second half of the nineteenth century, the powerful influence of lyric poetry led artists to believe that their work had to suggest some kind of narrative direction. From the beginning, realism had to mean something. Titles therefore became hugely important. Frequently they would make some kind of reference to temporality. Typical examples such as Arkhip Kuindzhi's *After the Rain* (1879) or Ivan Shishkin's *Before the Storm* (1884) create an implied relationship between the landscape depicted in the painting and an imagined past or future. In this context, a simple path or muddy track renders the temporal spatial. It translates the relationship between past, present and future into a three-dimensional configuration in which a narrative can unfold.

The Russian title of Savrasov's painting is in fact *Grachi prileteli* – not 'The Rooks Have Returned' but 'The Rooks Have Arrived'. The verb *priletat'* means 'to fly in', 'to land', 'to touch down' or 'to arrive'. Unlike Fyodor Vasilyev's 1868 painting *The Return of the Herd* (*Vozvrashcheniye stada*), there is, a little crushingly I admit, absolutely no allusion to 'return' in the title of Savrasov's painting, however appropriate to the subject matter and the whole spirit and ethos it might seem to be. Savrasov's variations and sketches mostly bear the same title too. The exceptions have titles such as *Landscape with a Church and a Bell Tower*; *Early Spring*; and *Landscape with a Church*. The return is not emphasised by Savrasov himself: it seems instead to be an interpretation by Anglophone translators.

In 2019, I made my own return to Savrasov. Once again I stood in the Tretyakov Gallery as multiple tour groups entered, paused in front of the famous rooks, nodded, took photographs, and left. I took the time to get up close – not only to the star attraction but also to the other, less celebrated paintings by Savrasov hanging in the same room. Many of these works have a similar tone: quiet, undemonstrative depictions of quiet, undemonstrative scenes. Little peasant houses are nestled into landscapes of thawing snow. But there are no peasants in them.

The foregrounds are blotched with boggy puddles. Muddy tracks meander into the distance.

I find myself drawn towards a small, scrappy little painting called *A Small Yard, Winter* (1870). Even looser and sketchier in its technique than *The Rooks Have Returned*, this shows – as the title suggests – a small outside space enclosed by a wooden fence and the back of a little wooden house. For a moment I too see this scene from the perspective of the Russian peasant: this little yard is suddenly my yard, my little patch of Russian land. Pigeons peck for grain in the snowy earth. They are so loosely painted that one is evoked with just a single quick smear of the brush. It's all that's needed. Next to the pigeons, stretching from the bottom to the top of the composition, right in the centre, is a slender young tree about the height of the house. Dark grey and white, it might simply be part-covered in snow. To me, of course, it's a birch tree. I'm home.

> Art says to its spectator: I am not what you think I am (in stark contrast to: I am what I am). The desire for nonidentity is, actually, a genuinely human desire – animals accept their identity but human animals do not.

This is theorist Boris Groys writing in a 2017 essay entitled 'The Truth of Art'. As an aside, I think Groys is wrong about animals. What is the playful bite of a young wolf but an act that says precisely: 'I am not what you think I am'? In play, a bite communicates both what it is (a bite) and what it is not (a *real* bite). But Groys is right about art. And the truth he pinpoints is especially acute in times of political repression, such as that which Russian artists endured during the nineteenth century. Everything means something else, or might be seen to. To the censors, everything was potentially a coded criticism of the

regime. Sometimes it was, sometimes it was not. And sometimes, like Schrödinger's cat, both at once. Who could ever
really know for sure?

In this context, when even the most playful of bites might
(wilfully) be construed as a genuine attack, to paint a Russian
landscape is to take a significant risk. To paint poor peasants,
muddy roads, badly managed estates could, to the regime's
censors, seem like a criticism of Tsarist economic management.
To urban elites, however, these things might seem more like a
celebration of the Russian landscape as humble and authentic –
in which case, to choose to paint them is to celebrate Russia, and
by extension the regime that rules it.

For Russian artists to depict distinctly Russian nature in this
way was therefore never simple. Savrasov may have caught the
eye of the Empress with *The Rooks Have Returned*, but until as
late as the 1850s it was believed that only those scenes already
designated aesthetically significant by European culture could
make for worthy artistic subject matter. Troops of Russian
artists dutifully plodded off to the mountains of Switzerland
or the coasts of Italy before plodding home again with their
plodding paintings. It was in opposition to this prescriptive
approach that the desire for an identifiably Russian landscape
painting began to grow, but it was not immediately obvious
what a Russian artist – conditioned to appreciate the value in
a limited range of views – should actually paint. Russia's landscapes seemed to Russian artists so different to those they had
been trained to depict. By comparison with Europe, Russian
landscapes seemed to come up short. The discovery of a specifically Russian nature took time and it was not always successful.

It is this early stage in the development of Russian landscape
painting that Nikolai Gogol mocks in his short story 'Nevsky
Prospekt', first published in 1835. 'Almost all of them use grey-
ish, muddy paint,' comments the narrator about the artists of

Saint Petersburg. He goes on to poke fun at the very idea of a Russian artist in a place so ill-suited to landscape painting:

> Is that not strange? A Saint Petersburg artist! An artist in the land of snow, of Finns, where all is wet, smooth, flat, pale, grey and misty!

The narrator cannot resist an unflattering comparison between Russia and Europe and the effects upon artists of their respective climates:

> If only the fresh winds of Italy were to blow on them they would surely blossom as freely, luxuriantly and brightly as a potted plant at last taken outdoors into the fresh air.

Gradually, however, the 'fresh winds of Italy' came to be seen as shallow and superficial in comparison to the authenticity evoked by the 'wet, smooth, flat, pale, grey' landscapes of Russia. Russian beauty was an inner beauty and the greyer and more muddy the scene, the more authentically, gloriously Russian it came to be. From the 1870s, birches began to proliferate. Arkhip Kuindzhi, an artist responsible for some of the most extraordinary landscape paintings of the era, also painted a diversity of birches: they are chunky and even a little ungainly in an undated *Birchwood Sketch* that I come across in a museum vitrine; in the more famous *Island of Valaam* (1873), a fallen birch is brushed with a single stroke of blue. To the right of the painting, a bird flies over shallow water and the surrounding scrubland is blue-yellow. In the background, the trunks of the evergreens fade from russet down to pale grey.

The birches are slim and elegant in E. E. Volkov's *In Spring* (1880). They grow in a dainty trio outside Ilya Repin's *The Ukrainian Hut* (1880). They are struck by the bright new rays of the sun in Fyodor Vasilyev's *After the Storm* (1889) while a horse and wagon are silhouetted on the wet road. Birches are tied with horses in Viktor Vasnetsov's *Waving Cornfield* (1892). In Viktor Borisov-Musatov's *Birch Trees* (1903), the birch branches have been picked out in white with the finest of brushes. Behind them the grain of the canvas shows through washes of green and grey-blue. In Stanislav Zhukovsky's *Spring* (1913), by contrast, the paint is thickly applied. A dirt track leads through a snowy forest and the birches have been scraped on with a palette knife.

For all their apparent timelessness, these multiplying birches cannot properly be understood without reference to the social, political and economic context which produced them and which they, in turn, helped to produce. The nineteenth century was the age of nationalism. But both Groys and Ukrainian-American historian Serhii Plokhy draw a distinction between the way that nationalism developed in Europe and the way it developed in Russia: in Europe, the Enlightenment – and later the nationalism that grew from it – provided a vital critique of existing power structures; in Russia, they both argue, nationalism and Enlightenment thinking were employed from their very beginnings not as a way to critique power but to serve it. Plokhy writes:

If in Europe the idea of nation, closely associated with the principle of popular representation, challenged political autocracy, in Russia it was supposed to support the traditional Tsarist regime.

In a 1992 essay, 'Russia and the West', Groys identifies Russia's victory over Napoleon and the arrival of the allied forces in Paris in 1814 as key moments in the early development of Russian national identity. Military success inspired waves of patriotic fervour. But what did this new love of Russia really stand for? Groys cites the 1829 'Philosophical Letter' by Russian philosopher Pyotr Chaadayev who expressed the fear that Russian culture, in Groys's words, 'entirely borrowed and imitative, has therefore no inner roots within the country itself'. Groys continues:

> Russian culture appeared to be exclusively imitative and contained no elements which could be considered as its original contribution to the universal world culture; religion in Russia appeared to be entirely Byzantine, and its secular culture entirely Western European.

Stuck somewhere between East and West, neither quite one nor quite the other, Russian elites were increasingly asking themselves: what do we stand for? In the nineteenth century, this self-questioning affected not only depictions of Russian forests in art and literature, but the very forests themselves. For the question of national identity was not asked only among the urban elites; it echoed also in the very depths of rural Russia.

During the late nineteenth century, Russia's woodlands bore witness to a series of concerted attempts by the state to impose rationalised management methods borrowed from Germany upon a peasantry with a very different set of values. The state was concerned with productivity and valued predominantly hardwoods. But for Russia's peasants, softer trees such as aspen, alder, linden and birch were more important for their local economies because of their multiplicity of uses. As Stephen Brain puts it in *Song of the Forest*: 'peasant forests, bereft of pine, spruce, and oak ... seemed from the point of view of the exchequer mere wasted land'. To paint birches was, in one sense, to take the side of the peasant against the state; in another, it was to privilege aesthetics over economic practicalities.

Out of this growing fascination with forests and their representation, emerged Georgii Morozov, regarded by some as the father of Russian forestry science. Morozov, a central figure in Stephen Brain's book, is best known today for his theory of 'stand types', which looked beyond individual species of trees and their monetary value in order to argue that different forests ought to be managed according to their own unique ecosystems, including soil, geology, relief and hydrology. Much of what Morozov argued would strike a chord with ecologists today. At the time, however, Morozov was radical: his writing employed populist peasant terminology and his ideas flew in the face of the modern, European-influenced approach to forest management. In short, Morozov appealed to the uniqueness of the Russian forest. He wrote:

> Our slowly evolving science of forestry arose in Western Europe, beginning with the Germans ... but our forestry, without discarding ... the idea[s] of the West, will make an attempt to allow for the unique properties of our forests and our country.

Despite these appeals to Russian exceptionalism, it was some time before Morozov's theories started to be adopted at state level.

What strikes me, however, is the way that Morozov's writing, laced with national Romantic ideas, chimed with wider thinking in art and literature around 1900. By this time, landscape painting had emerged as a valid artistic genre in its own right. Painting had long been tightly controlled by the Imperial Academy of Arts in Saint Petersburg, which was founded in 1757. For most of the eighteenth and nineteenth centuries, artists came from the lowest ranks of society. A full term of study at the Academy took no less than fifteen years. Even then, those who graduated did so as members of the fourteenth and lowest of the social ranks that had been instituted by Peter the Great in 1722 and that had contributed to the rigid stratification of Russian society ever since. Semyon Shchedrin, who painted *The Stone Bridge at Gatchina* that I examined before visiting the Gatchina estate, is a typical product of the Academy: classically trained, technically proficient, and resolutely unimaginative. Perhaps that's unfair. It was effectively impossible to be an artist outside of the Academy and therefore painters had to paint what the aristocracy wanted them to paint. Originality was not exactly a trait to be nurtured.

'There was almost no labour market for free artists,' writes art historian David Jackson in *The Wanderers and Critical Realism in Nineteenth-Century Russian Painting*, at least until after the emancipation of the serfs in 1861. In the 1840s, Count Vorontsov, for example, one of the richest men in Russia, owned one million acres of land and 80,000 serfs. 'Why buy paintings,' asks Jackson pointedly, 'when one could own a painter?'

It was for this reason, among others, that landscape painting could not find its feet until later in the nineteenth century. For it relied in part upon the emergence of a new middle class who could afford to buy art and wanted to demonstrate their taste not only in art but in Russian art. Tretyakov is the major figure here: the great collector, who arguably did as much as any critic or artist to bring about the rise in Russian landscape painting. Influenced by philosopher Nikolai Chernyshevsky and art critic Vladimir Stasov, Tretyakov embraced an aesthetics that sought to celebrate the apparently humble, overlooked Russian landscape – in contrast to the familiar grandeur of the Swiss Alps or the much-painted vistas of Italy. 'Give me even a dirty puddle,' Tretyakov is frequently quoted as saying, 'and in it will be poetry and truth.' It was just thirty years since Gogol ridiculed artists working in the wet, grey lands of Saint Petersburg. In that time Russian aesthetics had shifted significantly.

It was in the 1860s that things really began to change. In 1863, frustrated with the control exerted by the Academy, a group of artists founded the Peredvizhniki (the Wanderers). These artists travelled throughout the Russian provinces, painting scenes of rural life, putting on exhibitions and selling their work. In so doing, they managed to establish a degree of financial – and therefore artistic – independence from the state. These first Wanderers were generally poor and their landscapes were often subtly critical of the inequalities of the Tsarist regime. They created works that sought to document the realities of Russia – for better or, very often, for worse. Ilya Repin is the best-known of the group. Although his work ranged from portraits to history painting, perhaps his most important contributions to Russian art history were his large-scale depictions of everyday Russian life. Works such as *Barge Haulers on the Volga* (1870–73) or the later *Religious Procession in Kursk Province* (1880–83) were at once clear depictions of simple scenes and also vastly complex in how one might interpret them.

In *Religious Procession in Kursk Province*, dozens of Orthodox believers make their way along a sandy path, and as they walk they kick up dust into the air, creating a haze that clouds the horizon. In the foreground a bearded man beats a young girl on crutches. Further back a mounted policeman is about to strike a woman with his riding crop. To the left the earth is dry and spiked with severed tree trunks.

It's not obvious to me, but to art historians such as David Jackson and Jane T. Costlow, this famous painting is a forthright critique of Russia's mismanagement of its forests during the late nineteenth century. It is, for Costlow, 'the starkest image we have of nineteenth-century deforestation in Russia'. She also draws an analogy between the whip used by the policeman and the axe of the forester. Following Costlow, I would be tempted to draw a further analogy between the innocent female victims of police violence and the felled forest, itself an innocent (and during this period frequently feminised) victim. Repin's 1881 painting *Summer Landscape* lends support to this interpretation. Costlow notes that the work, also a depiction of a hillside of severed tree trunks, was a study for *Religious Procession*, which Repin was working on at the same time. What Costlow does not mention is the presence of a girl in white, left behind on the dusty path as a male figure strides forwards. The girl is mirrored by the one remaining tree to have escaped the axe: a slender birch just on the edge of the path. Prefiguring the pop lyrics of Yevgeniy Ross by over one hundred and twenty years, the girl, like the birch, must wait for a man to return. Costlow imagines that the felled forest in *Religious Procession* might have been oaks; as I look closely at the painting I notice in the background just the barest trace of birches. The girl may have been removed in the finished work, but the birch, her double, remains.

Where Repin's finest works are paintings of people first and foremost, many of his contemporaries largely eschewed human subjects altogether. The first major name in this history was Ivan Shishkin. Famous for his large-scale woodland scenes, Shishkin was known as 'the accountant of leaves' for his obsessive attention to every single detail in the forest. Shishkin, writes art historian Vladimir Lenyashin, 'makes no distinction between images that are worthy or unworthy of depiction'. Like realist novels, in attempting to account for everything, such paintings fail to convey what is actually significant. The great mystery then with Shishkin is what all this painstaking realism is *doing*. Is this tree important? Does this leaf matter?

Repin may be ambiguous but you know there is meaning there. With Shishkin, who knows?

Shishkin painted from the backwoods of remote rural Russia. Birch trees may have been important for many landscape painters of the nineteenth and twentieth centuries, but Shishkin largely shunned them. Or rather, his love of the deep forest took him to places dominated by other species, where the birch could no longer survive. One exception is *Tree Felling* (1867). In the artist's typically detailed style, it shows a broken birch stump in the foreground, the severed trunk stretching out beyond the right-hand edge of the painting. Along its surface, if you get up close, you can see the bark peeling back on itself just like a scroll. Nearby sprout the fly agaric mushrooms that are so characteristically associated with birch trees, all bright red and spotted white.

As far as I have discovered, Shishkin only ever painted landscapes – no genre scenes or still lifes, no portraits or history scenes or cities. For anything apart from trees and fields he often enlisted the help of other artists. The much-loved *Morning in the Pine Forest* (1889), for example, is populated with bears painted in by Konstantin Savitsky. Despite its technical limitations, this painting operates today like a shorthand for the impenetrable Russian backwoods full of charismatic danger. As a depiction of the animal most associated with the nation, it functions for Russia as Edwin Landseer's 1851 painting *Monarch of the Glen* does for Scotland: an instantly recognisable puff of sentimental patriotism. If Russians made shortbread, Shishkin's bears – or rather, Savitsky's bears – would be proudly printed on every tin.

One of Shishkin's most famous works is *A Rye Field* (1878), the painting reproduced on the desk of artist Maria Kapajeva and on the walls of her father's apartment. The composition is shaped by a muddy track which takes us from the foreground into the heart of the painting before disappearing quickly among the golden rye. Towering pine trees provide the vertical-ity often missing from Russia's flat agricultural lands or endless steppe. It is an easy image. It feels familiar but fresh rather than academically stale, humble rather than thematically complex. It guides us along a path. In addition, rather than wild, wasteful woods, *A Rye Field* is an image of agricultural productivity and the fertility of Russian lands. It is not surprising therefore that its popularity was encouraged during the Soviet era.

It is only on viewing the original painting in Moscow for the second time that I noticed a number of little details that are easy to miss in reproductions – certainly in those as small and dark as Maria Kapajeva's. The foreground, for example, is full of bright flowers: little blobs of yellow and white and red. In the middle of the field there are two figures I had not seen before – half-submerged in the golden crop, a head and a red hat just visible above the rye. These two figures are echoed by a pair of swallows, flying low along the dusty path at the base of the painting. They are, I'm sad to admit, clumsy and leaden. Shishkin had his skills as an artist – the lightness and move-ment of living creatures was not among them.

Gradually, as his style developed, Shishkin focused on landscapes stripped of human or animal life, except here and there a trace – a road or a wheel track, the clean slice of a tree trunk or a muddy path between the trees. These later paint-ings can be more difficult to read. Unlike, say, *A Rye Field*, in which convenient sightlines lead you by the hand, in these later paintings Shishkin picks you up and dumps you in the middle of the forest – alone. His forests do not create views, they block them. A fallen tree in the foreground bars the way forward. It is hard to see beyond the foliage. There is, at times, no sky. In such settings, birch trees rarely grow, crowded out by hardier broadleaf and evergreen trees.

For Christopher Ely, such paintings demonstrate the way that Shishkin

> conceived of nature as something external to the realm of ordinary experience. His landscape was not that of a rural inhabitant who saw land for its use value, but the landscape of an urbanite who saw nature as antithetical to life in the city.

This is, I think, one reason why Shishkin, who is technically a very limited artist, remains so hugely popular. As more and more Russians live in cities, the desire to view the country as an untouched wilderness has arguably grown stronger than ever.

Birch Tree Forest Artist Shishkin, Ivan Ivanovich (1832–1898)
credit © State Russian Museum/Bridgeman Images

One discovery that has continually surprised me is the popularity of artists like Shishkin even in the Soviet era. There is one particular moment that I can't help but find entertaining even in the most dreadful of contexts. Following the German invasion of Poland in 1939, Polish artist Józef Czapski served as an army officer in the struggle against Hitler. But, with Russia and Germany having undertaken a pact of non-aggression (the infamous Molotov–Ribbentrop Pact of 1939), Czapski, along with thousands of other Poles, was arrested by the Soviets and sent to a prison camp near Vologda, two hundred and fifty miles north-east of Moscow.

Czapski recalls his war-time experiences in *Inhuman Land* (1949), a book that threads together horror with absurdity. When Hitler invaded the USSR, Russia switched sides and these Poles, including Czapski, who had once been regarded as enemies – and treated as such by Russian soldiers and prison guards – were suddenly released and expected to join the war on the side of their former oppressors. This situation was patently absurd. But it was more than that: thousands of Polish soldiers never rejoined their regiments. Czapski's book details his search for these missing comrades in the face of frustratingly opaque Soviet bureaucracy. Eventually it is revealed that 22,000 Polish military officers and intelligentsia, captured by the Red Army during their invasion of Poland, had been executed by the NKVD in 1940 and their bodies buried in the forest. *Inhuman Land* tells of Czapski's heart-breaking failure to track down his countrymen.

Throughout the book Czapski, whose own paintings are full of bold colour, expresses his dislike of precisely the kind of Russian landscape painting that I have been examining in the Tretyakov. He mentions, for example, a war-time exhibition in which contemporary Soviet artists showed work that owed a clear debt to the paintings of Savrasov and Shishkin. Czapski is very sniffy about these 'distant echoes of the Peredvizhniki': 'This trend,' he writes, 'was for my generation so passé that it was only ever referred to in art criticism as a horror story.'

In the unlikely context of a Soviet prisoner-of-war camp, Czapski, the cultured European modernist, asks for reading

material, some art, something to look at, from the camp's commander, named Khodes. The commander's response is not
exactly what Czapski had hoped for:

> when I insisted on being able to receive books about art, he
> brought me from Moscow some shoddy colour postcards
> featuring pictures by Shishkin from the Tretyakov Gallery.
> Shishkin was a poor, once very popular, naturalist painter
> of pine forests, active in the second half of the nineteenth
> century. Khodes brought me the postcards as the last
> word in art.

I love this anecdote. You would think life could not get much
worse than a Soviet prison camp. And yet it is not starvation or
squalor or beatings that Czapski recalls here: it is bad art.

Czapski, who disparaged Shishkin as 'once very popular', would be aghast to learn that today the Russian painter
is maybe more popular than ever. I've visited rooms full
of Shishkin paintings at art museums in Moscow, Nizhny
Novgorod and Kyiv and, ironically for a painter of such empty
landscapes, these rooms are always the busiest. On the day
I visited the Museum of Russian Art in Kyiv, Ukraine, many
of the rooms were empty. But not the Shishkin gallery: it was
packed. Shishkin, it seems to me, shows the Russian landscape
as Russians want to see it. Even the most art-historically or
ecologically aware people that I have met in Russia view their
own country, to a significant extent, through his eyes. Beyond
the cities they want to believe that Russia remains ancient, wild,
untouched. And yet, what can Shishkin mean here in Kyiv? In
the capital city of a country at war with Russia? People of all
ages are here in the gallery gazing at Shishkin's paintings –
what do they see? A shared cultural inheritance or a point of
radical difference?

As I ask myself these unanswerable questions, I notice something amiss. It's hard to be sure; the work is hung up high and the lighting is terrible. But I think that one, just up there, might not be a painting at all. *Twilight* (1874) is a murky old thing: in the foreground, dark puddles and broken tree stumps; in the background, darkly silhouetted trees turning russet in the setting sun. I think as I look that in fact it's not a painting but a reproduction – and nobody seems to have noticed. I keep looking, right up on tip-toes to try to see for sure. I'm the one getting odd looks now. But I'm increasingly certain: that's not a painting but a photocopy masquerading as a painting. Perhaps Benjamin was right all along.

To really understand the importance of the birch in nineteenth-century Russian painting, the artist I need to get to know is Isaac Levitan. Levitan was orphaned and homeless as a young man, but because of his talent, the Moscow School of Art waived his fees in 1873. Influenced by Impressionism, but never content to portray the effects of light simply for their own sake, Levitan developed into the most technically accomplished of the nineteenth-century Russian landscape painters. And Levitan loved birch trees.

When thinking through the reception of Levitan's work, it is vital to remember that he was Jewish. He was born in a *shtetl* (a small town with a predominantly Jewish population) in what was then Congress Poland, once a sovereign state, but by the time of Levitan's birth forcibly incorporated into the Russian Empire. Today Levitan's birthplace lies within Lithuania. After an assassination attempt on Alexander II in 1879, the Tsar ruled that Jews be deported en masse from cities across the empire (even though the would-be assassin, Alexander Soloviev, was not Jewish). Levitan's family were among those forced to move from

Moscow to a suburb. However, there was an art world campaign on Levitan's behalf and he was allowed to return. The reason Levitan's Jewishness should not be forgotten is that it would not be long before the white birch – which Levitan arguably did more than any other artist to popularise as a worthy subject for Russian landscape painting – would be used by antisemitic nationalists to convey a very narrow image of the nation they claimed to represent. Rarely has this irony been acknowledged.

What kind of artist was Levitan? Art historian David Jackson encourages the image of Levitan as a kind of artisan – technically accomplished, working to meet market demand. But Russian curator Joseph Backstein has argued that we ought to engage with Levitan on a more intellectual level. 'In Russia, art has always been conceptual,' wrote Backstein in response to Levitan. So which is it? Levitan the artisan or Levitan the proto-conceptualist? Or is it possible that he was in fact both?

To answer these questions, one key work in Levitan's oeuvre is *The Vladimirka Road* (1892). The painting is an utterly typical, commonplace landscape: a flat, green, empty anywhere with a dusty road stretching into the horizon. There is a figure in the middle ground. A golden field of rye and a tiny white church are just about visible in the distance. Two things set the work apart: the first is Levitan's handling of colour (russets and mauve among the low grasses) and texture (dappled marks suggestive of tiny plants sprouting along the road itself). This suggests perhaps that we think of Levitan as artisan: well-trained, technically skilled, and materially dependent on creating work to please a paying client.

On the other hand, the second distinguishing feature is the work's title. Many of Levitan's birch paintings had much more generic titles: *Birch Forest* (1885–9); *March* (1895); *Golden Autumn* (1895); or *Spring, High Water* (1897). But Vladimirka Road, as would have been immediately familiar to Russian audiences, was the route down which gangs of shackled prisoners were driven to the Tsarist penal colonies of Siberia. Suddenly, this piece of knowledge radically changes how we view the painting: it becomes a scene powerfully charged not by what we can see but by what we cannot. Levitan's art is both political and conceptual: this is a landscape full of ghosts.

Levitan was great friends with the playwright Anton Chekhov. They met while Levitan was studying at Moscow School of Art, where Chekhov's brother, Nikolai, was also a student. In the mid-1880s Levitan spent long periods at the Chekhov family estate near Babkino, where the two would discuss art and literature and Levitan would act in pantomimes put on by Chekhov to entertain guests. Chekhov wrote about Levitan's work several times – in letters to his sister and also in the 1895 story 'Three Years'. It is said that Levitan's melodramatic behaviour inspired *The Seagull*.

For both Chekhov and Levitan, birches were an important feature in a distinctly Russian landscape. Take *Birch Grove* (1885–9), often cited as one of the finest examples of Levitan's handling of light. The work delicately evokes the dappled, warm dancing glow of a birch wood in the summer sun. There is a kind of multilayered horizon broken repeatedly by white birch trunks and a deep soft grassy green underfoot. A few years later, in 1892, Levitan painted *Evening Bells*, a vision of a small country church nestled among birches just the other side of a river. Art historian Averil King has noted how Levitan preferred to paint at dusk, in contrast to Monet who favoured dawn. In 'Levitan and the Silver Birch', she describes Levitan's love of birches: 'As a motif, it was lyrical, expressive and, above all, calculated to evoke feelings of affection for the Russian Motherland.' In *Evening Bells*, the birches are not the centre of the composition but a kind of support act. The evening light catches yellow-pink and mauve on the white of the church wall, echoed by the reflection in the water and by the slim birch trunks to the left as you look.

For Chekhov too the birch is an important motif of Russian landscape. But unlike landscape painting, theatre cannot be depopulated. And one of drama's enduring mysteries is that it is never quite possible to equate the views espoused by particular characters with those held by the playwright. Chekhov is a master of exploiting this feature of theatre: deep-held sentiments or earnestly argued philosophies can be undercut by a moment's action or by the behaviour of the speaker. In his 1900 play *Three Sisters*, Chekhov presents the audience with two characters embodying quite different understandings of nature. Olga, the eldest of the three titular sisters, lives in the countryside and sees the environment in prosaic and practical terms: she complains of the cold and the mosquitoes where they live. 'Oh, you mustn't say that,' replies Alexander Vershinin, representing here the aesthetically minded visitor from the city, 'you've got a good healthy climate, what I call a real Russian climate. There are woods and the river, and you've silver birches too. Charming, modest birches, they're my favourite tree.'

In *Uncle Vanya* (1898), another male character expresses his love of birch trees. This time it's middle-aged country doctor Mikhail Astrov and there's just the subtlest irony undercutting Astrov's professed love of the forests, a suggestion that perhaps it's the sound of his own voice that he loves more than the trees themselves. Early in the play, Astrov gives a long speech about the importance of valuing forests for their aesthetics over their use value: 'wonderful scenery disappears,' he laments. Towards the end of the speech, Astrov says with a note of pomposity:

When I plant a young birch and later see it covered with green and swaying in the breeze, my heart fills with pride and I—

And just as Astrov reaches his rhetorical apex, a labourer brings in a glass of vodka and interrupts him in full flow. The proximity of booze – and of the working class – contrives to ruin the fantasy. He takes the vodka, drinks it, and leaves. The freshly planted young birch is forgotten, along with all its symbolic potential.

On a cold, bright, January morning, I stroll through Edinburgh to the botanical gardens, where I've arranged to meet Max Coleman, who works in public engagement. Elms are his area of expertise more than birches, but 'trees in general are an interest', he told me via email before we meet. Over hot, weak coffee, Max and I talk about gardens, about his role in communications, and about birches. It is Max who first warns me about the complexities of identifying different species of birch; Max who tells me about the way that clumps of birch seem to move around, appearing and disappearing across the hillsides of Scotland.

During our conversation, Max raises an intriguing possibility – one tinged with excitement and dread (for me at least; I'm not sure if he gives it a second thought). In trying to explain my interest in Russian birches I tell him about Savrasov's famous painting, *The Rooks Have Returned*, in the Tretyakov Gallery. I try to convey something of the painting's cultural significance, its familiar representation of homely, humble, nostalgic, rural Russianness. Max nods from time to time, but I think he's just being polite: he's not the only person I speak to who seems rather uninterested in nineteenth-century Russian landscape painting.

When I mention the rooks themselves, however, and their nest-building, his attention picks up. I talk about how their return denotes the arrival of spring and of new life, and how this symbolism chimes with the importance of the return journey in so much Russian art and literature.

In my foggy memory of our conversation, Max looks a little quizzical.

I pause.

'I'm no expert on birches,' he says, or something like that.

'But?'

'Do rooks really build nests in birch trees?'

'Um . . .'

'I don't think I've ever seen it. The branches are surely too thin, they would bend too easily.'

'Um . . .'

'I haven't seen the painting,' Max continues, I seem to recall, unaware of the century and a half of art-historical interpretation that is about to be cast unceremoniously out the window. 'But it's possible that what looks like a bird's nest is in fact a witch's broom.'

'A what?' I whisper breathlessly.

Max patiently explains the phenomenon of the witch's broom: an unusual pattern of branch growth caused by the presence of a fungus, insect or virus in the tree. In birches the cause is usually a sporing fungus – either *Taphrina betulina* or *Anisogramma virgultorum*. These can lead to the release of a hormone that interferes with the tree's growth, causing a dense mass of shoots to sprout from a single point in the branch. Up close, the result looks a bit like the end of a witch's broomstick (hence the name); from a distance, it looks even more like a bird's nest.

This is not merely an interesting phenomenon; from the perspective of art history (at least the narrow part of art history that I'm currently wading through) it could be earth-shattering. What if this key work in the history of Russian art is actually wrong? Not only is the return a mistranslation but the entire narrative that underpins the work would be incorrect. In the bottom corner of the painting, Savrasov has depicted a rook gathering twigs. The implication is very clear: that the rook is building a nest or repairing an existing one. But what if this painting, one of the most famous examples of Russian realism, of a commitment to truth in depicting an authentic Russian landscape, was in fact, from the beginning, untrue?

After my meeting with Max I sit in the library at the botanical gardens, reading the minutes from an old botanical symposium; reading botanist Richard Hook Richens's multidisciplinary book about elm trees; and reading books by a Scottish missionary, John Croumbie Brown, who reported on the state of forests and forestry across northern Russia in the 1880s.

For the best part of the next week I find myself scouring the internet for information about rook nesting habits, and the suitability of birch trees for nest-building. There are suggestions that Max may be right, that birch branches are indeed too thin, too flimsy for rooks; that they prefer sturdier homes, high up in the branches of ash, beech, elm, oak, horse chestnut or sycamore trees. But there is nothing conclusive – yet.

Eventually, I find what I wanted to find, what I hoped not to find. On an obscure birdwatching blog, a close-up photograph of a rook, building a nest in the branches of what is, without doubt, a birch tree. The nest is clearly a nest, not a witch's broom; the rook is clearly a rook; and the birch, white and spindly, is clearly a birch. Proof!

I'm crestfallen. My chance to scribble a jotting in the footnotes of Russian art history has evaporated. But I'm also strangely relieved: realism remains real, for now. I excitedly compose a lengthy email to tell Max all about my find. And then I forget to send it.

VI.

ABRAMTSEVO

'Cut down the root, the lilac tree falls with a moan, the golden birch topples and the tulip is trampled, the secret glade is soiled.'

Tatyana Tolstaya, *The Slynx*, 2003

In retrospect it was predictable that I would take the wrong train to Abramtsevo. What I had not anticipated was that I would do so twice. The internet had given me one set of instructions; the hotel concierge another. Somehow I contrived to find a third way. Once aboard the first train, I was advised by the ticket instructor that it would not be stopping at Abramtsevo. So I did as I was told, swiftly disembarked at the next available station, and waited for the correct train. This I boarded and, feeling awfully satisfied with my virtuosic display of competence, sat gazing out of the window as we rattled straight through Abramtsevo station without stopping. 'Ah,' I thought to myself. 'Bugger.'

Abramtsevo is a vital place in my exploration of the developing relationship between nature and national identity in Russia. Perhaps it is *the* vital place: a country estate once owned by writer Sergey Aksakov (famous for his semi-autobiographical narratives and descriptions of hunting and fishing), it was visited by artists and writers such as Nikolai Gogol. But it was after its purchase by industrialist and arts patron Savva Mamontov in 1870 that Abramtsevo became a really significant centre of Russian landscape painting. During the 1870s and 1880s in particular, Abramtsevo was a home from home for many of the major names in Russian art, including Mikhail Nesterov and Mikhail Vrubel, Ilya Repin, and brothers Viktor and Apollinary Vasnetsov. It was at Abramtsevo that many artists cultivated their growing obsession with an idealised vision of medieval Russia influenced by a heady blend of myth, folklore and Russian Orthodox Christianity. And they were not content simply to evoke this vision in paintings, but instead sought to make it a reality in the world itself. They made furniture and ceramic tiles, they printed textiles and dabbled as architects. One of Abramtsevo's best-loved buildings is a small church designed by Viktor Vasnetsov. It looks like it has emerged from one of Vasnetsov's own fairy-tale paintings. Not insignificantly, Abramtsevo is full of birch trees.

I alight at Khotkovo station. I don't own a smartphone, and I haven't brought a map. I have only some written instructions that tell me where to go from Abramtsevo station. But I'm nowhere near Abramtsevo station. I wander back in the direction I have just come on the train, trying to track as close to the railway line as possible. I'll walk for an hour, I think to myself, and if there's no sign of Abramtsevo, I'll retrace my steps and take the train back to Moscow in defeat.

As I walk along busy roads, through anonymous suburbs, I wonder how important it really is for me to get to Abramtsevo. I think about hailing a taxi but I can't seem to extract cash from any of the ATMs. I think perhaps they're not ATMs. There are birches everywhere here: on the edge

of this car park, in a line by the side of that road, just over
there beyond the roundabout. I could always pause by *these*
birches just here – I mean, what's wrong with these ones? A
row has been planted by a low-rise residential block from the
Stalin era. Why are these trees any less significant than those
at Abramtsevo?

A scene just like this one is depicted in a 2006 photograph
by Alexander Gronsky. Born in Tallinn, Estonia, when it
was part of the Soviet Union, Gronsky worked as a press
photographer across Russia. Since then, his personal projects
have documented life and landscape in the apparently
peripheral places beyond the urban centres of the former
USSR. In two ongoing series entitled *Pastoral* and *Pastoral
Revisited*, Gronsky's crisply composed photographs show
the life and landscapes of high-rise suburbia, out-of-town
building sites, overgrown car parks and power plants. But as
the series titles suggest, Gronsky keeps finding moments of
incongruous beauty: a sandy beach in the shadow of unfinished skyscrapers; a girl in a floral dress somewhere in the
urban undergrowth; picnickers by a grubby river. Like the
painters of the nineteenth century, Gronsky seeks to convey
an authentic image of Russia by turning his gaze towards
that which has been overlooked or deemed ugly or insig-
nificant. Gronsky is a photographer of the edgelands. I can't
work out if his photographs flicker with hope or are simply
unbearably depressing.

The image I'm thinking about on the way to Abramtsevo
is from an earlier body of work, the series *Less Than One*, produced in some of Russia's most remote regions. It shows a view
of the city of Komsomolsk-on-Amur in the Russian Far East,
not far – on the map at least – from Vladivostok. (The internet
tells me it is in fact a fourteen-hour drive.) The image is a wall
of white birches, bare-branched, and cropped at the top. It is a

composition of parallel verticals, dark and white, like a barcode. The sky is as white as the tree trunks – it makes the image difficult to read at first. Then you notice through the trees a line of low-rise Stalin-era residential buildings. They too are predominantly white. Only the brown leafy ground provides a tonal contrast – and the splashes of acid blue-green painted on three of the buildings. It must be spring: the trees are bare but the ground is free from snow. If there are signs of new life, however, I cannot find them.

A similarly quotidian scene is shown more than once in the 2018 film *Sea Buckthorn Summer*, written by Olga Pogodina-Kuzmina and directed by Viktor Alfyorov, about the life of Russian playwright Alexander Vampilov. Vampilov's family live in a period-perfect 1960s Soviet residential estate in the Siberian city of Irkutsk. Here, the aspiring playwright happily returns from his stressful trips to Moscow where he attempts, with little initial success, to persuade the Soviet cultural authorities to produce his plays. These return journeys are emphasised by close-ups of Vampilov on a near-empty bus and by long, slow aerial tracking shots showing straight roads slicing through endless birch forests.

Watching the film at a festival in Vladivostok, there is one moment in particular that has my heart beating fast. At home in Irkutsk, Vampilov's family and closest friends have taken the kitchen table outside into the yard for lunch. Around them are low-rise concrete housing blocks, birches and a small playground. After eating, the group start playing a game of charades, in which each person takes it in turn to act out a famous painting for the others to guess. If I remember correctly, it is Vampilov himself – who has only just completed the exhausting return journey from the capital – who mimics the actions of a bird coming in to land. The painting is guessed immediately: Alexei Savrasov, *The Rooks Have Returned*. The group laugh. In the darkness of the cinema I laugh too. This feels like a very Russian joke – and, after many trips to the Tretyakov, I am in on it.

As a museum reserve, an extensive site conserved for posterity and open to the public, Abramtsevo has been designated as significant by the state: inside the fences, the trees are culturally valuable, worth paying to see. The implication is that those outside the fence are not. But is this really true? Gronsky's photography renders even the humblest of housing estate birches significant. So did *Sea Buckthorn Summer*.

Perhaps I should stop here a while, spend time with these Khotkovo birches. I could observe the greying whiteness of their trunks, a little blackened where they face the road. I could note their uniformity, the even spaces between each tree. When were they planted? After the housing was built, maybe in the 1960s? Perhaps more recently, to act as a screen as the road grew busier. I could pause and ponder the birch under socialism and in the years that followed the end of the USSR. What changes have these birches seen?

The birches of Abramtsevo are famous, depicted over and over again in drawings and paintings and photography from the nineteenth century right up to the present day. Tourists and school groups gather daily at Abramtsevo to check that the landscape looks like the paintings of the landscape, to confirm that their cultural heritage is as it should be. But if the lesson from the Russian realist paintings of the nineteenth century – some of them at least – is that the true Russian landscape is the humble, overlooked, unloved landscape, then maybe it is this line of birches by an anonymous housing block that I should really be writing about – and it is this elderly couple, whom I notice now, pausing at the end of a path to scatter grain for the pigeons by the side of the road, who would provide the necessary detail of authenticity to my descriptive sketch. And then, notes taken, observations made, perhaps I wouldn't need to keep walking to Abramtsevo (whichever way it is) after all. This is a persuasive idea – or perhaps I'm simply justifying my inability to read a departures board or bring a map.

But I don't stop here in Khotkovo. I keep walking. And after an hour or two, much to my own surprise, the signs are telling me that I've arrived. Welcome to Abramtsevo.

Influenced by the realist paintings of the early Peredvizhniki, came a generation of artists who adopted a quite different aesthetic relationship with Russian landscapes. Where Shishkin, Levitan, Kuindzhi and Savrasov sought inspiration in humble puddles, artists at the close of the nineteenth century and into the twentieth, such as Mikhail Vrubel, Nikolai Roerich and Ivan Bilibin were influenced by myth, folklore, Christian and pagan spirituality. In bringing such influences together, these artists sought to define a distinctly Russian sense of national identity. In contrast to their predecessors, they were less interested in documenting the hardships of the present than in diving headlong into an imagined past. The results were often quite bizarre. Vrubel, for example, painted strange shimmering demons inspired by Romantic poetry and Byzantine art; Roerich embedded giant skulls and Buddhist deities into fiery red mountains; Bilibin produced vivid illustrations for publications of Russian fairy tales, in which lean white birches often stand out starkly against the blackness of the forest behind; Viktor Vasnetsov painted stock folk-tale characters like the heroic Bogatyr knights or Ivanushka retuning home from his adventures, sailing above a misty Russian landscape on a richly woven flying carpet. Artists interested in Slavic folklore were often also influenced by Christianity. Vasnetsov, one of the key figures at Abramtsevo, painted frescoes in Saint Vladimir's Cathedral, Kyiv, among several commissions for the Russian Orthodox Church.

The most successful of these artists was Mikhail Nesterov. Nesterov was among the later generation of Wanderers, who often came from more prosperous families. His paintings characteristically depict stories from Russian folklore or tales of Orthodox saints embedded into the landscape. As historian Evgenia Kirichenko has written, the 'orthodox notion of the essential spirituality of daily life ... was the unique feature of the Russian peasantry, the *narod*'. It was this all-pervasive peasant spirituality that imbued so many of Nesterov's paintings, often shimmering images of humble rural devotion. Stylistically, his work shares significant qualities with the likes of Gustav Klimt of Austria (who also painted several beautiful, jewel-like birch forests), Finland's Akseli Gallen-Kallela, Sweden's Carl Larsson and the Norwegian Harald Sohlberg.

One of Nesterov's typical compositional techniques is for the landscape to mirror human narratives. This is done most obviously with trees. *The Hermit* (1888–9), for example, Nesterov's first great artistic triumph, depicts a wizened old man wearing woven birch-bark *lapty* and walking with a stick. In the work of another artist, this hermit might be handled very differently. Repin, for example, might use him to critique the material conditions of the rural poor. But Nesterov shows him seemingly untroubled, content to walk his own path. Repin's art carried the potential for political change; Nesterov was deeply conservative. Just behind the hermit stands a young fir tree. Both are content in their solitude.

In Nesterov's paintings the birch mostly mirrors a female presence. There are exceptions: in *Wayfarers Beyond the Volga* (1922), two men walk a riverside path with two slim birches rising behind them; in *Holy Rus* (1901–6) a cluster of birches stands behind Christ himself, clad all in white in a snowy Russian landscape. But for the most part birches stay close to women: a young girl pining by the water (*The Nightingale is Singing*, 1918), for example, or a group picking flowers by the river bank (*Girls by the River*, date unknown). In *The Taking of the Veil* (1897–8) a procession of nuns make their way through a Russian forest village. The white trim of their cassocks and the long pale candles they carry are echoed by the long white birches in both back- and foreground. Nesterov hoped his art could reconnect Westernised elites with the traditional values of the Russian peasantry. '[This] frustrated desire for contact with traditional Russia came to be expressed in overtly mystical and gendered terms,' writes professor of Russian literature Ellen Rutten. Arguably it was Nesterov who did more than any other visual artist to cement the relationship between femininity and the birch.

There is an irony here, however. The actual biology of the birch contradicts the gendered symbolism attached to it by Nesterov and by so many other artists and writers. As ethnobotanist Anna Lewington notes, 'Birches are hermaphrodite and are mostly self-infertile.' Birches grow catkins which allow their pollen to be shaken easily by the wind and carried away to other trees. Such effective wind pollination combined with easy hybridisation means that birches are, according to Lawrence Banks, owner of Hergest Croft Gardens in the UK, 'amongst the most promiscuous of trees'. For Nesterov, birches may be the very image of chaste Russian femininity, but the actual tree itself refuses this kind of interpretation.

In Nesterov's paintings, landscapes are like stage sets: the land confirms each religious scene as timeless, natural and, above all, Russian. *The Vision to the Youth Bartholomew* (1889–90) is one of Nesterov's most sophisticated paintings. It is the first in a series of five works he produced between 1889 and 1899 that depict scenes from *The Life of Saint Sergius* by Epiphanius the Wise, a medieval monk from Rostov. Today four of the works hang in the same room in the Tretyakov (including a truly dreadful painting of Sergius with a bear) while the final work, an icon-like portrait of Sergius, is in the collection of the Hermitage in Saint Petersburg.

Saint Sergius, also Sergius of Radonezh, is one of the most venerated figures in the Russian Orthodox Church. He founded many monasteries, including Trinity Lavra a few miles from Abramtsevo. In Nesterov's painting, he appears as a young boy approaching an old monk on the outskirts of a rural village. The landscape is humble but, typical for Nesterov, it shimmers like enamel. Nesterov covers the world in jewels. Wildflowers twinkle blue and yellow in the foreground. The autumn leaves glow with warming fires. Russia shines with holiness, with ancient tales, with a glory that is humble and quiet. But there are dark undertones, as I will soon discover, to all this gentle light.

Across the painting, multiple mirrorings are taking place. The most obvious is the ancient oak to the right, which reinforces the presence of the aged monk. Both are dark and old, reliable and Russian. Not only do their basic forms double one another, but their relationships to their immediate surroundings do too: the brown and green oak leaves overlapping the dark grey bark at the top-right of the painting are echoed precisely by the brown and green ground-level foliage overlapping the monk's dark grey cloak at the bottom-right of the painting.

Look closely and everything here is doubled: the twin blue onion domes on the village church; the twin little wooden huts in the field, golden rye piled up outside. To the left of the painting is another natural mirror. A young, slender birch tree, its leaves bright gold in the autumn, is a precise parallel of the young Sergius, so fair-haired and wide-eyed in his white over-shirt. And there's more: further left is another young white birch bracketed by two darker trees. This double reflection is like a hall of mirrors: a cyclical echoing between (Russian) man and (Russian) nature that could last for eternity beyond the frame of the painting. In the background yellowing larch and rich green firs stretch away across the hillsides.

Then came communism and everything changed. Many of the prominent names in Russian landscape painting – Shishkin, Levitan, Savrasov – went abroad. Bilibin left Russia to settle in Paris. Roerich was in Finnish Karelia when revolution broke out, and he and his family soon moved to London, then the US. The avant-garde flourished and, for a time, it seemed like Russian landscape painting would be consigned to the scrapheap of art history, remembered merely as a relic of a Tsarist past.

But the revolutionary wheel would turn full circle. The conceptual complexities of the avant-garde did not make for effective propaganda. Defending the realist approach to art was the Association of Artists of Revolutionary Russia (AkhRR), which had grown directly out of the Wanderers. They argued against the avant-garde, stating in 1922 that 'Our civic duty before mankind is to set down, artistically or documentarily, the revolutionary impulse of this great moment in history.' In short, for art to serve a revolutionary purpose it need not be revolutionary in form. AkhRR eventually triumphed and, as Stalin consolidated his grip on power in the 1930s, Socialist Realism became the dominant mode of artistic creation across Russia. For all its emphasis on modernity and progress, the regime would come to identify itself with an aesthetic that had largely been defined during the second half of the nineteenth century.

The post-revolutionary career of Nesterov is a case in point. A painter whose subjects were saints, rural churches and supposedly ancient stories of Orthodox belief would seem an obvious target for the regime's repressive apparatus. Yet Nesterov did not merely survive under Soviet rule, he thrived. Nesterov, whose anti-modern, anti-industrial images were so characteristic of the Russian fin-de-siècle, was awarded the Stalin Prize in 1941. He was one of the first artists to receive such a prestigious accolade. In part, this suggests remarkable ideological and stylistic flexibility on Nesterov's part. After the revolution, he designed propaganda posters for the state and painted portraits of prominent intellectuals while continuing to work on paintings of rural Orthodox piety all through the 1920s. That the Soviets not only accommodated but actively celebrated Nesterov points towards the highly conservative approach to culture eventually embraced by the communist regime.

The continuing prominence of nineteenth-century landscape painting throughout the twentieth century continues to surprise me. Across Russia there were artisanal workshops making reproductions of the most popular of nineteenth-century landscapes – Shishkin's *Rye Field* (1878) in particular. The aesthetics established by the likes of Levitan and Savrasov were major influences on the Socialist Realist painters espoused by the state under Stalin. Birch trees featured in Soviet-era paintings with the same familiar connotations of Russianness, femininity and purity. They helped to make the new world familiar. Especially in the second half of the twentieth century, rural scenes such as birch groves were a common subject for artists. But while their nineteenth-century predecessors were often bleak and grey, twentieth-century birch paintings by the likes of Arkady Rylov, Viktor Popkov and Vasily Baksheev were invariably sunny and bright. If landscape had once had something of a critical edge, this had long gone.

Put simply, in the Soviet era, the birch became a cliché. This cliché has not faded: from children's cartoons to war movies to countless bad paintings, the birch is so often there. Painters today churn out thousands of little birch-filled landscapes just as they did in Soviet times. Only now they serve the market not the state. The birch has become shorthand for a soppy kind of sentimental nostalgia, one that slides all too often into a narrow form of nationalism.

Within the fenced-off boundary of Abramtsevo museum reserve the world has come to life. I spot a nuthatch upside down on a tree trunk. And then another, two in fact, feeding on scraps of bread laid out on a little metal tray. There are birds everywhere, tapping away at the wooden beams of the quaint little nineteenth-century buildings or rattling the metal gutters of the Abramtsevo art museum.

Inside many of the buildings are displays of folk art collected in the nineteenth century: carvings, brass samovars, birch-bark containers, a straw cat. There are objects made by the artists who lived and worked here: sculptures and tiles, vases and fireplaces. Mounted on one wall is a green majolica head that looks like a pagan Green Man but labelled 'theatrical mask'. Made by Mikhail Vrubel, whose paintings hang in the Tretyakov, the figure is nestled among stylised green leaves with a green beard swirling like malachite.

Outside, I stroll through the grounds, chuckling at preposterous structures like the hut of folk witch Baba Yaga, with its bat-shaped wooden cross-beam. Abramtsevo feels sometimes like a place built for children – or even by children. Having spent so long looking at Russian landscape paintings, my experience of Abramtsevo is, at first, one of contented déjà vu. Everything is so familiar because this landscape has been depicted so many times by Russian artists, a synecdoche for the entirety of a nation. This little estate, just fifty acres, has again and again been used to represent the whole vast Russian land with its huge, diverse population. Walking through Abramtsevo is like looking at a model of a place or seeing the nation through a fish-eye lens.

I walk down towards the lake, where three little arched bridges connect a narrow curving promontory with water on both sides. This is, I'm fairly certain, the same location that Nesterov depicts in his 1905 painting *Two Harmonies*, in which a pair of lovers in elaborate medieval attire are echoed by a pair of swans, gliding together smoothly across the water. The narrow peninsula of white birches is exactly the same; the water reflects the autumn trees just so. There are differences between 1905 and today but, aesthetically at least, they are only minor. Instead of Nesterov's pair of swans, two ducks glide past. Instead of Nesterov's folklore fairies, there are couples taking photographs of each other: Russians eager to record themselves against this most Russian of Russian landscapes. The relationship between landscape and representation has come full circle once again. A man in a camouflage-patterned hoodie rows by in a dinghy.

It is only some time later that I remember one of the first inspirations for this book was in fact a painting of Abramtsevo. And it is only even later that I realise the troubling political implications of the painting and, by extension, Abramtsevo itself. In 2017, the Royal Academy of Arts in London held an exhibition entitled *Revolution: Russian Art 1917–1932*. It celebrated the diverse flourishing of artistic styles in that intense, creative, violent period of Russia's history. Surprisingly, it was not only the avant-garde Suprematism of Kazimir Malevich or the powerful realism of Ilya Repin or even the oddball visions of Pavel Filonov that lingered so strongly in my mind; it was also the piercing conservatism of Nesterov.

The painting on show was *The Philosophers*, a 1917 double portrait in which two men walk side by side deep in thought. One is dressed in contemporary clothing: black suit and tie, black overcoat, a broad-brimmed black hat held by his side in his right hand. He has short hair and his brow is deeply furrowed as he scrutinises the distance. This is Sergey Bulgakov: theologian, philosopher, economist, priest.

By Bulgakov's side is another man, dressed in long white robes and a small, box-shaped, black velvet hat called a *skufia*. His hair curls out onto his shoulder. This is Pavel Florensky: like Bulgakov, a theologian, philosopher and priest, but also a mathematician and, in the terminology of the Russian Orthodox Church, a 'neomartyr'. Sometimes compared to figures like Goethe or Leonardo, Florensky is seen as one of the great Russian thinkers of the pre-revolutionary era, whose love of geometry manifested itself through writings on a diverse range of subjects, from religion to politics, physics and electrodynamics.

In Nesterov's painting, both Bulgakov and Florensky are shown with their heads tilted downwards. But where Bulgakov's face betrays fierce worry over the future, Florensky's eyes are cast calmly towards the earth. In his right hand is a tall wooden staff, his left hand touches his heart. Bulgakov has strong features and a dark pointed beard; Florensky is altogether softer. *The Philosophers* is one of Nesterov's less elaborately bejewelled works. I wonder if it's because he was treating contemporary, living subjects rather than those of folklore or religion. Or whether it's simply the date: 1917. That gilded age of fin-de-siècle symbolism was coming crashing to a close. The background is simple and dark. No wildflowers, no glimmering birch trees, just fields and a hillside forested with evergreens. These are the fields and forests, I now know, of Abramtsevo.

Abramtsevo was an apt choice. Nesterov was living here while working on the painting in 1917 and both Bulgakov and Florensky visited too. For Florensky, in particular, Abramtsevo was a vital place not simply because of the aesthetics of the landscape but because of its proximity to the holy site of Trinity Lavra. Founded in 1337, the monastery had for centuries been home to communities of monks. It was also home to relics of Saint Sergius and the burial place for several Russian tsars. 'The Abramtsevo landscape was seen by Florensky as the main element in the spiritual structure of the Lavra's grounds,' writes art historian Nicoletta Misler.

When I first saw Nesterov's painting, however, I knew little about either Bulgakov or Florensky. I was taken by the sense of tension, a deep concern for the future, and what I fuzzily felt to be the sheer great Russianness of it all. The visual language of the painting suggested to me the need to make a choice, a fork in the road for Russia. What I misunderstood was the

The Philosophers Artist: Nesterov, Mikhail Vasilievich (1862-1942)/Russian. Credit: Location Tretyakov Gallery, Moscow, Russia/Bridgeman Images

nature of that choice. Because they are dressed so differently, their facial expressions in clear contrast, I read the relationship between Bulgakov and Florensky as somehow oppositional: one modern, secular, worried; the other traditional, pious, calm. I was too quick to read the painting as an allegory for the debate between Westernisers and Slavophiles over Russia's identity and destiny. By the time I visited the painting again, this time in the Tretyakov in Moscow, I felt it was best read as a story of personal ethical choice. The future is coming. How ought one to face it? After the revolution the two experienced contrasting fates: frowning, black-clad Bulgakov went to Paris where he founded a theological institute and continued working until he died of throat cancer in 1944. Florensky, already depicted by Nesterov with the tranquil acceptance of a martyr, remained in Russia. He was arrested several times, sent to labour camps, and eventually, on 8 December 1937, he was taken with 500 others to a wood outside Saint Petersburg, and shot.

But even this interpretation is limited. For both Bulgakov and Florensky were, it is now thought, deeply antisemitic. Nesterov was close friends with both and was also at one time reportedly a member of an ultra-nationalist proto-fascist group known as the Union of the Russian People. It is not unlikely therefore that Nesterov held similar beliefs.

In her 2013 book *The Moscow Pythagoreans*, historian Ilona Svetlikova goes into detail about the extreme right-wing views of a group of mathematicians calling themselves the Moscow School, with whom Florensky was closely associated. Members of the school, in particular Pavel Nekrasov, argued that mathematics could provide an argument for absolute monarchy. 'Mathematics seems to deal with stable unchangeable laws,' writes Svetlikova in an attempt to explain the rigidly authoritarian politics of this group of mathematicians. Florensky, she notes, wrote in a letter to Vasily Rozanov (the antisemitic writer who described all Russian philosophy as 'that of the flogged man') that 'the only effective way of solving the Jewish question would be to castrate the Jews'.

Historian Dominic Rubin's book *Holy Russia, Sacred Israel* includes a chapter entitled 'Bulgakov and the sacred blood of Jewry'. It seems that it was after his exile from Russia that Bulgakov's own hatred of Jews frothed to the surface. It is likely that Bulgakov blamed Jewish people for the revolutions that saw him exiled, but it is also evident that antisemitism had ebbed and flowed in his writings long before he put, in Rubin's words, 'the guilt for the Russian Revolution onto Jewish treachery and parasitism'. Florensky, for his part, was already writing in support of Zionism that Jews should

> get for themselves some sort of territory somewhere on the earth and arrange for themselves their kingdom, their ghetto, any of them that want to, but just let them leave us in peace.

In reading about Bulgakov and Florensky I find it difficult to know whether antisemitism was an avoidable supplement to their ways of thinking or a structural component of their worldviews. But what of Nesterov? Can we read his paintings without reference to this political history? Can we separate the man from the art? In *Heart-Pine Russia*, art historian Jane T. Costlow admits that Nesterov's later paintings, especially those produced in the decade leading up to the 1917 revolutions, were among his least successful. These works 'don't just fail', she writes, 'but become monuments of oppressive, kitschy national-ism'. It was during this period, Costlow does not mention, that Nesterov joined the extreme nationalist Union of the Russian People. If Nesterov's art is inseparable from such politics, then it fails for more serious reasons than being simply 'kitschy'.

In a preceding chapter, Costlow discusses Pavel Melnikov's pseudonymous 1874 novel *In the Forests*, which describes the region around the upper Volga and was a huge influence on many of the Abramtsevo artists. She quotes his descriptions of a 'mythic Rus'' and his disdain for Batu Khan, 'the godless Tsar Batu', one of the Mongol rulers whose Golden Horde had con-quered the lands of the Rus' in the thirteenth century and ruled the region for 250 years. 'It's Old Rus' there,' writes Melnikov in a purple paragraph from which Costlow has borrowed the title of her fascinating book: 'time out of time, heart-pine Russia'.

Melnikov continues: 'It's a kindhearted land, though it looks with anger on the stranger.' Melnikov, it seems, is not only referring to 'godless' Mongol rulers here. So what strangers does he have in mind? Costlow glosses these unwelcome interlopers not as 'non-Russian inhabitants of the woods but a *Russian* from Petersburg or Moscow'. Costlow seeks to exonerate Melnikov from any revisionist accusation of xenophobia by shifting the dividing line between friend and stranger away from the nationalist opposition of Russian/non-Russian to less historically charged distinctions between the urban and the rural or the local and the tourist. However, by stressing the word 'inhabitants', Costlow leaves open the wider possibility of a xenophobia based not on ethnicity or nationality but on what it means to live in a place.

One hundred and forty years on from Melnikov's description of rural Russia, what has changed? A 2018 essay by curator Georgy Nikich describes comparable attitudes among the village population of Kaluga, ninety miles south-west of Moscow. He writes of a 'rigid border of mistrust between the locals and all others, businessmen, managers, artists, tourists (i.e. outsiders, "not ours")'.

Such examples beg the question: what does it mean to call a place 'home'? Who decides and when? For, as history has shown many times, 'home' is a concept that may always be exploited and weaponised or uprooted and walled-off. Not everyone gets to choose where they call home – and defining what 'home' means is not simply a question of individual choice, but one that also involves local communities, nation states, the police, the law … It is therefore not so much who gets defined as 'us' or 'them' that matters as the urge to impose a rigid border between them. To attribute xenophobia not to (mortal) people but to the (immortal) land, as Melnikov does, suggests precisely this desire to fix division.

At the very least, Melnikov's Rus' is a place willing to exclude those not deemed local enough. And I now see something similar in Nesterov's paintings too. Sat at home at my computer, I look again at an image of *The Philosophers* and it is, all of a sudden, a totally different painting. I see Nesterov, lovingly painting his two close friends, united by their fawning love of absolute power and their hatred of Jews.

In digging into this dark history I start to find out more. It was not only Nesterov whose politics seemed to align with those of the far-right. Fellow Abramtsevo artist Viktor Vasnetsov was a member of a pre-revolutionary movement known as the Black Hundred – an ultra-nationalist group that advocated Tsarist absolutism and Russia for Russians only. The Black Hundred counted among their number some of the most influential names in Russian society: from leading figures in botany, history and philology to prominent members of the Church and aristocracy. This was not some group of cranks railing powerlessly from the fringes of Russian politics; they stood right in the very centre. Members of the movement assassinated Jewish politicians and incited pogroms against Jewish people in the early years of the twentieth century. In the 1890s, my own Jewish ancestors fled from such pogroms taking place in Poland, then ruled by the Russian Tsars. It is hard for me not to think of this family history when I look now at the work of Nesterov or Vasnetsov.

This era of Russian landscape painting, and by extension the continued obsession with Abramtsevo, is, it now seems to me, tainted by the politics of an extreme conservatism that also embraced antisemitism. The reason I cannot now overlook Nesterov's politics is because his landscapes always served a political programme. If the very earth, the flowers and the birches are eternally and exclusively Russian, then where does this leave those who are deemed not to be Russian enough? By imbuing the land itself with Orthodox religion, such art allows no place for difference or dissent. It fixes a natural law, a narrow, unchanging Russianness as a law of nature. Jews were welcome to do the same – just so long as it was somewhere else. As Florensky puts it, they should 'get for themselves some sort of territory somewhere on earth' and 'leave us in peace'. '*Zemlya moya,*' as Yevgeniy Ross sang in 'Birch Trees of Russia' that accompanied Maria Kapajeva's film: the 'my land' of private property or the 'my land' of xenophobic ethno-nationalism?

Antisemitism was hardly new in Russia during that period, nor was it new in many other countries. Here is Fyodor Dostoyevsky expressing fears over the destruction of Russia's forests in 'My Paradox' (June 1876):

> Now the Yids are becoming landowners, and people shout and write everywhere that they are destroying the soil of Russia. A Yid, they say, having spent capital to buy an estate, at once exhausts all the fertility of the land he has purchased in order to restore his capital with interest. But just try and say anything against this and the hue and cry will be at once raised: you are violating the principles of economic freedom and equal rights for all citizens.

Costlow quotes this exact same passage from Dostoyevsky in *Heart-Pine Russia*. She notes that Dostoyevsky's 'implication that Jewish landowners are exhausting not just the soil but the peasant himself is incendiary' but she then moves swiftly onwards to deal with her primary interest in the chapter: deforestation. I, however, cannot move on quite so quickly. As I re-read this passage, I notice a number of things.

Firstly, Dostoyevsky does not admit the criticism of Jews as his own but as that of unidentified plural others – '*people* shout and write . . .', '*they* say . . .' In so doing, Dostoyevsky gives voice to these perspectives (real or merely employed rhetorically) at the very same time that he adopts the 'Don't shoot me!' hands-in-the-air pose of the innocent messenger. He is then able to claim for himself the status of persecuted victim for merely daring to voice this criticism. There is also a contradiction: on the one hand, everyone is complaining about the Jews; on the other hand, nobody is allowed to complain about them. Well, which is it?

The text continues in a similar vein: Dostoyevsky imagines a 'Talmudic *status in statu*' (a secretive Jewish state within a state); he rages over the 'exhaustion of the soil'; that these new Jewish landowners have 'sucked the juices from the peasants of western Russia'; and that they are not only buying up the land with all that capital but have 'also begun to buy up liberal opinion'. Exploitative, vampiric, rich, powerful, shadowy and somehow in control of a liberal European left: nearly one hundred and fifty years later, such attacks on Jews have returned once more. Dostoyevsky's text might have been dredged from the darker corners of alt-right internet discussion boards. Instead it is from one of the most celebrated writers Russia has ever produced.

Dostoyevsky, incidentally, loved a birch forest. In 'The Peasant Marey' (February 1876) Dostoyevsky goes foraging for mushrooms and wild berries in a birch wood. There, he undergoes an encounter with the titular peasant that affirms his belief in the 'almost feminine tenderness' that 'fill[s] the heart of a coarse, bestially ignorant Russian serf'. Following this encounter, Dostoyevsky cites writer Sergey Aksakov (the owner of Abramtsevo until 1870) and his praise of the apparently 'advanced level of development of our Russian People'. In this scene, the birches are not simply an incidental backdrop but an enduring presence and influence: 'And even now, as I write this,' continues Dostoyevsky, 'I can catch the fragrance from our stand of birches in the country: these impressions stay with you all your life.'

At Abramtsevo, which to my knowledge Dostoyevsky did not visit, the tiny Church of the Saviour that Viktor Vasnetsov designed in collaboration with fellow landscape painter Vasily Polenov, is packed with visitors. People make the sign of the cross, stand quietly in prayer or contemplation. In the bottom right-hand corner of the church's iconostasis is a tiny portrait of the venerated Saint Sergius of Radonezh, who founded the nearby monastery of Trinity Lavra, so beloved by Florensky. Sergius is strongly associated with the idea of Holy Russia, the medieval image that nineteenth-century Slavophiles attempted to rekindle. 1892 marked the five hundredth anniversary of Sergius's death and he was celebrated by the Tsarist authorities and the Russian Orthodox Church as a timeless embodiment of religion and autocracy. Florensky described Sergius as 'the guardian angel of Russia'.

Saint Sergius, whose earthly name is Bartholomew, is the boy depicted in the Nesterov paintings I was looking at in the Tretyakov. Vasnetsov's 1882 portrait in the Abramtsevo iconostasis and the fifth and final work in Nesterov's series are both strikingly like icons. The composition in both is simple to the point of austerity, but there are differences: Nesterov shows a more expanded view of the surrounding Abramtsevo landscape; Vasnetsov's painting is embroidered by a patterned border and, in the top right corner, what looks like a representation of Andrei Rublev's *Trinity*, a celebrated Russian icon commissioned for Trinity Lavra in the fifteenth century. Sergius stands still in the centre of the frame facing straight out towards the viewer. He holds a scroll in his right hand and is making the sign of the blessing with his left.

There is one striking similarity between these two paintings, however: the presence in both of birch trees. In Nesterov's painting, the young birch mirrors the presence of the young Bartholomew. In Vasnetsov's portrait there are in fact three birch saplings. But what do they mean? Perhaps they allude to Sergius's eternal youth; perhaps they provide a visual short-hand for Russia; perhaps they are an echo of the Rublev *Trinity* or Trinity Lavra itself. The power of the symbol is that it can be all at once. On the other side of Sergius is a small white church that looks a little like Trinity Lavra but also very similar to the Church of the Saviour, designed by Vasnetsov, in which this painting hangs. Not for the first time the birch seems to be growing inside a hall of mirrors.

To enter the Abramtsevo art museum visitors are required to don blue plastic overshoes. The floor is pristine and shiny and white.

There are many second-rate paintings hanging here. The late nineteenth century was the estate's art-historical apex and Tretyakov bought most of the better pieces. As a result, the museum contains a high proportion of works from the first half of the twentieth century. After the estate had been nationalised, it remained to varying degrees a retreat for artists. There are later works too: in particular, a pair of paintings by husband and wife Nikolai Andronov and Nataliya Egorshina, each a portrait of the other against a backdrop of birches, as well as many luminous watercolours by Alexei Shmarinov, several of which show wavering birches reflected softly in water.

But there is one painting in the museum that I especially wanted to see: *Birches* (1918) by Robert Falk. I find it hung in a corner by a still life, *Bottles* (1912), also by Falk, and partly obscured from certain angles behind a bronze bust by Vera Mukhina (best known for her famous Socialist Realist monument *Worker and Kolkhoz Woman*). As the title suggests, the painting depicts birches. Painted at Abramtsevo, where Falk produced a number of works, it is quite unlike the slender, fairy-tale nationalist birches of Nesterov or Vasnetsov. Instead, Falk, who was a great admirer of Paul Cézanne, employs swooping curves, angular lines and planes of colour. The houses are simple fields of red, orange and yellow, the sky an undulating blue like one of Vrubel's glazed ceramic tiles. Every surface is textured by the marks of the brush and gradients of blended colour.

There are two trees in the painting: a large birch filling much of the centre of the composition and a smaller one off to the left as you look. Both are predominantly grey-white; the slimmer tree on the left has a rippling line of pink running up the left side of the trunk, while the larger tree blends from grey-white to purple, to dark mauve and brown in the upper branches. When you get nearer, you can see an array of further colours down the trunk: subtle traces of dark blue, mustard yellow, flushing sunset pink, green, grey, purple, black.

Unlike, say, Ivan Shishkin, Falk is not a painter of details: no lenticels, no delicately curling birch bark, no individually delineated leaves. And unlike Nesterov and Vasnetsov who sought to fix an image of an eternal, unchangingly religious Russia, Falk's painting is characterised by its gusting sense of movement. Falk's birches are not slender and ethereal. They are angular and strong. But most striking is the sense of lightness and movement in the foliage – possible precisely because Falk has avoided the careful rendering of individual twigs and leaves. Instead, the painting is the result of the movement of paint in swatches, in waves, from left to right, up and down. The brush creates movement in the group, not the individual. There is a gentle sense of a jostling breeze, a rustling of birch moving. You can hear it if you listen right up close.

Falk, incidentally, was Jewish. I wonder what he must have felt while he was at Abramtsevo, staying in the same buildings as Nesterov (maybe they even met there?), walking past

Vasnetsov's silly little church. What must he have thought of such a place? This birch painting gives nothing away.

What intrigues me about *Birches* is the way that Falk takes a subject so close to that of Nesterov – a tall white birch and the self-consciously traditional wooden huts of Abramtsevo – and carves something completely different in tone and implications. The huts look not timelessly medieval but makeshift and temporary. Painted in 1918, the year after the revolutions, with Russia having exited World War I only to find itself mired in a civil war that would last even longer, it is a painting above all of movement. What this movement might mean is much harder to know.

Historian Musya Glants has compared antisemitism in Russia in the later years of the USSR to the way that Jews were treated earlier in the twentieth century. She writes:

> In the 1970s and early 1980s, the arbitrary behavior of the authorities, which affected everyone in the country, was aggravated by antisemitism where Jews were concerned. The situation had not changed much from the mid-1940s when a Party boss came to the studio of the great Soviet artist Robert Falk, looked at one of his landscapes, and declared: 'This is not a Russian landscape. Our Russian birches are tall, straight and well-proportioned while these are birch trees from the *shtetl* (*mestechkovye*) and they are all crooked.'

'Our Russian birches are tall, straight and well-proportioned': where could this Soviet boss have received his aesthetic values from if not from the landscape paintings of the Socialist Realists, who had in turn taken theirs from the birch tree paintings of the nineteenth century? And yet the key artist of that era was Isaac Levitan, the Jewish painter born in exactly the *'shtetl'* that this art-historically ignorant Party boss is so keen to deride.

And what of the painting itself: could this be the same

painting that I am looking at in Abramtsevo? Falk certainly
painted other birches. *Landscape, Crimea* (1905) shows a white
birch leaning unsteadily from the right side of the painting
towards the centre. *Young Trunks* (1907) depicts line upon line
of grey-white birches against a murky grey-green forest. Where
the regular vertical lines in Alexander Gronsky's photograph
reminded me of a barcode, Falk's painting looks more like
prison bars. The birches are crooked in the centre: if these are
bars, it would not be difficult to escape through them.

When Falk painted *Birches* in 1918, the communists had just
come to power and repealed a host of antisemitic legislation that
had existed under the Tsars, circumscribing where Jewish people
could live, where they could conduct business and what work they
were allowed to do. In the late nineteenth century, long-standing
repressive policies and antisemitic attitudes were exacerbated
after several assassination attempts on Tsar Alexander II, events
falsely blamed on Jews. The fabrication of *The Protocols of the Elders
of Zion*, a text purporting to be a secret Jewish plan to take over
the world, took place in Russia in the early years of the twentieth
century. Fake, but disseminated as genuine, it helped fuel suspicions that Russia was somehow being run by a secret Jewish state
within the state (to borrow Dostoyevsky's phrase). Although the
Bolsheviks repealed many officially antisemitic policies, their
attitude towards Judaism was often contradictory. With Stalin's
rise to power, antisemitism reared its head once more. Falk left
for Paris in 1928 and refused to return for a decade. By the 1950s,
once again living in Moscow, Falk was feted by a new generation
of Russian artists. He died in 1958.

Tiring of birches, I walk back to the railway station. I'm
increasingly conscious of Abramtsevo not as an idyllic home
for some innocent reconnection with the natural world but
as a place in which antisemitism was nurtured as if it were
an inseparable part of Russian identity There is a walkway

through the woods, punctuated every dozen yards or so by information boards telling passers-by about the history of the estate. No mention is made of the far-right ideology of Nesterov or Vasnetsov – nor is there in any of the guide books or many of the art history books I have read on the subject. To one side as I walk are high metal fences, demarcating private property. Along the walkway are lamp-posts and, as I draw closer, I hear music rattling obtrusively through sinister-looking speakers. First Tchaikovsky, then something from, I think, *Evita*. By the time I get to the station I can't wait to leave this weird place, but instead I must sit and wait. The next train back to Moscow is not for hours.

VII

BORDERS, BIRCHES, WAR

'I saw myself walking through the camp gates ... they slammed shut behind me with a loud clank. I'm free ... I walked a little way and saw a birch tree by the road ... just a regular birch ... I ran up to it and put my arms around it, pressed my whole body against it.'

Anna M., quoted in Svetlana Alexievich,
Second-Hand Time, 2016

The deep quiet of a birch grove is broken all of a sudden by the sound of banging. A Ukrainian man is smashing trees with his head. A second Ukrainian approaches him.

'What's the matter with you?' asks the second Ukrainian.

'A Russian man just walked by,' explains the first Ukrainian, 'and he said out loud: "What a purely *Russian* landscape."'

When Daniel Rancour-Laferriere tells this little joke in his psychoanalytic study *Russian Nationalism from an Interdisciplinary Perspective*, he includes the respective ethnic slurs: the Ukrainians are *khokol*s (derogatory Russian slang for Ukrainians) while the Russian is a *moskal* (derogatory Ukrainian slang for a Russian). The joke is supposed to illustrate

Rancour-Laferriere's exploration of the hugely complex relationship between the peoples of the two nations, who are in certain areas, he says, ethnically indistinguishable. The point he is making is that ethnicity and nationality are not always neatly aligned. Historically, this has led not only to conceptual complications for those who think – or wish – them to be so, but also to persecution and worse for those seen as failing to fit into rigidly imposed models of identity. Ukrainian-American historian Serhii Plokhy has pointed out that, in the nineteenth century, many of the intellectuals promoting the idea of a Russian nation were in fact Ukrainian. Rancour-Laferriere mentions numerous Russian nationalists from the nineteenth century onwards 'who believe that Ukrainians are really just Russians'.

Such beliefs have informed systematic repression of attempts to establish a Ukrainian identity separate from a Russian one. The Ukrainian language was banned in schools from 1804 to 1917. After the exile and death of poet Taras Shevchenko who wrote in Ukrainian and advocated Ukrainian independence, Russia imposed even tighter restrictions on the use of the language, many of which continued under the Soviets. According to Rancour-Laferriere, one high-ranking Tsarist official 'even declared that the Ukrainian language did not exist'. And it is not only Ukraine: children in Poland were banned from speaking Polish in the nineteenth century. In Chechnya, a very different context, the Russians also attempted to impose their own language from above. Even Chechen literature was taught, if it was taught at all, in translation.

Another feature of Russia's treatment of the so-called 'near abroad' from the Tsars to Stalin has been mass deportations. In a phenomenon that has become known as the 'memory hole', Soviet publications simply stopped mentioning places like Chechnya and the Crimean Republics after 1946. These countries were removed from official maps, their existence denied altogether. 'Not only was each nation's present obliterated,' wrote historian Robert Conquest in *The Nation Killers*, 'but its past as well.'

Historic divisions such as these may be felt in the landscape. But not always. The humour of Rancour-Laferriere's joke – if there is any – is that, while the Russian feels the birch grove to be a 'purely Russian landscape', for the Ukrainians, it only signifies as Russian once a Russian has claimed it as such. Until then it was just a birch grove. We're not even told which country it is actually in. There is nothing intrinsically Russian about such a place. And yet, the act of claiming ownership, in this case by a Russian man, leads very quickly, in the joke and sometimes also in reality, to violence.

When I set out on this journey I expected to be spending a lot of time in art galleries and landscape gardens, in forests and libraries. I did not expect to be writing about war. But war and nationalism have so often fed one another, and in Russia's case, it is during war-time that the symbolism of the birch tree has been at its most ideologically charged.

In his 2015 series *Line of Site*, Russian artist Mikhail Tolmachev explores the way that war shapes the aesthetics of landscape and vice-versa. The series is based upon photographs published by news agencies on both sides of the conflict between Russia and Ukraine in Crimea. Tolmachev collects these images, then rephotographs the backgrounds and produces greyscale photo-etchings from the results.

In so doing, *Line of Site* asks us to focus not on the events of war but on the backdrop against which these events take place. And the backdrop, as Tolmachev suggests, is never simply a backdrop; it is the land that is being fought over. In every sense of the phrase: the earth upon which the fighting takes place; the landscape against which it is depicted; but also the territory that is being fought for in the name of power, the nation, its people. And yet, in Tolmachev's images, these lands – apparently so vital that ten thousand must die to win them – have almost no distinguishing features.

Tolmachev's work therefore stands in marked contrast to the war-time art and literature of the Soviet era. In the 1940s, many Russian artists and writers sought to emphasise fundamental differences not only between Germans and Russians but also between German land and Russian land. 'Nature itself is for us and against Hitler,' wrote Nobel Prize-winning author Mikhail Sholokhov (famous for his four-volume novel, *And Quiet Flows the Don* (1925–40), about the lives of Cossacks living along the Don River) in a war-time short story called 'Cossack Collective Farms'. 'Everywhere in Germany nature is different,' says the narrator of another short story, 'One Man's Destiny', published in the same collection.

The land in Tolmachev's photographs could be almost anywhere. But it is not anywhere; it is a very specific area of land laden with psychological significance. Crimea was annexed by Russia in the 1780s, its landscapes experienced as a parade of picturesque idylls by the plant-loving Catherine the Great. But the idealised views shown to the Empress have not been borne out by subsequent realities. Part of the difficulty, as Masha Gessen has noted, is that in 1944, Stalin embarked on a process of ethnic cleansing, deporting Tatars and many others from the region to be replaced with ethnic Russians. Then in 1954, Khrushchev redrew the borders to make the newly Russified Crimea part of Ukraine.

'Thinking takes place in the relationship of territory and the earth,' wrote Gilles Deleuze and Félix Guattari. I wonder if that is precisely where war takes place too. Incidentally, *Line of Site* has been exhibited in both Moscow and Kyiv, on both sides of the dividing line that war scrawls across the earth.

Rancour-Laferriere likens national identity to marital status: it is binary (a person is either married or not married, Russian or not Russian); performative (confirmed through linguistic acts guaranteed by the appropriate authorities – church/state); and strongly felt by those involved. Marriage, like national identity, may be a social construct perpetuated by patriarchal forces but that doesn't make it any less powerful, emotionally and therefore also, from time to time, politically. 'Russia is an illusion,' writes Rancour-Laferriere:

> One cannot see her – unless one believes that the very earth enclosed within the borders of Russia is Russia, or that the birch tree standing before one's eyes is Russia, or that the tricolour flag of white, blue and red is Russia.

Few things are more powerful than dreams. And it strikes me as significant that Rancour-Laferriere chooses these three emblems of Russianness: the earth, the flag and the birch tree. The earth is the ground we walk upon and, as Tolmachev shows, the ground that is fought over. The flag is pure symbol, unsullied by materiality (unless you should undertake the provocative act of burning one). The birch is a visual link between the two: a vertical line, just like a flag pole, from the earth beneath our feet to the flag fluttering in the sky. The earth has always been here, the flag must arrive: whether it's the hammer and sickle or the Tsarist tricolour, back in use from 1993. If the earth is nature, the flag is culture, and the birch tree the bridge between the two. The birch is therefore both dream and reality, or the dream made real. Rancour-Laferriere continues, citing Vamik Volkan, a Turkish-Cypriot psychiatrist known for his work in conflict resolution:

> Earth, birch trees, the tricolour flag – these are just physical objects at one level. But they can function as what Vamik

Volkan terms 'reservoirs' or 'suitable targets of externalization of one's feelings'.

I like this idea of the birch as a reservoir, a place where meaning is stored like water, to be drawn upon in times of drought. Reservoirs can supply entire populations. They are controlled by municipal administrations or, increasingly, private corporations. In what dry times is the birch most needed? And has it too been privatised?

In 1951, a propaganda poster was issued that depicted Stalin as 'the best friend of children'. The poster, designed by Elena Melnikova, includes a portrait of the Soviet dictator looking remarkably youthful for a sixty-three year old. The portrait hangs behind a group of children, all clad in the white shirts and red neck scarves of the Young Pioneers. The five children on the front row have their right arms raised in salute. The rows behind them are waving red flags in dutiful exuberance. It is a multi-ethnic group and they all have bright smiles on their faces. There is something of the matinee idol about Stalin behind them, his hair and moustache glossy, his eyes twinkling bright.

The backdrop to the entire image is a leaf-like green, interspersed with clusters of sketchily drawn white birch trees. The black and white tree trunks certainly lend a pleasing verticality to the composition. But they also serve another function – only, I'm having trouble deciphering exactly what that is. On the one hand, the birches might be read as symbols of Russia, in which case the smiling children would represent some of the many ethnicities that have long called Russia home. On the other hand, perhaps the children represent not different ethnicities but the fifteen constituent republics that made up the USSR at the time, Russia being just one of them. '[T]he Soviet Union,' writes Thomas Meaney, 'was the first modern state to make no reference to any national or ethnic connection in its name. But as much as Lenin and Stalin believed in transcending the nation-state, they did not see it happening anytime soon.' This tension between an ideological internationalism and a pragmatic politics of power meant that questions of ethnicity and nationalism were invariably complicated. As Masha Gessen explains in *The Future is History*:

> All Soviet citizens ... were aware of their ethnicity, which was never neutral information – it could confer advantages where vestiges of affirmative action remained, or open one up to official discrimination or persecution if one's ethnic group was currently suspect ... In other words, the Soviet system of managing both the republics and the various ethnic groups who populated them was inherently contradictory.

This fraught complexity is also embodied by the confusion between the terms 'Russian' and 'Soviet', between Russia as a nation and the USSR as a group of nations or empire. These two terms were sometimes in alignment, but not always. 'There was a tendency,' writes Rancour-Laferriere, 'to equate or conflate "Soviet" (*sovetskii*) with "Russian" (*russkii*) both in the Soviet Union and in the West.' Rancour-Laferriere also notes the way that Russia imposed its language and culture on other nations in much the same way as the British Empire. 'Soviet and pre-Soviet Russian imperialism thus had the same linguistic side-effect as British imperialism: many Russian-speakers today are no more "Russian" than English-speakers are "English".' At the same time, the conflation of Russian with Soviet also meant that very few specifically Russian institutions were created. 'Geoffrey Hosking is quite correct,' he continues, citing the venerable historian, 'in saying that the Russians were thereby "disadvantaged in the very culture they dominated".'

This conflation between Russia as a nation and something altogether larger not only pre-dates the Soviets but outlives them too. I'm concerned that my own thinking may not be able to escape these problems: to say 'the Soviets did …' is to allocate agency to an ideology; to say 'the Russians did …' is to do so to a nation. Very often, neither is quite right. Like Rancour-Laferriere, Ukrainian-American historian Serhii Plokhy also quotes Hosking, who wrote that: 'Britain *had* an empire, but Russia *was* an empire – and perhaps still is.' Plokhy is explaining the historical confusion at the heart of Russian identity, but such sentiments are also used as justification for expansionist authoritarianism by Putin-era demagogues such as Aleksandr Dugin, the fringe intellectual whose fascist philosophies have gradually been embraced by the Kremlin. 'Russia is unthinkable without an empire,' Dugin has said in a classic sleight-of-hand that blurs 'is' with 'ought'; conflating what may be historically true with what is ethically justifiable.

But back to the birches: in the poster, it's noticeable how the lines of the trunks and branches provide an echo of the wooden sticks upon which the Young Pioneers wave their little red flags. In the centre of the image along the line of where a horizon might be, these red flags are waved over and across the white trunks of the trees. The juxtaposition of red against green and white is a striking one for it lays, one on top of the other, two significant 'reservoirs' (in Vamik Volkan's terminology) of Soviet symbolism.

But there is more, I think. Aside from the green background, the trees are shown leafless, so it looks sometimes as if, instead of foliage, these birches have sprouted communist flags, which are now fluttering in the breeze. As in the landscape paintings of the nineteenth century, there is a merging of human symbolism with natural imagery. The intention, I think, is to draw upon nature's apparent timelessness in order to shore up a particular political position. The problem is that, while nature is presented as fixed, politics is always on the move.

In a pristine white café on the top floor of an oligarch-funded art centre in Kyiv, I chat about birch trees with Anna Gidora, founder of a Ukrainian festival of land art. Founded in 1997, the festival takes place every summer in Mogritsa, just a couple of miles from the border with Russia. 'Some people think of land art as some kind of intrusion,' Anna tells me through a translator, but she explains that most of the contributions to the festival are only temporary. Artists have made circles of fire, cairn-like sculptures, and floated branches through clear green streams. That said, plans are afoot for a more permanent land art park, the first in Ukraine. 'Land art enjoys state and private funding in civilised countries,' reads a text on the website of a Ukrainian foundation that is helping to finance the project. 'In our country, this movement survives only thanks to enthusiasm born by sincere love for land and its inexhaustible resources.'

As we drink bitter sea buckthorn tea, Anna tells me about the Holodomor, the 1932–3 famine in Ukraine that was deliberately induced by the Soviet authorities, during which up to ten million people are thought to have died. The horrendous famine, which many consider to be a form of genocide, was for years denied by the Soviet authorities and covered up by Western journalists. 'People were dying with hunger and eating the dead,' says Anna. 'Just a few miles away, the shops were full of food. People were shot if they tried to take any of it back across the border.'

One recent summer in Mogritsa, an artist threaded lengths of red fabric between the birch trees on the Ukrainian side of the border in an act of remembrance. In so doing the artist was designating a tree growing within Ukraine as a symbol of Russianness and therefore historic oppression. As in Rancour-Laferriere's joke, the artist shifts the resonance of the landscape by drawing attention to different political and historical associations. 'The birch trees are associated with Russia,' says Anna, 'the red with aggression and blood.' After the festival the fabric was taken down; the border, of course, remains in place.

The Soviet Union was bookended by wars: World War I signalled the end of the Tsars; the war in Afghanistan hastened the end of the USSR. In between, the civil war that engulfed Russia in the aftermath of revolution ensured that, whatever intentions the Bolsheviks started with, in order to hold on to power only the most militarised command structure could succeed. Then came World War II, the Great Patriotic War as it is known in Russia. Each of these four wars reshaped how Russia understood itself: the first destroyed a dynasty, the second reshaped a continent, the third made Russia great (again); the fourth ground greatness into dust.

For the UK and US, war is mostly fought far away. The Battle of Britain saw the UK subjected to sustained bombing campaigns, and the Nazis occupied the Channel Islands from 1940 to 1945, but ground fighting has generally been seen as something that happens overseas: an activity for the colonies or mainland Europe. Britain likes to think of itself as gallantly intervening, its borders never breached. For Russia, however, like the other countries of Europe, war has not only been waged in foreign climes (in Turkey or Afghanistan or Syria), but has also left its mark at home. Mother Russia was invaded by the Mongols in the thirteenth century, by Napoleon in the nineteenth and by Hitler in the twentieth. In particular, war has marked those lands at the peripheries of Russia – Crimea, Chechnya, Georgia … – not only physically, in the form of death and scarred landscapes, but also in the very sense of what these regions signify in relation to Russia. Just as the results of war have shifted Russia's borders, so the processes of war have muddied distinctions between Russian and non-Russian. Where does Russia begin? Or more accurately, where does it end?

Tolstoy's 1886 short story 'How Much Land Does a Man Need?' tells the story of a peasant, Pahom, who buys some land, works hard, and makes a more comfortable life for himself and his wife. However, having made a pact with the devil, his attitude to the land changes and he becomes greedy, possessive and desirous of more and more. Eventually he goes to buy yet more land from a group of Bashkirs, a semi-nomadic people living between the Volga River and the Ural Mountains. For a thousand roubles, they say, he can have however much that he is able to walk around in a day. In trying to enclose as much as he possibly can, Pahom exhausts himself: he makes it back to the beginning and so wins the land, but he immediately drops down dead.

There are a number of ways one could read Tolstoy's parable. One is perhaps a human lesson: be wary of greed and over-reaching; know when enough is enough; embrace the modest life. Such a reading can easily slide into a very conservative interpretation: peasants, know your place. And it's certainly easy for Tolstoy, owner of the estate I visited at Yasnaya Polyana, to lecture the poor about restraint. However, I wonder if the parable can be read in a different way too: as the story of a nation. Perhaps it is to be read as a caution to those powers within Russia, as elsewhere, for whom bellicose expansionism is not only a psychological bent but a political strategy. If so, then perhaps Tolstoy is also trying to tell us that there will always be friction at the borders, there will always be calls to expand and conquer, no matter how large the territory. The devil will always encourage us to ask for more.

War changes the land. And it changes how we see the land.

In 1941, the Nazis invaded Russia. Leningrad was blockaded until 1944. Over the course of the city's 872-day siege, at least eight hundred thousand civilians were killed, mostly from starvation or exposure. Throughout that time, poet Vera Inber kept a diary, which was published in Russian shortly after the war and then in English in 1971. One of the very first entries, from 23 August 1941, describes Inber's journey by train back to Leningrad. Near the town of Mga she records the scene from the train window:

> we are moving now, and we pass dead woods, all the earth scorched by explosives. In one place all the trees are torn out, and their roots point upwards ... and there is the bark of a small birch tree – all tiny dots, stripes and spots – it makes me think of a shorthand record – here is the whole history of its life, and now this history is cut short in the middle of a sentence. Everything is split, charred, dead.

There is, I think, something of Nikolai Gogol in Inber's description: in its parallel between the real world, out there, and the written word of history or journalism, bureaucratic records and documents. In 'The Overcoat', Gogol's central character, Akaky, is a low-level functionary in the state administration. The entire focus of his life is copying official documents. Even in the streets of Saint Petersburg, 'all he ever saw were rows of letters in his own neat, regular handwriting'. It was only if something out of the ordinary were to occur to him, such as unexpected physical contact, that he could be stirred from his administrative introspections:

> Only if a horse's muzzle appeared from out of nowhere, propped itself on his shoulder and fanned his cheek with a gust from its nostrils – only then did he realize he was not in the middle of a sentence but in the middle of the street.

I love this moment in the text: 'not in the middle of a sentence but in the middle of the street'. While Gogol exploits the inter-penetration of language and reality for comedic effect, for Inber it points to something more ominous. Gogol writes of a city full of life; Inber's countryside is marked by death. The birch here, unlike so many of those I will encounter in Russian war-time writing, does not seem to serve a nationalist agenda. Primarily, it is a witness to its own life and death. If it is also a bearer of a collective history, it is not one limited by ethnic or national borders. Instead, the visual similarity between the bark's distinctive lenticels and abbreviated, encoded forms of writing suggests a greater significance: it is as if the destruction of the tree threatens not just Russian culture but all forms of communication, indeed the very possibility of meaning itself. 'Everything is split, charred, dead': nature, language, culture, everything.

In the twentieth century so much damage has been wrought by war, through mines and rockets, missiles and grenades, the digging of trenches, the felling of trees, the building of roads and railways, the destruction of crops and villages and human lives. Taking a plane from Moscow with photographer Robert Capa in 1947, John Steinbeck looked down upon the land below and observed the 'zigzags of trenches', 'the scoops of shell holes', and the 'black patches of burned buildings' over the 'flat grainlands' of Ukraine ('as flat as our Middle West,' he notes with his American readers in mind, 'and almost as fruitful'). The statistics vary considerably, but one estimate has Russian fatalities during World War II at nearly seventeen million people. Estimates for Ukrainian losses are somewhere between eight million and fourteen million, most of them civilians.

Amid such loss and devastation, the birch tree somehow survived. Another Vera Inber diary entry, this time from 27 February 1942, reads:

> We dined in the Divisional Commander's dugout. It was so warm there that in two or three places birch shoots were sprouting in the earthen wall ... a fragile stem and tiny leaves, weak and pale but still alive.

Inber seems simply to be recording a surprising observation. This is a diary: if these little birch shoots are alluding to something wider, it is not an official Soviet propaganda message but a more general faith in the possibilities of regrowth. Among the writers I have encountered from this period, this is an anomaly. In fact, World War II and its aftermath constitute one of those periods during which the symbolism of the birch tree clicks into the clearest focus. I've already learned how the war against Napoleon in the early nineteenth century coincided with waves of patriotic fervour. Something similar took place during World War II. In this context, it is precisely the perceived vulnerability of the birch – the way its outward fragility belies an ability to endure the harshest of conditions – that, for those in search of galvanising national symbols, made the tree irresistible.

By the 1940s the birch's medieval associations with fertility rituals, water spirits and the decorating of rural chapels had long gone (at least in official discourse). Instead, in the approved art and writing of the Soviet Union the birch became, like the flag and the earth that Rancour-Laferriere mentions, a focal point for a resurgent war-time nationalism.

So far in my explorations, the birch has been at its most fertile, symbolically speaking, when it has been multidimensional, able to harbour many different meanings, even or especially when those meanings might be at odds with one another. I'm thinking of Maria Kapajeva's film about 'mail-order brides' or the birch-bark notes in Novgorod or the myriad ways it's possible to interpret the paintings of Alexei Savrasov. During World War II, however, the many possible meanings that had accrued around the birch were reduced and simplified in the service of the war effort. Vera Inber's beautiful, strange description of the dots and dashes of the lenticels is an exception. In most of the writing that I have come across from the war, the birch's range of potential signification narrows to the width of its slim white trunk.

But sometimes the least sophisticated art and writing can be the most informative. Mikhail Sholokhov is one example. As a writer who rarely strayed from Soviet orthodoxy, Sholokhov offers the chance to track the regime's changing attitudes. He wrote numerous articles and stories in support of the Russian war effort and, from World War I to World War II, there is a notable shift in the way that his writing characterises Russia's enemies.

In the 1920s, while working on the first volumes of *And Quiet Flows the Don*, Sholokhov also published a number of short stories, including 'The One Language'. The narrative describes how Russian and Austrian soldiers would shout to each other in Polish across the front line. Sholokhov advocates solidarity with the enemy rank and file: 'those Austrian soldiers,' he writes, 'were just the same as us. We'd all been driven off the land, like children from the titty.'

Leaving aside (for now) this crass feminisation of the land, Sholokhov's text is interesting to me because it offers the possibility of seeing the enemy not simply as a single mass, but as a multiplicity of people with their own identities and differences. Such an understanding draws a distinction between the ruling classes and the German or Austrian soldier-proletariat, the former being the true enemy, the latter a potential ally. This was Bolshevik orthodoxy during World War I: that the war was a product not of national differences but of the greed of the capitalist class.

During World War II, however, it was felt that Marxist-Leninist structural analysis was insufficiently inspiring. Instead, the language of nationalism, often suppressed since the Bolsheviks had come to power, took precedence over internationalist communism, and Sholokhov – again attuned to official policy – no longer felt compelled to empathise with the proletariat the other side of the front line. At the height of war, Sholokhov (whose own mother was killed by a German bomb in 1942) knew the purpose of his writings: no longer were the communists opposed to war as they had been in 1917; now they had to galvanise popular support in hatred of all Germans regardless of complicating factors like class or the Molotov–Ribbentrop Pact. In 1939, the two powers, so opposed ideologically, had not only made a pledge of non-aggression but also agreed to a secret carve-up of Eastern Europe that only came to light at the Nuremberg Trials. In 1939, Germany invaded Poland from the west; the USSR from the east. The Soviets then annexed Finland, Estonia, Latvia, Lithuania and parts of Romania.

In contrast to the earlier war, Sholokhov's World War II writing repeatedly employs bestial imagery in its depictions of the enemy. His 1942 short story 'A Lesson in Hatred' includes a description of the German soldiers as 'degenerate mongrels maddened with blood'. In another story, 'Prisoners of War' (1944), the narrator describes a Nazi as 'hardly human: No, he is not a man, but a poorly cooked dumpling with an evil-smelling stuffing.' He 'stares with the eyes of an envenomed, blood-thirsty polecat'. Nazi soldiers are 'bands of beasts and gallow-birds', as worthless as 'filthy fungus growing on a dung heap'. The German is 'stupid', 'false', 'hideous', 'hopelessly perverted by Nazi propaganda', and 'blind'.

There are at least two ironies about this vehement anti-German sentiment. The first is that the Soviets had been more than happy to co-operate with the Nazis when it was in their own interest. It was only after Germany broke the pact by invading in 1941 that Russia entered the war and Germany was all of a sudden its sworn enemy. The idea that the war against the Nazis was somehow one of good against evil, civilisation against barbarism, is therefore more than a little hard to stomach.

The second irony is that, while Sholokhov is so scathing about the impact of Nazi propaganda upon German troops, he does not acknowledge the dehumanising role played by Soviet propaganda, to which his own writing contributed. I've seen Soviet propaganda illustrations of the same period in which Nazis are depicted as sharp-clawed wolves, as fat pigs, blind moles and monkeys. I've seen a German tank illustrated as a mechanised reptile with a semi-human face but crocodile jaws and tail. I've seen one series of images in which animal-bodied Nazis – led by Hitler as an arrogant wolf – come across an animal skull and imprison humans inside it. Fortunately, they are defeated by a single mighty punch from a Red Army soldier – unmistakably manly, unmistakably human.

The birch makes a memorable appearance in 'A Lesson in Hatred'. Throughout the story, as with much of Sholokhov's writing, he is at pains to emphasise links between nature and nation. The landscape is alive like a person, and people are rooted in the earth like trees. From its opening page, 'A Lesson in Hatred' draws explicit parallels between the destruction wrought by war upon the landscape and its devastation of a people: 'In a war trees are like human beings, they each have their destiny,' he writes, before detailing the impact of artillery fire on pine trunks, 'their bodies, torn to shreds'. Here nature is not simply a witness, but a fellow victim of violence.

'Death ruled majestically and silently over a glade which had been created and ploughed by our shells,' he writes. However, amid this scene of destruction is a quite different image altogether:

> right in the very middle of the glade stood one birch tree, miraculously spared. The wind swayed the shattered stumps of its branches and rustled among the glossy, sticky young leaves.

This birch is the very model of war-time Russian birch trees: it has endured great suffering and somehow – 'miraculously' – survived against the odds. It is always encountered with surprise. The text continues:

> We had to pass through this glade. A Red Army liaison man who was walking in front of me touched the birch trunk gently with his hand, and asked in genuine, kindly amazement: 'But how did you manage to escape, my dear?'

Here at least four notable things happen at once. Firstly, the soldier touches the tree 'with his hand': this shows that the tree – in the world of the text at least – is not simply an illusion, but a real tree that has really survived. The birch offers the possibility of the dream made real. Secondly, it is not only Sholokhov, or even the story's narrator, who is moved by the presence of the birch. So too is another soldier, in this instance a Red Army liaison man. By spreading responses to the tree across several actors, Sholokhov attempts to conceal the way that propaganda acts from above and from the centre; instead he suggests that such feelings are widely held and that he is simply reporting them. Thirdly, the tree is addressed as a person ('But how . . .?'). Fourthly, as Mother Russia, the birch is gendered female. I've already quoted Sholokhov's description of the land as 'titty'. Here, the soldier touches the tree 'gently', he speaks in 'kindly amazement', and addresses it as 'my dear'.

Even though this image of Russia as suffering woman, humble but beloved nonetheless, was not one associated with official Soviet discourse, it had never really gone away. In Vladimir Zazubrin's 1923 short story 'The Chip', for example, the narrator thinks of Russia as

> a pregnant woman, a fat-bottomed Russian peasant woman dressed in a torn, lice-ridden, dirty sackcloth blouse. And I love Her as she is – a real, living thing, not a figment of anyone's imagination.

Tone aside, in terms of the sentiment expressed, this could have been written in the 1880s, not the 1920s. It speaks of precisely the same conception of Russia: motherly, suffering, grubby, real and deeply, deeply loved – not despite the flaws but because of them. What I find most intriguing is that at the very moment in which Zazubrin presents the Russia of his imagination (a fat-bottomed Russian peasant woman), he emphasises in the same breath his commitment to reality and rejection of the imagination. The imagination denies itself as such. What strange paradoxes underpin national identity.

Incidentally, there is a fascinating moment in Zazubrin's 'The Chip' in which the narrator – a secret police executioner – describes the effect of seeing so many dead bodies lying in the basement of the Lubyanka headquarters in Moscow:

> It wasn't corpses that were lying on the floor – they were white-trunked birch trees. Birch trees have resilient bodies. The life in them is very stubborn and never gives up without a fight.

Zazubrin's description strikes me as a precise inversion of a scene in Ivan Turgenev's *Hunter's Sketches*, in which the great nature writer of nineteenth-century Russia recalls the sight of fallen trees lying rotting on the ground in the forest 'like corpses'. Turgenev, who does not specify the species of tree, compares the death of the trees to the death of humans in order to emphasise the evils of woodland mismanagement. Zazubrin's Soviet narrator, on the other hand, is so inured to the sight of dead bodies that it is only when they are described in terms borrowed from nineteenth-century nature writing that they really signify as something truly tragic. For such a professionalised killer, outwardly cold and inwardly sentimental, the white birch speaks more deeply than any mere human ever could. This is not a good omen.

Sholokhov's short stories demonstrate that the Soviets were willing to open the Pandora's Box of virulent nationalism. In the writings of Mikhail Bubennov I can start to see a little more clearly what that might mean. Bubennov's major work is a two-volume war-time novel entitled, appropriately enough, *The White Birch*. It is, I'm afraid to say, long-winded, predictable and sentimental, but, for somebody like me, fascinated by the multiple meanings of Russian birch trees, very significant. The first volume of *The White Birch* was published in 1947 and awarded the Stalin Prize. The second volume appeared five years later and both volumes were then translated into English and published in 1954. This was a book the Soviets wanted the world to read.

The novel tells the story of Russia's defence against the invading German army, with particular focus on the character of Andrei, a young man from a village called Olkhovka in the countryside near Moscow. As the title forewarns, the novels are full of birch trees. And, in my eyes as much as Bubennov's, these birches are never not symbolic. It is true that birches are sometimes put to material use. One wounded man walks with the aid of a heavy birch stick; another is carried to safety on a stretcher made from birch poles. In one scene, the soldiers roll their cigarettes out of birch bark and newspaper.

But it is as a symbol that the birch means something important. And primarily it is a figure of suffering. I've already encountered antisemitic writer Vasily Rozanov describing all Russian philosophy as 'the philosophy of the flogged man' but he is not the only one for whom suffering is a central part of how Russians conceive of themselves. Daniel Rancour-Laferriere characterises Russians as submissive masochists with a 'national inferiority complex' in relation to the West. He diagnoses Russia as a nation with long-repressed feelings of shame, the inability to admit to which has engendered a tendency to define those perceived to be other (such as Jews, Georgians, Chechens etc.) as shameless or haughty or arrogant. In relation to birches, Rancour-Laferriere notes that

Many Russian folk practices involve the birch in acts of ceremonial violence, such as: tearing off branches, peeling off the bark, chopping the birch wood into pieces, inflicting corporal punishment with birch rods, beating oneself or others with birch switches (*veniki*) in the *bania* etc.

In Bubennov's war-time novel, birch trees are very rarely the instrument of torture (although they are used to hang a man); more often they are themselves subjected to extremes of pain and suffering. As the army marches east towards Moscow, for example, we're told that 'A biting wintry wind blew from the swamp. The birches and alders writhed in anguish.' A description of the effects of war upon the landscape culminates in the image of 'a crippled birch', on top of which 'by some miracle, hung a sheet of dented, rusty roofing'. The occupying Nazi forces hang all the dogs in the village of Olkhovka. Then the soldiers cut down 'several thin young birches in the middle of the village' and use them to make fences 'without stripping the bark'. Following the destruction of the birches, the village, we're told, 'immediately lost a little of its soft, radiant glow'. I wonder which of these two crimes – the murder of the dogs, or the felling of the birches – the author deems the more heinous.

Bubennov, I found out after reading *The White Birch*, can be added to the growing list of Russians who hate Jews as much as they love birch trees. In the immediate aftermath of World War II, with patriotic nationalism now the official state position, people like Bubennov felt empowered to try to put down what they saw as the growing influence of a pro-Western intelligentsia. Despite the fact that an estimated 500,000 Jews fought in the Red Army, Soviet Jews were now accused of 'rootless cosmopolitanism' and Bubennov wrote vicious reviews of books by Jewish writers. He also led a campaign to ban the use of pseudonyms, worried that writers were trying to conceal their Jewish origins by assuming more Russian-sounding names. Bubennov, a heavy drinker, was involved in a public brawl outside the Tretyakov Gallery in Moscow with several other literary figures. The episode was the subject of an anonymous satiric verse circulated among Moscow literary circles. It describes Bubennov as *pevets 'Berezy'* – singer of birch.

After Bubennov's denunciation of the use of pseudonyms by Jewish writers, poet Konstantin Simonov published a rebuttal in *Literaturnaya gazeta*, of which he was the editor. Who leapt to Bubennov's defence? None other than Sholokhov, who by this stage was one of the major names in Soviet literature. Simonov was subsequently the subject of a sustained smear campaign that accused him of being secretly Jewish. In December 1952, according to Orlando Figes's *The Whisperers*, a book that is in large part about the life of Simonov, Stalin told a meeting of the Central Committee that 'every Jew is potentially a spy for the United States'. 'The country seemed to be returning to the atmosphere of 1937,' writes Figes, 'with the Jews in the role of "enemies of the people"'. Antisemitism was ramped up even further by the so-called Doctors' Plot, in which a group of Moscow doctors were falsely accused of attempting to assassinate high-ranking Soviet officials. It was arguably only Stalin's death in 1953 that averted mass deportations of Russia's Jews.

Bubennov, who clearly hated the possibility that he might be deceived by a pseudonym, liked things to be nice and clear. Heroes are heroes, Russians are Russian, and, in the case of the birch, Bubennov is not shy of spelling out exactly how to read its symbolism. The first volume of *The White Birch* closes with a predictably heroic last stand in the countryside outside Moscow. The description is suspiciously similar to that given by Sholokhov in 'A Lesson in Hatred'. Bubennov's novel was published five years after Sholokhov's short story and, given the esteemed writer's public support for his less celebrated colleague, it is fairly likely that he would have read it.

In the build-up to the climax, Bubennov describes the landscape near the enemy lines through the eyes of the novel's hero, Andrei:

> On a rise in the very centre of the field stood a slender white birch-tree; it seemed to be standing there undecidedly, wondering where to flee from that dangerous spot. For some reason it reminded Andrei of the one on the roadside just outside Olkhovka, although both before and since he had seen many such solitary birches that autumn.

At first this birch is therefore of local, personal significance, a reminder for Andrei of the village he has left behind and, by extension, the place he is fighting to protect. But it soon becomes clear that this birch signifies a little more than that. In conversation with one of his comrades before the battle Andrei describes the tree as a 'landmark', and then just a few lines later as a synecdoche for the entire nation. 'It's a birch,' says Andrei, 'a little white birch-tree, that's what it is. When I look at it I can see the whole of our Russian land.'

Throughout the thirty pages of the volume's final battle, the birch is a recurring presence. With the battle finally won, we are given a panoramic description of a scene of death and destruction. 'The entire field has been ploughed up by shells and mines.' Against the odds but completely inevitably, the birch tree survives – exactly as it does in Sholokhov's short story. On the book's closing pages Bubennov is in full flow, brushing the tears from his cheeks as he chugs back vodka after vodka:

> And just as in the morning, on the naked little rise in the midst of that shambles where fire and steel had raged throughout the day and where death had trampled everything, stood the lone white birch, glowing softly in the twilight.
>
> 'Still there?' Andrei whispered in amazement.

Just as in Sholokhov, the (female) birch is viewed through the eyes of a male narrator and addressed out loud by a male central character. Not content with such cinematic schmaltz, Bubennov lays it on even thicker:

> And Andrei felt that there was something very significant and portentous in the fact that like some sacred thing this birch – the beautiful tree of song – had survived such a furious battle in that unsheltered place. Nature herself had set it there to adorn the drab field, and hence nature herself had endowed it with immortality.

The book continues just a little bit longer. Bubennov pauses and takes another drink. Suddenly he is very serious. The tears have stopped and he sits bolt upright at his typewriter. In these closing lines the voice of the narrator merges once again with Andrei's own thoughts. It is exactly the same strategy that Sholokhov employed:

> He kept his rapturous gaze on the birch for a few seconds, and then, placing his hand on the ledge of the trench, said with great solemnity and rejoicing in his heart, as though making a vow to the earth itself, 'And it will always be there!'

A female personification of nature, a blurring of the way things are with the way things ought to be, an attempt to fix a certain conception of the landscape forever: this reminds me of the paintings of Mikhail Nesterov. Where Nesterov sought to fix an Orthodox, Tsarist Russia, Bubennov attempts to fix an atheist, Soviet Russia. Both, ultimately, served the interests of power.

Arkady Plastov's 1942 painting *The Fascist Plane Flew By* is oh-so-nearly bucolic. The painting is in the Tretyakov collection, but I've never seen it on display. Instead, I sit at home, squinting at my computer screen, and try to imagine the original from a number of poor-quality digital reproductions. From what I can tell, the work is painted in the artist's scruffy, brushy style. This owes a debt, I think, to Alexei Savrasov, painter of *The Rooks Have Returned*, but it was also a feature of Socialist Realism: noticeable brushmarks made visible the labour of the artist. The scene depicts a landscape of fields and sheep and rolling hills. A large cow is shown emerging from a grove of young birch trees, their leaves (in most reproductions) bright golden yellow. In the foreground lies a boy, a dog by his side. The hills in the distance are blue-green.

But this is not a bucolic scene. Or, at least, it is not any more. The boy is not asleep but dead, a small patch of red visible through his hair. The loyal dog howls into the sky, where the titular Nazi plane flies small and blue into the distance.

A comparable moment is described in Svetlana Alexievich's *The Unwomanly Face of War*, a book that brings together multiple first-person accounts to form a kind of mosaic impression of the war-time experiences of just some of the half a million Soviet women who fought against the Nazis alongside their male counterparts. But this time the outcome is quite different to that depicted in Plastov's painting. 'At Zhmerinka station we came under a terrible bombardment,' recalls Vera Vladimirovna Shevaldycheva, surgeon and First Lieutenant in the Red Army:

The train stopped and we ran ... We sat in the forest all night ... In the morning German planes began combing the forest. Where to hide? I couldn't burrow into the ground like a mole. I put my arms around a birch tree and stood there: 'Oh, mama, my mama! ... Can it be I'll perish? If I survive,

I'll be the happiest person in the world.' When I told people afterward how I held on to the birch tree, they all laughed. I was such an easy target. Standing up tall, a white birch ... Hilarious!

Where Alexievich gives us unexpected humour, Plastov emphasises unforeseen horror. And he does so quite subtly by borrowing from the conventions of nineteenth-century landscape painting. It is easy to look quickly at the painting and see a simple rural scene. It is only when you look a little closer and notice the blood, then follow the gaze of the dog to the plane, then read the title, that you realise what has just happened. But even that title, which seems so clearly of the 1940s, owes a debt to the nineteenth century with its allusion to a moment just passed and therefore a relationship to time and to narrative.

By sticking to long-established conventions (not that in the era of Socialist Realist hegemony Plastov had much choice) the work draws attention to the one thing that does not fit: the Nazi plane, which not only shatters the quiet Russian landscape, but also the illusion of timelessness that such paintings seek to convey. Modernity, violence, the foreign enemy: these have no place in this immortal Russian landscape of peasants and birches. The Nazi plane – anonymous, already far away – is therefore presented not only as an enemy of Russia but of art itself. The birches on my screen bear witness to what has taken place.

In *The Cranes Are Flying*, one of the best-known Soviet war movies, a young man goes off to fight the fascists; his fiancée must endure great suffering, all the while waiting for his return, which never comes. When I let slip my fascination with Russian birches, several people told me to watch this film. Over sixty years on from its release, it continues to shape the way that many Russians think about their country. This is not a film about glory: the man, Boris, dies almost exactly halfway through; it is his fiancée, Veronika (played by Tatiana Samoilova), who is the centre of the narrative. The camera lingers on her dark eyes, her retroussé nose, her white skin as she suffers repeatedly: her parents are killed by German bombs, she is pursued aggressively by Boris's cousin (there is a suggestion of rape), and she must relocate to Siberia along with Boris's family who continue to judge her for what they see as betrayal.

Even when Veronika is not shown directly, she is being looked at. Boris carries a photograph of her with him to the front and quarrels with a fellow soldier over her beauty. He is then sent out on a reconnaissance mission with the same soldier. The latter is wounded and Boris carries him to the safety of a patch of wood. The land is a sea of mud; the trees reflected in the knee-deep water. In my eyes at least, the landscape in this pivotal scene precisely echoes a painting made sixty years earlier: *Spring, High Water* (1897) by Isaac Levitan.

Spring, High Water is a late work and one of Levitan's most influential. Between the viewer and the watery horizon, most of the painting's middle ground is composed of birches, their slim verticality emphasised by reflections in the spring floodwater. The composition is gently sinuous, framed by a curving line of land to the left and a bending birch to the right. A wooden boat in the foreground and wooden huts in the distance provide the only traces of human presence. This humble scene could be anywhere in rural Russia – and that was precisely the point.

In *The Cranes Are Flying*, the subject matter is the same, the composition the same: clusters of thin, spindly white birches elongated by their reflection in the deep seasonal flooding. The difference is the addition of a pair of soldiers and the sounds of war.

Spring. High Water Artist Levitan, Isaak Ilyich (1860-1900)/Russian. credit Bridgeman Images

At the film's emotional apex, birch trees are inescapable. Boris pushes through the branches with the other soldier still on his back, lays him down at the base of a birch tree. But then, just as he stands upright, takes a breath and reassures his comrade that all will be well, Boris is shot. His head arches back, his eyes wide to the sky. He lurches, becomes dizzy, and grabs an upright birch tree for support. The camera takes us inside the mind of the dying soldier as his vision flits between the immediate surroundings (a spinning shot of the birch canopy above his head) and a projection of his never-to-be-realised wedding to Veronika, dressed all in white, her veil enveloping them both as they kiss. The last thing he sees is Veronika's smiling face overlaid with the leaves of the birches.

Boris dies on Russian land, defending his nation from European invaders. And he does so in the name of a country whose aesthetic identity has been defined, in large part, by the landscape paintings of the late nineteenth century. But, in overlaying the Levitan-influenced landscape with an image of the soldier's beloved, the film's director, Mikhail Kalatozov, takes the image of Russia one step further than Levitan did: Russia is not only associated with humble birch trees but also with the beautiful bride and the heroic death, with suffering and sacrifice. The bright future dreamed of by Boris and Veronika will never be realised. But the film was released in 1957: the audience knew that, while Boris may have been killed, Russia did survive against the odds, just like those birch trees, slim and white as in Levitan's painting, reflected in the muddy water and pointing to the sky.

On a recent visit to Moscow, the following lines of poetry were lodged in my head:

I, the Kitezh woman,
Have been called home.
One hundred thousand birch trees
Pursued me . . .

Over and over these lines repeated themselves, every time giving me the shivers as I wandered through parks, attended gallery openings and press conferences, sat on a bus to a suburban housing development. It's the same when I read them back to myself now. There's something about the rhythm, I think, of Richard McKane's English translation: slow, ponderous, and I'm not quite sure where the stress ought to land in those first two lines.

The lines come from a long poem entitled *The Way of All the Earth*, written in 1940 by Anna Akhmatova, one of the great tragic figures of Russian history. Akhmatova rose to prominence in the early twentieth century and chose to remain in Russia after the revolution even though many of her friends emigrated or were killed. Throughout her life, much of her writing was censored and she periodically produced work in praise of the Soviet regime in order to save members of her family from the authorities. It rarely worked. Her first husband, poet Nikolai Gumilev, was shot by the Soviet secret police in 1921. Her son, Lev Gumilev (a significant influence on current right-wing thinking in Russia), and her subsequent partner, art critic and museum director Nikolai Punin, both spent many years in labour camps. Punin died in the gulag in 1953.

Given this existence, it is hardly surprising that Akhmatova's poetry is etched with sorrow and loss. Her writing navigates an irreconcilable conflict between the desire to remember and the desire to forget. 'The expected outcome of grief,' is how one Russian curator described Akhmatova's poetry to me, with a barely perceptible shrug of her shoulders, as we drank together in the shadowy glow of a Moscow basement bar. In the introduction to a recent edition of her work, translator Richard McKane expresses it a little differently: 'Akhmatova's voice,' he writes, is 'a better translation for the Russian word *tuska* – more anguish than longing, and more longing than anguish – than any dictionary definition'.

If Akhmatova's overriding tone is unsurprising, her work nonetheless contains unexpected moments. Birches make their presence felt from time to time, although pines, poplars and willows are, I think, more frequent, at least until the outbreak of World War II. From the 1940s, at least from the collections I have read, more and more birches may be found in her writing. For the most part, they are quite conventional: there are dancing birches 'Throwing off their transparent attire' in 'Three Autumns' (1943); birch embers whispering – 'barely, barely heard' – in 'Cinque' (6 January 1946); and 'the birches and the mushrooms' of a Moscow autumn awaiting her return ('Three Verses', 1944–50). Sometimes, as in 'Victory' (January 1942), Akhmatova's language reads like propaganda.

> *The glorious labour is gloriously begun,*
> *In the menacing thunder, in the snow dust*
> *Where the purest body of the motherland*
> *Lies, defiled by the enemy.*

> *The dear birch branches*
> *Stretch out to us and wait and call,*
> *And the powerful grandfather frosts march*
> *In tight formation with us all.*

Here, labour is predictably heroic and Russia is a figure of feminine innocence defiled by the foreign invader. Just as in the propaganda writings of Mikhail Sholokhov, nature is on the side of the Russians, not only as a homeland to protect (the 'dear birch branches' waiting and calling) but also as the 'powerful grandfather frosts', themselves a part of Russia's defensive capabilities.

Before the war, however, Akhmatova's few birches grew at the margins of tolerability. In 'I Know There's No Moving' (1939), Akhmatova imagines herself back in the seventeenth century, fusing Christian and pagan beliefs: 'in church at Whitsun / With a fragrant birch branch'. At first the poem seems like a vague nostalgic reverie ('Oh, to escape back / Into some sort of seventeenth century,' it begins), but it swiftly takes a darker turn. Akhmatova imagines herself as Feodosia Morozova, the wealthy Old Believer who rejected reforms made by the Russian Orthodox Church, was arrested in 1671, inter-rogated and tortured. But she refused to abandon her beliefs and was starved to death in prison. It's not hard to see why Akhmatova, hounded by the Soviet authorities, was drawn to such a figure.

It was in the following year, 1940, that she wrote those lines I can't seem to shake: 'I, the Kitezh woman ...' But what do they mean?

It is months later that I find out Kitezh is not simply one provincial Russian town among others. It is, in fact, a city of legend. It is said that in the thirteenth century Georgy II, Grand Prince of Vladimir, founded Kitezh on the shores of Lake Svetloyar, eighty miles north-east of the city of Nizhny Novgorod. When Batu Khan and the Golden Horde invaded the region, the inhabitants of Kitezh did not attempt to defend their city; they simply knelt and prayed. This gesture of submission reminds me of the Christian missionary, referenced by Jane T. Costlow, who refused to protect himself against the 'enraged heathen' and was venerated as a result. Likewise at Kitezh, as the Mongol army prepared to attack, the devout inhabitants did nothing. Miraculously, fountains of water spouted up into the air and the city gradually sank below the waters. No wonder the psychoanalysts associate Russian identity with masochism. I look up the supposed location on Google Maps and come across an avenue of birch trees that leads towards the lake. In calm weather, if you listen closely, you might just hear the sounds of bells and singing.

The legend has inspired not only poets but artists, composers and even the makers of computer games. There is a depiction of the city by Russian Post-Impressionist Konstantin Gorbatov, a hazy blue dream world framed by ancient white birches, flame-leafed in autumn. Nikolai Rimsky-Korsakov based an opera upon the story, Werner Herzog made a film, *Bells from the Deep* (1993), about it, and Lara Croft visits a version of Kitezh in 2015 game *Rise of the Tomb Raider*.

It is only after reading Akhmatova that I realise Mikhail Nesterov produced a number of scenes of Kitezh too. Several of those paintings I have been looking at were depictions, I now know, of Kitezh. In Nesterov's vision, Kitezh is an enamelled place, a devout place. In *The Taking of the Veil* (1898), nuns process with lit tapers serenely through town streets. In *The Legend of the Invisible City of Kitezh* (1920), they pray by the edge of the water against a backdrop of birches. How comforting in times of turmoil to imagine a secret place of retreat, accessible only to those who think the same as you.

It is those paintings that are in my mind now when I re-read Akhmatova's *The Way of All the Earth* (1940). And yet they don't really seem to fit.

> *I, the Kitezh woman,*
> *Have been called home.*
> *One hundred thousand birch trees*
> *Pursued me . . .*

Nesterov's paintings present scenes of great harmony: traditionally clad figures exhibiting their devotion against backdrops of wooden houses and slender white birches. But Akhmatova's lines are very different. For her there is no such harmony, no such peace. For Nesterov, timelessness offers the relief of peaceful stasis; for Akhmatova it is to be condemned to repeat the same actions, to fear the same fears over and over again. Eternity is a blessing for those who imagine themselves in heaven; not so much for those who see hell all around.

So far, I've been pursuing the idea of the return in Russian culture as something to be embraced: from the expansionist policies of Catherine the Great ('I *restored* what had been torn away'); to the rooks returning home for spring in the art of Alexei Savrasov; or the pop songs of Yevgeniy Ross (in which the birch waits 'with womanlike patience'). But for Akhmatova the idea of the return is more ambiguous. Her return, it seems, has been demanded by an external force. She has been 'called home', summoned against her will. She flees and is pursued. But where is this home? Kitezh is just a legend, a place that no longer exists, that can only be visited, according to legend, by the pure of heart. In the poem, Akhmatova need not prove her faith but show her papers. This is Soviet Russia now. 'Here's my pass, comrade, / let me through round the back.'

Later in the poem, Akhmatova is forewarned by 'a cunning voice':

> 'You will return here,
> return many times,
> and you will strike
> the resistance of the diamond.
> Better go past

> *better go back,*
> *cursed and praised*
> *to your father's garden.'*

'return', 'return', 'go past', 'go back': among so many prophesied returns, what intrigue me most, unsurprisingly, are the birches. So often they have been a passive presence, patiently awaiting the return of an active narrator. Here, however, the relationship is reversed: it is Akhmatova who is passive and the birches in active pursuit. The birches chase her, hunt her down like an animal. It is a striking image. And there are just so many of them: one hundred thousand birches on the move, a symbol of home found now so far from home. They exemplify, like the legendary city of Kitezh, a conception of Russia not confined to a real place. Rather, home is an idea that pursues you wherever you go. For Akhmatova, it seems, there is no possibility of escape.

A patch of dense forest to the south-east of the Latvian capital Riga is a place that has borne witness to atrocity. Today we are asked to remember what happened. And we are told exactly how this remembering ought to take place.

In July 1941, the Nazi army captured Riga, which had only recently been annexed by the USSR as per the secret terms of the Molotov–Ribbentrop Pact. They quickly set about recruiting collaborators to form a new auxiliary police unit, Arajs Kommando. Over the course of nine days that winter, these volunteers, mostly students and former Latvian army officers, supported Nazi Einsatzgruppe A in the killing of 25,000 Jews in the Rumbula Forest. The pine trees would have rendered the killings all but invisible. The sandy soil made grave-digging easy.

While these killings were taking place in one forest, the Nazis were building a concentration camp in a second patch of woods nearby: Salaspils. One thousand people, mostly Jews, are thought to have died in the construction of Salaspils; at least another thousand died while imprisoned there.

I visit Salaspils on a little tourist minibus en route from Riga to Vilnius. Our guide is a young woman from Lithuania, whose ebullience oscillates between entertaining and insensitive. We enter the site down an avenue planted with birch trees and flag poles, slim and straight and white like the birches. There is a Latvian flag and the flag of the European Union. There is a museum, formed like a huge, angled slab of concrete, floating heavily across the entrance. It is closed for repairs on the morning of our visit and the sound of drilling vibrates through the early summer sun and the silence of the surrounding pine woods. Outside is a flat expanse of grass, parched and brown, a clearing carved from the forest by slave labour, now maintained, I imagine, by municipal workers. Surrounded by trees, this feels not only like a dark place but also, unexpectedly, like a sacred place.

The clearing is dominated by groups of enormous concrete figures. To the right as you stand is a cluster of four: a figure with a clenched fist; a figure with arms raised aloft; and a third figure leaning back upon a fourth. Each is the personification of an idea, I later read: Protest, Solidarity, Red Front. But I'm not totally sure which is which. In the foreground, some yards away from those four, another figure performs a one-armed press-up: Unbroken. Away to the left is a mother figure protecting her children. She pushes forwards in defiance, her arms swept strongly back to form a kind of wedge: not the figurehead of a ship but its very prow. Is this supposed to be Mother Russia? In which case, do the children represent states such as Latvia?

The implication of the Salaspils memorial is that the Red Army liberated Latvia from the clutches of Nazism, and in so doing put a stop to the atrocities taking place. But when the Soviets annexed the Baltic States in 1940, they organised sham elections and killed or deported hundreds of thousands of people. Even after the subsequent Nazi invasion, it is unlikely that many Latvians would have looked upon Russia as their maternal protector. The return of the Red Army to Riga in 1944 was not a precursor to Latvian liberation but, for many Latvians, simply the replacement of one occupying force by another. Latvia was not finally independent until 1991. Such historical complexities are not revealed but obscured by memorials such as Salaspils. The entire complex was designed in 1967 by Latvian-Soviet architect Oļģerts Ostenbergs, who was awarded the Lenin Prize in 1970. Not only are the figures physically huge, and therefore suggestive of power and permanence, but also sculpted in that monumental Soviet style that makes them even more formidable. They bespeak their symbolism with the loud voice of a fragile authority. This is propaganda modernism.

There is one other statue at the memorial site that I am especially interested in: *Pazemotā*. It means the humbled or humiliated. It is a female figure with a strong, square face, her arm across her mouth, a pointed elbow jutting into the sky. Up close you can see spots of yellow lichen on the surface of the concrete. And just next to her, perhaps a solace in suffering, or an accompanying familiar, is a tall tree, rising up above the figure, its leaves cascading down like a fountain: *Betula pendula*, the silver birch. It is the only tree in the central section of the memorial complex, so I'm fairly certain its presence is no accident. When it was planted I'm not so sure. The memorial is over fifty years old and I guess the birch must be about the same. It looks to have been trimmed too, so that its foliage does not obscure the figure of *Pazemotā*.

But what does the birch mean here in this context? The birch, as I have mentioned, is not only important to Russians. Many other countries, including Latvia, have strong attachments to birch trees. In Nora Ikstena's novel *Soviet Milk* (2015), for example, birch trees are a symbol of new life, optimism and homely familiarity. The novel tells of two unnamed Latvian women, a mother and daughter, each struggling to forge their own identities under Soviet rule. When the mother attempts to make a new start in the Latvian countryside, we're told that 'The birches were still in that brilliant, bare greenness that dazzles one's eyes.' At the end of the book, when the daughter looks forward to a life free from Soviet rule, the trees reappear, almost word for word as they did before: 'The birches still showed that bright, bare greenness that dazzles one's eyes.'

The chief architect of Salaspils, Oļģerts Ostenbergs, studied at the State University of Latvia until it was dissolved by the new Soviet government and he continued his studies at Leningrad Institute of Civil Engineering. Is the birch here aligned with Latvia? In which case, is Ostenbergs suggesting that Latvia has been humiliated (by the Nazis presumably)? To me the birch suggests a Russian ownership of this place, of the histories and memories attached to it, and even of nature itself. Hidden in the woods, Salaspils would therefore be a Russian story, with the Russians claiming that it should be they who tell it.

Adding to the complexity of interpretation are Latvia's changing demographics under Soviet rule – the result of both large-scale Russian immigration and deportations of Latvians to Siberia. In 1935, according to journalist Jonathan Steele, Latvians comprised 77 per cent of the republic's population, but by 1989 they were only 52 per cent. When it came to Latvia's independence referendum in 1991, many of these Russian immigrants joined with their new countryfolk and voted to leave the USSR. Could this Salaspils birch then in fact be a symbol of unity? A motif of shared culture and history, of shared suffering, between two war-torn (Soviet) nations? If propaganda modernism is characterised by its lack of ambiguity, then why am I having such trouble understanding what it means?

One final possibility: perhaps it is simply a birch tree. As I turn to leave, its branches rustle as the wind blows towards the east. Birds chatter in the pines around the edge of the clearing. On the way out, I notice again the flag of the European Union. None of this is Russian – or Soviet – any more. And yet these histories and identities linger in the landscape and in the memories of the people who live here. We pass an elderly couple on their way to visit the memorial. What histories have they witnessed? They look sadly at us as our guide laughs and jokes. I feel only embarrassment. What could we ever understand? Back on the little bus everyone is silent. Then somebody asks a question and our guide starts to sing.

VIII.

CHERNOBYL

'How does one pass through what does not pass, does not become a past?'

Michael Marder (with Anaïs Tondeur),
The Chernobyl Herbarium, 2016

In December 1985, from a prison cell inside a Soviet labour camp at Barashevo in Mordovia, three hundred miles south-east of Moscow, poet and writer Irina Ratushinskaya tried to imagine the future. In Ratushinskaya's future, as in the many pasts I have been tracing, Russians would sing of birch trees. Ratushinskaya had been arrested in 1983, the day before she turned twenty-nine, and sentenced to seven years' hard labour for 'anti-Soviet agitation and propaganda'. During her years in labour camps she continued to write, using a matchstick to etch letters into a bar of soap before copying them later onto scraps of paper. Next to each poem she would write the date and often the location in which it was written: PKT for the prison inside the camp; SHIZO for the isolation cell.

During her imprisonment, some of Ratushinskaya's poetry was smuggled outside and published, unbeknownst to the poet herself. One of her poems embodies the paradox of writing words that may never be read. 'Pencil Letter' begins:

> *I know it won't be received*
> *Or sent. The page will be*
> *In shreds as soon as I have scribbled it.*

Where Anna Akhmatova sought (and failed to find) refuge from the Soviet authorities via a temporary retreat into the seventeenth century, Ratushinskaya by contrast looks straight ahead. But in 'To the Children of Prison Warden Akimkina', the future offers as little respite as the past. The poem's opening lines throw us forward thousands of years into the future, before looping back round to a distant past:

> *In this year – the year seven thousand*
> *Five hundred and ninety four*
> *Since the beginning of time –*
> *It snowed continuously.*

In parts of Russia, when all is cold and dark it can feel as if winter will last forever: 'the season when nature falls asleep', as a Moscow-based curator phrased it to me in a gloomy January email, when 'sleep is more like limbo'. No wonder Alexei Savrasov's *The Rooks Have Returned*, for all its downbeat realism, evokes such jubilation. For somebody enduring temperatures as low as $-40°C$ in nothing but a prison smock, the endlessness of winter is unimaginable. What changes there are – the cycle of night and day, for example – only confirm the inescapable repetition. Time is a monolith; all space has fused into one:

> *Each morning the sky's blade hardened*
> *With a particular glare.*

The sky and earth's white rim
Were a single entity.

Later in the poem, Ratushinskaya extends this sense of the natural world as unyielding, as an inescapable prison around the
agency of the individual. To Ratushinskaya, the architecture of
the camp is a product of this unforgiving natural environment,
and just as permanent:

In this place, fences are grown,
Watch-towers stick up like splinters,
And, under the wind, the bales
Of wire sound like dried-up reeds.
Wild animals also roam –
Snarling dogs, trained for service.
Without them, there'd be no camp,
No transport, no prison sentence.

This is a very different conception of the wild to all those I've
encountered in Russia so far. For Ratushinskaya, the wild is
not a spirit-filled forest to be feared (or felled). It is not a symbol
of economic backwardness or of natural (national) beauty.
It is not a resource to be tapped or a place of freedom ... In
Ratushinskaya's conception, the wild is not something defined
by its ability to evade human control. Quite the opposite: here
the wild is in league with the authorities. The Soviets never
quite did master nature in the way many of them dreamed
of with their huge ambitions to reroute rivers or replant the
steppe. But maybe they did achieve it in the gulag. In Anne
Applebaum's extensive study of the subject, she describes
camps that were so remote they didn't even need the fences
or barbed wire mentioned by Ratushinskaya. In the depths of
Siberia, where would anyone escape to?

From her far-imagined future, Ratushinskaya looks back upon a moment from the past, and in that moment she sees birch trees:

Russia was where it happened –
Mordovia, to be exact –
The nation, which joined with Russia
Five hundred years ago.

It was Ivan the Terrible who subjugated Mordovia in the fifteenth century when he defeated the Golden Horde. So Ratushinskaya's imagined far future is, it seems, the present.

For this most distinguished act
She received an Order of Merit
Which is still being talked about
And discussed on the radio.
And they sing about lyrical groves –
Birch-groves, naturally.

In the poem's earlier lines, the snow and the cold, the watch-towers and fences and dogs demonstrate the fusing of the natural with the architecture of incarceration. But here the birches signify very differently: they are shorthand for the unchanging – indeed, unchangeable – content of state propaganda. Birches have always been sung about, and this will never change, even though the identity of the 'they' who are doing the singing remains unclear. In my copy of Ratushinskaya's book, the English translation is by poet Carol Rumens. Rumens casually appends the word 'naturally', after the comma at the end of the line. It is the perfect choice of word: at first, I just read it literally (birches as the natural choice for lyric verse) but then I notice the possibility of a wry edge (an arched eyebrow at yet another clichéd birch grove). I'm not sure if this effect is there in the original Russian, which the internet translates as:

> *And they sing songs – about the groves*
> *With lyrical birches.*

This carries a very slightly different sense. The birches are described as *liricheskimi* – lyrical: they are both a fitting or *natural* subject for lyric verse but also they are themselves lyrical. Or perhaps there's no difference either way. And how ironic is Ratushinskaya's use of the word *liricheskimi* in Russian?

The dichotomy of the poem is between a state that sings of lyrical nature on the radio while exploiting a cruel, unyielding nature against its own people. Both seem eternal. Ratushinskaya imagined a future fixed for all time, for that is the reality that stretched out before her.

And then, suddenly, it all splintered into pieces. Ratushinskaya wrote these lines in December 1985. Within a few months an event was to take place that – for many historians, if not necessarily for those who experienced it directly – would mark the beginning of the end for the Soviet Union. On 26 April 1986, reactor number four at Chernobyl Nuclear Power Plant exploded.

Just weeks later, after significant international pressure, Ratushinskaya was transferred from Mordovia to a KGB prison in Kyiv, eighty miles south of the power plant at Chernobyl. In October, she was released.

Exactly how Chernobyl contributed to the end of the Soviet Union remains a contentious subject. Some have argued that the disconnect between events and the official coverage of those events pushed popular distrust in the Soviet system to breaking point. Others maintain that, because of the international nature of the catastrophe, with radiation clouds spreading rapidly across Europe, the USSR's isolationism simply became untenable.

Many debates centre on who knew what when, and therefore who was lying and who was simply ignorant. Journalist Jonathan Steele has written that, due to pressure from the West to receive accurate information on the spread of radiation, 'Gorbachev realised that the accident could not be covered up'. In *Russia's Stillborn Democracy?*, by contrast, historians Graeme Gill and Roger D. Markwick argue that the deception was in fact coming from the ground up: an instinctive response from Soviet officials accustomed to manipulating results to meet and exceed targets.

Either way, the result was the same: *glasnost* (openness), Gorbachev's relaxation of the strict controls previously imposed on freedom of expression. For Gill and Markwick, *glasnost* was 'a means of checking on the presentation of misinformation by lower level officials'. For Steele, the result was a rapid loss of control, with an increasingly free press playing a vital role:

> The opening-up on Chernobyl led to demands for information and action on the whole spectrum of environmental pollution in the Soviet Union. The press began to report other accidents. Crime and prison statistics, a long-held secret in the Soviet media, were published. Soon Soviet journalists were writing about all the seamy aspects of Soviet life, concentrating with relish on everything that had long been forbidden.

Glasnost, combined with the policy of *perestroika* (restructuring) which sought to solve the economic malaise of the Soviet

Union by introducing market reforms, led quickly to the unravelling of the Union altogether. Political reforms created a power struggle, economic changes failed to bear fruit, people began openly to question the system and the leadership, while several countries jostled increasingly for independence. After a failed military coup, Gorbachev's authority was at its nadir, and the opportunistic Boris Yeltsin was quick to harness the separatist nationalism growing in the republics. On 8 December 1991, from a state dacha in rural Belarus, Yeltsin, along with Ukrainian president Leonid Kravchuk and the leader of Belarus, Stanislav Shushkevich, announced the end of the Soviet Union.

The 1990s for Russia and the other post-Soviet nations was a chaotic time. While Yeltsin set about strengthening the position of the presidency (paving the way for Putin), the rapid move to a market economy under economist Yegor Gaidar was devastating. Millions were plunged into poverty while a few in privileged positions (often members of the old *nomenklatura* bureaucracy) seized state assets during the privatisation frenzy. In the countryside, fences went up as publicly accessible land was suddenly declared private property.

Western leaders encouraged Gaidar's reforms, in part to drive a stake through the corpse of communism. But they also feared a possible resurgence of Russian nationalism. Steele notes that 'In fact, Russians abandoned their empire with remarkable ease', especially when compared with the British in Rhodesia (which became Zimbabwe in 1980) or the French in Algeria. But with the end of the USSR came a period of great confusion over national identity. 'The Russian imperial paradox,' argues Steele, 'was that Russians did not feel the Soviet Union was an empire.' Steele maintains that, in this period, national patriotism was comparatively weak and that growing regional sentiments were more of a threat to the break-up of the Russian Federation: 'With the iron hand of central control removed, the tendency for disintegration was very strong.' In such a period of insecurity, however, it is not surprising that those who offered simple answers might hold significant appeal. Nationalism, in various forms, would return again, not as a challenge to power but as a means to hold on to it. Steele's analysis of Russian nationalism in the early 1990s was that it was not directed against other ethnic groups, who were seen as allies against the USSR. Instead, the notion grew that Russia, far from being a colonial power, had itself been colonised – by the Soviets. 'Now it was time to liberate Russia,' writes Steele. 'De-Communization became decolonization.'

Like an idiot, I went to Chernobyl with a clear idea. It didn't take long to unravel. I had thought Chernobyl would demonstrate the limits of a predominantly aesthetic approach to landscape. I was wrong.

Up to this point in my research, one particular question has been whirring away in the back of my mind: how do we visualise and communicate that which, ultimately, cannot be seen with one's eyes? I'm thinking of abstract ideas like the glory of Russia, for example, or the dignity of labour; faith or inner beauty or heroism. But I'm also thinking of things or places that are not what they seem: the surface of a lake that hides a legendary sunken city; the folk-tale birch trees that are actually women transformed by witches.

Artists have developed a number of strategies in order to make the invisible visible. An accompanying text is one possibility: Isaac Levitan made deft use of a title – *The Vladimirka Road* – in order to alert us to the convicts who had died en route to Siberia along an otherwise unidentifiable road. Another possibility is to make use of pre-existing visual conventions:

Saint Sergius, for example, is always depicted in a brown cloak.
That is how we know it is him. More generally, a halo depicts
holiness; height or prominence within a composition conveys
importance. The birch tree is one such visual convention, but
the more it is used, the more meanings accrue around it: a
symbol of fertility in Slavic folklore; a sacred Russianness
in the nineteenth-century paintings of Mikhail Nesterov; an
image of femininity or chastity in the 'mail-order bride' portrait photographs collected by Maria Kapajeva ...

In Chernobyl, that which cannot be seen is radiation. It can
be heard on the click-clicking of a Geiger counter. It can, by
some accounts, be tasted. It can be measured and mapped but
it cannot be seen, and this invisibility leaves questions that
cannot be answered. 'It's a new world now,' says one of the
women interviewed in Svetlana Alexievich's *Chernobyl Prayer*.
'Everything is different. Is it the radiation to blame, or who is
it? And what's the stuff like? ... Is it white, or what does it look
like? What colour?'

Time and again, Alexievich's interviewees speak of the
world as if nothing had changed – visually at least. One recalls:

> The orchards were blossoming, young grass sparkling
> joyfully in the sun. Birds were singing. Such a profoundly
> familiar world. My first thought was: everything here is as
> it should be and carrying on as usual. Here was the same
> earth, the same water and trees. And their shapes, colours
> and scents were eternal.

Despite this apparently idyllic, timeless world, the people of
Chernobyl were being told that, suddenly, everything had
changed. That which once looked beautiful was now poisoned.
And yet, visually there was no difference. The testimony
continues:

But on the first day, I was warned: don't pick the flowers, don't sit on the ground, don't drink the water from the spring.

With sight no longer trustworthy, other senses become more important. Tony Parker's *Russian Voices* – a book comprised of dozens of interviews carried out by the British journalist in 1990 – includes five testimonies from people living near to the reactor at the time of the catastrophe. Each of them tells us what they did not notice. None heard the explosion, which took place at 1.23 a.m. None could see anything specifically different when they woke up and first went outside. And yet ... 'I was aware at once something was wrong,' says a newspaper editor. 'I could feel on my face a tingling as though it was raining although it was not. I felt also a taste of metal in my mouth ...'

In the National Museum of Russian Art in Kyiv hangs a still life painting by Ivan Khrutsky, a successful if not especially interesting artist of the nineteenth century. The painting shows a rectangular birch-bark carton overflowing with freshly picked ceps. Their stems glow brown, their undersides are milky white and black soil still clings to the bases where they have been plucked from the earth. The basket has been placed on the ground against a backdrop of dark trees. Baby turnips and five fat little cucumbers loll on the ground nearby. Painted in 1842, this is not a landscape painting; this is a still life set outside. But Khrutsky nonetheless conveys a very particular understanding of the natural world. It is not a wild place or even a place of labour: it is simply a source of bounty, a place that provides delicious things to eat.

Despite Stalin's appalling treatment of rural Ukraine – first collectivisation in the late 1920s, then the Holodomor famine in the early 1930s – the region around Chernobyl was regarded as an idyllic one by many of those who lived there. The town of Pripyat was a model Soviet town, with some of the best living conditions in the USSR. But the countryside too was seen as a perfect timeless place. 'It was such a beautiful area,' recalls one of Alexievich's interviewees. 'The trees were not recent plantings but the original, ancient forest. Meandering streams ... green grass ... People calling to each other in the forest.' Visually, at least, it was as if nothing had changed.

'The elderly people didn't believe in an invisible enemy,' recalls a military commander in a Discovery channel documentary that I watched on a minibus from Kyiv to the exclusion zone. This idyllic landscape – the one that for a hundred years artists had been glorifying in the name of Russia, that looks exactly the same as it did yesterday – was no longer plentiful, fertile, bounteously Russian, but suddenly a place of poison and undetectable treachery. 'Something had gone wrong with nature,' says a woman interviewed in *Chernobyl Prayer*.

Throughout the book, animals sometimes sense what humans cannot. Cows refuse to enter a contaminated river, cats stop eating mice, worms burrow deep underground, bees and wasps hide inside their nests. At other times, the nonhuman world seems completely unaffected by the catastrophe that has taken place. One former resident recalls a moment in which the sight of a line of ants 'crawling along a tree trunk' provides a vivid contrast to the chaos of army vehicles, soldiers and helicopters all around.

We had stopped in the forest, I got up to have a smoke near a birch tree. I stood there, leaning against it. Right up close to my face were those ants crawling on the trunk, deaf to our presence, not paying us the slightest attention. Stubbornly following their path. We could vanish and they wouldn't notice.

Chernobyl is a tragedy arising out of a combination of human technological power and our inability to control that power. As such, it prefigures discussion of the Anthropocene, the dawning realisation that there is no such thing as untouched nature any more. But this striking image of the line of black ants against the white bark of the birch suggests something else: the indifference of the nonhuman world. The birch in this moment is not a Russian tree. For many who speak of Chernobyl, national borders between Russia, Belarus and Ukraine no longer mean anything. There is simply inside the zone, and outside. Chernobyl forces us to wonder whether life will always find a way to recover or whether we have already ruined the planet. When humans become extinct what kind of world will we hand over to the the ants and to the birches?

Painter-turned-photographer David McMillan has been visiting the Chernobyl exclusion zone since 1994: twenty-one times over a quarter of a century. In 2019, a glossy book of his images was published with an accompanying essay by art historian Claude Baillargeon. Aptly entitled *Growth and Decay*, the book captures the changes, both subtle and dramatic, that have taken place since McMillan has been visiting the zone: on the one hand, decay (peeling wallpaper, crumbling buildings); on the other, growth (lush vegetation, young birches, bright red rowanberries).

On his wanderings, McMillan often returned, deliberately or purely by chance, to the same locations. The resulting photographs provide the clearest examples of the changes taking place in Chernobyl. There are three such images that are of particular interest to me. Yes, they are photographs of birch trees.

The images show a single room inside the Polissia Hotel, which was built in the 1970s to house delegates and guests visiting the nuclear power plant. McMillan's book has been lavishly produced: there are several instances in which the pages fold outwards to allow the reader to view a series of three or four photographs at once. The three images of the Polissia Hotel are presented like this. The recto (or right-hand page) of the spread appears blank until you fold it outwards to reveal two further images. The result is a triptych of photographs, shot, left to right, in 1996, 2004 and 2013.

In his accompanying essay, Baillargeon provides an excellent description of differences from the first image to the third across the seventeen years that separate them:

> Back in 1996, McMillan pictured an invading blanket of greenery sustaining a young birch growing in the middle of one of the guest rooms. Eight years later, as the birch was thriving in the most unlikely of environments, two shoots of mountain-ash, along with a gooseberry tree, woodfern, a thin carpet of moss, and other botanical specimens had also taken root. Against all odds, the trees found enough nourishment to continue growing for a number of years, but their heroic struggle proved impossible to sustain and everything had died by the time the artist returned in 2013.

Baillargeon's description intrigues me for a number of reasons. I can't help but smile, for example, when he uses the same words that one might use to describe the hotel interior before the catastrophe: the 'blanket of greenery', the 'carpet of moss'. I'm also surprised by how similar his language is, in places, to that employed by the war-time Soviet writers such as Mikhail Bubennov and Mikhail Sholokhov. Like them, although for very different reasons, Baillargeon sees the growth of the birch as a 'heroic struggle', in which the young sapling is somehow 'thriving in the most unlikely of environments', its very existence a sign of life 'against all the odds'.

A botanist would see it differently. For it is in such apparently inhospitable places that birches often grow. Kenneth Ashburner, for example, has described birches as 'colonizers par excellence, prolific and ephemeral'. Writing in 1992, Ashburner observed that 'Man's urban activities in more recent times have opened up new habitats also, such as abandoned industrial sites – railway yards, old quarries etc.'. For birches, the irradiated interior of a Soviet hotel is just another new habitat created by humans. It is only those eager to bestow meaning upon every natural occurrence who seem so continually surprised by the birch tree.

Baillargeon makes an additional observation, however: that the 'heroic struggle' was 'impossible to maintain', and by 2013 'everything had died'. It is certainly true that, while the first two photographs are comparatively lush and green, the third shows a floor of dusty grey, the roots of the young trees exposed to the air, and most of the growth gone dull and dark. This observation is important. As Baillargeon puts it:

As the walls collapse while this organic matter decomposes and more seedlings are brought in by the elements, a new life cycle may well manifest itself.

Life in Chernobyl is filling the gaps made vacant by our departure. But McMillan's triptych suggests that the process by which the nonhuman might gradually replace the human is not likely to be linear. Within the great cycle are many little spirals. Chernobyl was not even forty years ago. The long-term future of the land remains uncertain.

Hotel Room, October 1996. By David McMillan

Hotel Room, October 2004. By David McMillan

Hotel Room, October 2013. By David McMillan

At a time of climate chaos and mass species loss, this is not simply a local observation. If the 1986 explosion at Chernobyl marked a moment when the USSR could no longer isolate itself from the world, then the regrowth in the ruins that McMillan documents suggests similarly that the importance of the birch – both real and symbolic – is not limited to Russia (or Belarus or Ukraine). The tentative regrowth of the birch in a site of unprecedented catastrophe might perhaps be a sign of possible global futures. If the apocalypse comes, the conventional narrative runs, we will have to get used to living (and dying) in the ruins. However, as professor of 'inhuman geography' Kathryn Yusoff has pointed out, many people already are. Many have been for centuries. Apocalypse, it turns out, is not an event but a process. For some, these ruins are philosophical or political; for others, they are literal and real (economic, environmental, colonial). And the birch is already here too, growing right beside us in the ruins. As Belgian philosopher of science Isabelle Stengers said recently about what the future may hold for today's youth:

> We cannot pretend to know the future but we can ask the question: What can we leave to these generations? We cannot leave them anything but ruins. They will have to go on living in ruins, because there is no other possibility. Gaia is here to stay.

In 2005, Mary Mycio, the Kyiv correspondent for the *LA Times*, published a book entitled *Wormwood Forest: A Natural History of Chernobyl* that expresses continual amazement at the animals and plants apparently thriving within the exclusion zone, despite high levels of radiation within their cells. She tells of the many people within the zone who continue to try to live as if nothing had happened, for example making moonshine out of birch sap.

A popular beverage in Ukraine, birch sap also concentrates radionuclides. A liter of the stuff in one 2003 sampling contained 1,800 becquerels of cesium. Birch sap, together with things such as nuts, falls under the 'other' category in Ukraine's list of radioactivity limits in different foods. The maximum permissible cesium level in a kilogram or liter of 'other' is 600 becquerels.

The exclusion zone is no longer a forbidden place. Tourism was officially sanctioned in 2002 and today it is a popular destination, mostly for international visitors. Among these visitors have been many artists and scientists and, in particular, photographers. Some artists have produced sensitive, thought-provoking responses. Art-architecture duo Metasitu have organised an artist residency programme in Slavutych, a town built after the 1986 explosion to rehouse workers and their families who had previously been living in Pripyat. Alice Miceli's *Projeto Chernobyl*, meanwhile, is a series of thirty radiographs produced over the course of four years through direct contact between specially treated film and the radiation still present in the region. Anaïs Tondeur's *Chernobyl Herbarium* consists of thirty-one rayograms, created by the imprint of specimens from a radioactive herbarium onto photosensitive plates. The resulting images show glowing roots and seed-heads among faded brown-black galaxies. 'Plants will gently gag the silent scream of things,' wrote philosopher Michael Marder in a text to accompany Tondeur's work. 'Where there was devastation and abandon, there will be a forest.' For now, as I discover when I make my own visit to the exclusion zone, that forest is predominantly birch.

Other artistic responses have been crass and superficial. In 2019, writer Megan Nolan was invited to a media view inside the exclusion zone of an artwork that included animations projected onto ruined buildings, a large silver star with screens

showing clips from Tarkovsky's 1979 film *Stalker*, and what
Nolan describes as 'a disarmingly jaunty Eurodance soundtrack'.
The project was part of a government initiative to 'rebrand'
Chernobyl and further attract international tourists to the region.
With Kyiv the nearest major city, Chernobyl is being cast by the
government as a Ukrainian story, even though, as Alexievich has
noted, one in five Belarusians lives in the contaminated zone.

With the worldwide success of the recent HBO television
series, tourism is already on the increase. In 2017, 50,000 people
visited Chernobyl, according to the Ukrainian government. In
2018, that figure had risen to 72,000. And with every tourist
comes a camera. Image-sharing websites such as Flickr and
Instagram show hundreds of thousands of results when I search
for 'Chernobyl'.

I had thought Chernobyl would show me the limits of the
visual. But it has become emblematic of the oversaturation of
imagery that characterises contemporary internet culture. Places
like Chernobyl are part of a wider fascination, bordering upon
obsession, with photographs of crumbling buildings. Where the
picturesque ruin merged with the surrounding landscape to
form an aesthetic whole (the naturalisation of history), today's
renewed interest in the ruin emphasises aesthetic contrast
(history versus nature). The postmodern ruin makes visible the
failure of all those Enlightenment grand narratives, while the
image-maker and viewer stand smugly outside the errors of history. Inside the frame, the clean hard lines of twentieth-century
modernist architecture are overrun by the sinuous growth of
roots and branches. Regularity and repetition crumble towards
chaos. Bright white modernity grows dirty with lichen and age.
Birches sprout through windows and floors. Paint invariably
flakes. Everything rusts.

At the entrance to the exclusion zone stands a pair of bright yellow kiosks, one each side of the road. They sell coffee and crisps and Chernobyl-related paraphernalia: badges, posters, respiratory masks. Music blares out as buses and coaches gather. There are just three songs on the playlist: two old classics and one I've not heard before that a later internet research reveals to be by Las Vegas band Imagine Dragons. 'Radioactive' is the name of the song. 'Welcome to the new age,' runs the chorus. 'Whoa, oh, oh, oh, oh, I'm radioactive.' It's not entirely clear why but our entry into the exclusion zone is delayed by about an hour. I must have heard that chorus line forty times. If I ever hear that song again I'll—

It's late November, cold with a scattering of snow. I'd risen early in the morning, hurried through slippery Kyiv streets. The skies are grey and hard. Our guide wears camouflage trousers with a pink fleece; her nails decorated with little radiation symbols. I have not told any of the people I know in Ukraine that I'm going to Chernobyl. What would they think?

Within an hour of our arrival inside Chernobyl I have taken an irrational dislike to the rest of our group: two Italians in pristine navy puffer jackets; a Chinese boy on a two-year journey to every country of the former Soviet Union ('I like visiting the markets,' he tells me, 'and bartering with the old ladies.'); a young English woman in a bobble hat, flared jeans and a bag adorned with pin badges, who describes herself as 'kooky'. There's a Belgian with a nose ring, wearing bright red socks and Reebok Classic trainers, hoodie, raincoat and cut-off jeans. He spends the day taking photographs, knees bent, legs thrust wide apart as he does so. I get the impression he is more interested in playing the role of the photographer than in the subject matter of his photographs – destruction, loss, death. The soundtrack to the day is the arrhythmic chirping of the Geiger counters.

We wander through an abandoned village, taking endless photographs. Fragments of patterned linoleum are littered across a floor; wallpaper peels like birch bark. Everybody wants their photographs devoid of people.

I stand perpetually to the side of the group, jotting in my notebook, disgusted, fascinated. If I scribble enough thoughts down, will that make my tourism different from their tourism?

As we drive to Pripyat I can hear what sound like chain-saws. I wonder what kind of forestry management can operate here in what seems like the epitome of a rewilding land-scape. It is only later I find out that illegal logging has been taking place within the exclusion zone for years. All logging is officially banned due to the high level of contamination. But irradiated trees are felled and sold anyway. How much wood and paper is dangerously irradiated? And where does it end up?

The most extraordinary sight in the exclusion zone was once known as the Russian woodpecker. Constructed in 1976, and still active three years after the Chernobyl explosion, it is a vast radar, an important part of the Soviet missile defence early-warning system. The nickname comes from the radar's tap-tap-tapping sounds that regularly interfered with short-wave radios across the world.

To stare up into the radar today is to suffer a kind of inverse vertigo: a perfect ruined sublime. It is made from dozens of interconnected pylon-like structures, dark grey and rusting brown, nearly 500 feet high. Trees grow up and around the base columns. My feet crunch in the snow as I gaze up, groggy, at the hundreds of horizontal metal struts and wires, repeating to infinity and fading into mist. The flat, grey, papery sky is lined with endless horizontal radio wires. A blank page, ready to be written upon. But what to say?

A few baby birches stand nearby. I spot a crow's nest, jolly like a fat dark pom-pom in a line of trees. Or perhaps it's mistletoe. Or a witch's broom.

Everywhere the forests are new growth. Nature, or something that looks like it, is returning – but what does that mean? The rewilding dream is a place where humans no longer exist, but maybe such a thing is impossible now: our traces are too wide, too deep. Landscape, by definition, requires an active viewer. After the apocalypse will the photographs survive?

We enter the main square of Pripyat as the light begins to fade. This had once been a town with a bright future, its population 50,000, the average age just twenty-six. In the snow the footprints of all the other tour groups lead down the same roads. We enter what used to be a café and tread gingerly down icy steps to the edge of the river. It flows from here into the Dnieper, from which Kyiv takes its drinking water. Birches line the river bank and the water is starting to freeze. As the grey day fades further, my camera runs out of battery.

IX.

MOSCOW TO VLADIVOSTOK

'... all that broke the almost straight line of the horizon were distant, small groves of birch trees with their rounded, tooth-shaped tips.'

Ivan Turgenev, *Kasyan from the Beautiful Lands,* **1851**

Outside the train window rolls an endless line of blue wagons, each carrying row upon row of birch trunks cut into identical lengths. We've paused for a moment at Kovrov station on the way from Moscow to the city of Nizhny Novgorod on the banks where the Oka River joins the Volga. It is the first leg of our journey to Vladivostok on the Trans-Siberian railway. We will stay in several cities along the way: after Nizhny Novgorod, there is Krasnoyarsk, Irkutsk and Ulan-Ude before our arrival in Vladivostok in about two weeks. By the side of the tracks are workmen wearing orange high-visibility vests layered over full camouflage. It's an outfit that rather sends mixed messages: do they want to be seen or not?

Inside the train our group is in high spirits. This first journey is a gentle introduction: six hours at most. There are five of us: Miina and Arttu, a husband and wife curatorial duo I've known since living in Helsinki; Iona, a British artist and film-maker currently studying in Helsinki; and Katja, a Finnish researcher as obsessed with Russia as I am and far more knowledgeable. At the front of the carriage a television is playing an old Soviet war movie. Iona films the film: men in military uniforms and women in cotton dresses blurry behind a foreground of grey seats and luggage racks.

Up to this point, my attempts to understand the multiple meanings of the birch in Russia have ranged unsystematically across history: from the earliest people to be known as the Rus' to medieval peasant customs, the landscaped estates of the Tsars, revolution, war, Chernobyl, and the anti-Putin environmentalism of the post-Soviet era. Geographically, however, the scope of my thinking has been much narrower. Rarely have I strayed too far from Moscow or Saint Petersburg. But Russia is a vast place. Today the Russian Federation encompasses eighteen sovereign nations, over 144 million people and thirty-five official languages. It covers 6,612,100 square miles across eleven time zones. In order to put together a fuller picture of the importance of the birch I need to start thinking beyond the limits of European Russia. I need to branch out, into the depths of Siberia, into Asia. I need to get out of the cities. I need to travel. And what better way is there to 'see Russia' than the Trans-Siberian? It is not until I'm sitting on the train, gazing at the endless forests of birch gliding past the window, that I realise the limitations of this whole endeavour. At the end of the line, in Vladivostok, a contemporary art curator is dismissive about the possibility of learning much from travelling the Trans-Siberian. 'It's just one thin line through Russia,' she tells me. By then, it's a bit too late.

There is another reason behind my desire to see more. Many people believe that it is only in the so-called provinces that one can hope to find an authentic Russia untouched by the corrupting influences of modernity or Europe. This is not a new phenomenon: the Slavophiles of the nineteenth century believed that Russia's true spirit should be sought in the countryside, in the day-to-day lives of the peasantry. Since the end of communism, this belief has been reprised, although on slightly different conceptual lines. No longer is the division one between the urban and the rural; today the line that cuts Russia in two is the line between the centre and the periphery, between the capital and the provinces.

The 1990s under Boris Yeltsin was an era of haphazard decentralisation, in which Moscow struggled to exert authority over regional administrations. Under Putin, this process has been reversed. In that time, the provinces have come to be seen as a repository of a new (or maybe an age-old) Russian national culture: 'home,' as professor of Russian and Slavic studies Lyudmila Parts puts it, 'to the true Russia, both past and future'. Through an analysis of recent films and television shows, Parts's book, *In Search of the True Russia*, traces this development not only as a psychological coping mechanism following the end of the USSR and Russia's loss of imperial dominance, but also as a strategy of communication and control embraced by a conservative, increasingly authoritarian centre. As Parts puts it, 'The myth of the provinces provides the contemporary cultural elite with a semiotic approach to formulating Russia's new postimperial identity.' This means Russia today is being symbolised through a narrow conception of the provinces and the (conveniently hyper-conservative) values supposedly innate to those who live there.

At the same time that the provinces are depicted as the home of timeless Russian values (patriarchal, Orthodox), they are also places of natural (Russian) beauty: increasingly associated with what Parts calls 'the concrete and marketable images of unspoiled nature, clean air and water'.

As in the nineteenth century and during World War II, affection for the natural world can be co-opted in the service of a nationalist agenda. That is why nature conservation can be so emotionally charged: such issues are perhaps unique in their ability to bring together the nationalist right with the radical left in a union against a fiscally minded 'centre' that seems only to understand value in terms of economics. Such unions are fragile, for the 'nature' championed by one group is never quite the same as the 'nature' of the other.

In the summer of 1956, Soviet writer Vladimir Soloukhin went for a walk through the countryside around Vladimir, an ancient town on the way from Moscow to Nizhny Novgorod. On the Trans-Siberian, this region passes by in a blur of birches. But Soloukhin took his time, exploring, in the time-honoured tradition of writers who walk, the interconnection between the people he met and the places he visited. The resulting book was translated into English and published as *A Walk in Rural Russia* in 1967.

In part, the book is the story of a return home (Soloukhin was born in a village in the Vladimir region) but it is also imbued with a sense of discovery, as if the writer is encountering aspects of his homeland for the very first time. There are discussions of land management, environmental conservation and the preservation of rural traditions. There are insights into Soviet-era debates on forestry management. Soloukhin pinpoints, for example, a conflict between foresters, who were tasked with ensuring the ongoing health of natural ecosystems, and timber-fellers, who were better equipped, better funded, and whose job was simply to chop down trees to feed the industrial economy.

Soloukhin was part of a group known as the 'village prose' writers. Writing shortly after the death of Stalin, in a brief period known as the 'Khrushchev thaw' in which censorship was a little more relaxed, they often presented idealised views of timeless Russian peasant life. The village prose writers had to strike a careful balance: on the one hand was their desire to glorify an unchanging Russia; on the other hand was the simultaneous necessity to celebrate the radical changes imposed upon the countryside under the Soviets.

Such difficulties are exemplified in *A Walk in Rural Russia*. In one section, Soloukhin meets the head of an icon-painting studio, who laments that all of the employees are tasked with knocking out reproductions of works by Ivan Shishkin and other nineteenth-century landscape painters. Soloukhin even dares to criticise realism, and by implication Socialist Realism. This is dangerous territory, and he treads very carefully.

Soloukhin also ventures to compare the communications strategies of the communists with those of Christianity. Soviet rural propaganda, he observes, struggles to compete against the heady smell of incense or the grandeur of church architecture. Several times he also notes evidence of the continuing material presence of religious beliefs. 'Among trees and funeral crosses stood a little wooden church, a survivor from the darkness of the ages, coming straight out of a fairy-tale.'

What does it mean for such things to linger in the landscape? Soloukhin answers: 'if external objects of the old world continue to exist, it must mean that inner traces of it live on in the hearts and minds of men'. If he were cleaving close to Soviet orthodoxy, he might have advocated for the destruction of these traces of former systems of belief. But he does not. He says nothing, and his silence leaves open the possibility that the old ways ought to be cherished after all. *A Walk in Rural Russia* was published in Russia in the 1950s; it was not until the late 1980s, with even further relaxation of press censorship under Mikhail Gorbachev's policy of *glasnost*, that Soloukhin became more outspoken. Following the lead of economist Vasily Selyunin, Soloukhin didn't simply blame the faults of the Soviet era on Stalin (as had become accepted discourse) but on Lenin too. Such a criticism was tantamount to saying not simply that the communists went wrong, but that communism *was* wrong. In publicly idealising the pre-revolutionary era, Soloukhin helped to pave the way for a new generation of Russian artists and writers. Some of these felt that Russia had been on the verge of adopting European-style liberal democracy until the Bolsheviks seized power; others argued for a return to Tsarist autocracy.

Before he even begins his journey, Soloukhin asserts that the countryside of Vladimir is 'as beautiful as any in the world'. He continues: 'I had always been convinced of that, because it is my native land.' In order to explain the appeal of 'native' beauty over that of other lands, however, Soloukhin recalls a memory not from home but from a botanical garden in the Caucasus. He remembers all the 'wonderful names' of the exotic plants: yucca, eucalyptus, *laurocerasus* (laurel). But such novelty quickly palls: 'After a time we grew tired of marvelling,' he writes. And then:

> Suddenly we saw a quite unusual tree, like no other in the whole garden. It was white as snow, a tender green like young grass, and it stood out sharply against the somewhat uniform colouring of the background. We saw it then with new eyes and valued it in a new way. The label told us that there stood before us a common birch.

I have not read the Russian original but in the English translation by Stella Miskin, the word order is quite perfect. We are first alerted to an 'unusual tree', but instead of being told what it is we are given tantalising clues: it is 'like no other', 'white as snow', 'a tender green'. The tree is an everyday sight but one that, in the context of a botanical garden with all its exotic species of plant, is appreciated afresh. It is only right at the end of the paragraph, after a pleasurable sensation of suspense, that the identity of the tree is revealed (for readers who had not guessed already): 'a common birch'. Soloukhin elaborates:

> Just try lying under a birch-tree on soft, cool grass, when only fragments of sunlight and the clear blue of the midday sky are glimpsed through the leaves. How the birch will whisper to you, bending softly to your ear, what tender words and wonderful stories it will murmur, and what a feeling of contentment it will bring!

Here, Soloukhin follows in the time-honoured tradition of feminising the birch tree. It bends down softly, whispering and murmuring tender words. In official discourse, the Soviet era was famously sexless, and here Soloukhin leaves unsaid what kind of love might exist between the author and the personified tree. What he emphasises is a sense of calm and softness felt to be unique to the birch. He continues:

> Then think of a palm-tree. One cannot even lie beneath it, for either there is no grass at all, or it is dry, dusty and prickly. The leaves of the palm rattle in the wind as though they were tin or ply-wood, and there is no caress nor feeling in the sound.

It is both interesting and ominous that Soloukhin expresses his love of the (Russian) birch by disparaging the (non-Russian) palm tree. At the end of this section, he admits to seeing the landscape through the lens of the same nineteenth-century painters that I have been looking at: Isaac Levitan, Ivan Shishkin and, co-builder of the Abramtsevo chapel, Vasily Polenov:

It may well be that all the beauty of lands beyond the sea yields to the quiet charm of the Central Russian countryside, painted by Levitan, Shishkin and Polenov.

Here Soloukhin seems to concede what I have been examining all along: that love of one's native land is not simply something one is born with, but the product of, among other things, art history.

In the Nizhny Novgorod city history museum a propaganda poster from 1925 shows a Russian peasant girl in a white skirt and red bandanna, striding arm-in-arm with her new communist boyfriend. She waves goodbye to her ex, a portly fellow, who drops his umbrella in surprise. Join the party, get the girl, seems to be the message. Behind the couple on the edge of the image is a bright white birch.

A café is playing an irritatingly catchy pop song, a paean to a life of middle-class nomadism. 'I've got no roots,' runs the chorus, 'but my home was never on the ground.' As we travel across Russia, there will be no escape from this song.

Inside the old city walls of Nizhny Novgorod, teenage army cadets are marching in formation by a marble memorial: 1941–1945, the years of the Great Patriotic War. Before the end of the USSR the marchers would have been wearing the white shirts and red scarves of the Young Pioneers. The uniforms may have changed, but the militarism remains. Around the white walls of the nearby Cathedral of Archangel Michael all is white: white gravel borders, white flowers in white municipal flowerbeds, the white neoclassical columns of the Belarus Embassy, the white grid of the Foreign Ministry. Among it all, scattered on grassy slopes or framing the city, young and staked or high and handsome, there are white birches everywhere.

On the train from Nizhny Novgorod to Krasnoyarsk I somehow secure pole position in our compartment: next to the window, facing forwards. Katja is opposite me; Iona filming as people pass by in the corridor; Miina and Arttu in their compartment next door. I watch and make a note of the passing birch trees, tightly packed and largely leafless, foliage only visible towards the tops. Some are just turning to yellow and brown. There is an occasional flash of fiery red. The trunks unfurl in an endless film-roll of parallel lines, irregularly interspersed. Running out of words, I draw them in my notebook:

|||| | | | || ||| | | | || || ||||| || || || | || || | |||| | | | ||| | | || |

Things rattle by: a rusted pylon; a plank of wood over a shallow winding stream; a long tin-roofed storage shed; fields; a road; a crossing; a waterlogged bog. I see tyre tracks through the red earth; workmen dozing under a trailer. I sit and open my book of Russian magic tales, snoozily hoping that all the birch trees will start to mean something, not yet worried that they don't.

Miina and Arttu head into our compartment. 'The landscape is very Finnish,' says Miina.

'It's not exotic enough,' laughs Arttu. 'I want water! And dramatic ravines!'

The sun hits the birches. They seem to glow white from within just like in the paintings of Savrasov or Levitan. It's not dramatic, but it is beautiful in its way. The landscape is appearing to me not only through the window of the train but also through the aesthetic lens of the late nineteenth century. I must try to snap out of it, see the landscape through a different filter. But how?

On the edge of a hamlet, a woman in black jeans stands with her children and watches as the train passes them by. A real rural Russian! Or just a compositional device.

In my book of Russian magic tales I notice a trope. Again and again I read phrases like 'A long time passed – or maybe just a short time' or 'he walked a long way, or maybe a short way' or 'he walked for many a day, or maybe less than a day'.

These phrases demonstrate a certain ambivalence to time and place – not dissimilar in that way to 'Once upon a time . . .' that begins so many folk tales in English. But instead of simply placing the narrative in the dim and distant past, these phrases carry a sense of duration that is both unknowable and unimportant. Sitting on a train, with nothing I need to do and nowhere I need to be, no meetings or deadlines, this vagueness of time and space strikes a chord.

We are on the way from Nizhny Novgorod to Krasnoyarsk. We depart at night and are due to arrive early morning three days later. Iona is frequently checking the time on her laptop, looking at the map to see what kind of progress we're making, adjusting her phone as we pass into each new time zone. Historically, this is appropriate behaviour for a train journey. Historian and essayist Tony Judt has described how railways changed the world in the nineteenth century, transforming the landscape and reshaping concepts of distance, but also laying the grounds for the development of bourgeois society. 'The conquest of space led inexorably to the reorganization of time,' he argued in a 2010 article for the *New York Review of Books*. This was not only a result of the speed at which trains travelled but also of the introduction of the train timetable. Judt continues:

It is hard today to convey the significance and implications of the timetable, which first appeared in the early 1840s: for the organization of the railways themselves, of course, but also for the daily lives of everyone else. The pre-modern world was space-bound; its modern successor, time-bound.

Since then, many people's lives have been conditioned by the train timetable and its correlate, the working day. Urban existence is characterised by a strange alternation between frantic rushing and aimless waiting, and the railways are, for Judt at least, the origin. In the Soviet era right up until 2018, the Trans-Siberian ran not according to local time but according to Moscow time. But the characters of the Russian magic tales were not concerned with timetables. The length of the working day was prescribed by the arc of the sun (and the lash of the birch rod).

Somewhere along the way we cross the fictional border that separates Europe from Asia. Soon the birches will visibly change. The Trans-Siberian is famously punctual, but for me, time and distance have already ceased to mean anything at all.

Russian folklore is full of birds. Katja tells me about Sirin and Alkonost, a pair of mythological characters with the heads of women and the bodies of birds. Both sing beautiful songs which cause mortals to lose their memories. Sirin is a figure of joy; Alkonost brings only sorrow. In my own books, I read of Finist the Bright Falcon, who transforms into a young man to woo the youngest of three daughters; of Gamayun, a bird of magical prophecy that lives beyond distant lands; and of the firebird, captured and brought home by Ivanushka, the youngest son of the Tsar. I ask Katja how Russian fairy tales differ from Finnish ones. 'In Russia, Ivan Tsarevich is a recurring heroic central figure,' she says. 'In Finland, we have fewer heroes.'

As we talk, the landscape continues to scroll past the window: golden onion domes and wooden villages, a hillside cemetery, a lake. Young birches recolonise a clear-felled forest. The larches turn yellow as we head east, as if travelling towards autumn, towards winter. A rail-side sign reads '1642km'. To where? From where? It doesn't say.

Occasionally, from a vantage point, I see a scattering of houses, a wet foreground, trees fading into the distance. A figure in red walks a winding path. In the early evening sun, six golden crosses gleam bright on the domes of a church. There is a cow trotting along a lane outside the village.

'This is so beautiful!' grins Katja.

To view the world from the train is to see but never know: all those lives just glimpsed. At Perm a workman rolls a stripe of fresh red paint along the base of the station building. A military jet booms overhead. Then another. At Kalachinska a young boy helps his mother across the train tracks.

A long time passed – or maybe just a short time.

My notes are all in diary form. But the dates no longer matter.

After Omsk, the birch forests seem less managed. The trees grow further apart from one another and there are more branches and foliage as a result: less good for logging. The landscape begins to open out – no longer an endless forest but patches of wood among farmland. Crimson grasses grow in boggy ground. The foregrounds are red with the fire of *Betula nana*, an Arctic tundra shrub known as dwarf birch. This is a new species to me: I'd never realised that the birch family included not only trees but shrubs too. With glossy red bark and little round leaves, *Betula nana* is well suited to tough conditions. It stretches along much of the route of the Trans-Siberian.

Today's major event is our half-hour stop at Barabinsk station. A friend of Katja's lives here: an old Russian woman named Lydia whom she lived with for a year near the palace and gardens I visited in Gatchina, but who has recently relocated to her home village near the trainline. 'Aunty' Lydia has arranged to meet us at the station. We're all very excited.

We come to a halt and it isn't long before Aunty Lydia bustles onboard and into our cabin, every inch the stereotypical babushka. I'm not sure how she has managed to carry it all but she has brought with her the most extraordinary array of food. She hands over boiled eggs and a fat slab of pale cheese, two litres of fresh milk, a big tub of *smetana* (the Russian crème fraîche), a sawn-off eight-litre plastic bottle filled with tomatoes and just-boiled potatoes, wrapped in tin foil and still hot. There are fat sweet buns, a chocolate cake, loaves of bread, a sponge roll filled with sweet and tangy rowanberry jam, plastic cups and cutlery. Aunty Lydia unveils each item in order with a detailed explanation – translated by Katja – of how best to enjoy it. The milk is natural, says Lydia, because you can see the cream at the top. These big potatoes are for the boys; these little ones are for the girls. This is how you take the top off an egg ...

Aunty Lydia's generosity is beautiful to witness. She knows Katja well but the rest of us are perfect strangers. We chat nonsense and pose for photographs. We warm to Lydia and she to us very quickly. Polish artist Józef Czapski wrote of the intensity of his encounters with Russian people in the 1940s: 'Once again I experienced that rare, so very Russian, instant contact with someone whom I had never met before, and will probably never meet again.' I feel something similar as Lydia reluctantly leaves the train. I still think so fondly of her and those fleeting moments.

The afternoon rolls by to the rhythm of the train:

... telegraph pole, rye field,

telegraph pole, rye field,

telegraph pole, birch grove,

telegraph pole, crow ...

At the 1900 Paris Expo, the Russians were keen to tell the world about the new Trans-Siberian railway. By then it had been nearly completed, the majority built by hand and as cheaply as possible. A mock-up carriage was constructed for visitors: far grander than those used today. But it was not just the interiors that were important; the Russians wanted to show off their landscapes too. According to Nicole Segre's history of the railway, 'A diorama of Siberian views, painted by set makers from the Paris Opera House, wound past the windows, foreground and background passing at different speeds to convey movement and perspective.' We've only been on the Trans-Siberian a few days but sometimes it feels like the landscape outside the window has also been painted by set makers.

... telegraph pole, rye field,

telegraph pole, rye field ...

And then, every so often, the landscape offers up a surprise. That evening the sun sets with a blaze of hot pink behind the red and white funnels of a distant power plant. We feast on potatoes and *smetana* from Aunty Lydia, bread and cheese, and a salad of cucumber, dill and lemon juice.

A long time passed – or maybe just a short time.

And on a morning of rain-saturated russets and greyed-out skies, we draw towards Krasnoyarsk, the third largest city in Siberia.

Krasnoyarsk is a city of wide, traffic-filled roads where wooden huts face off against Soviet residential blocks and unfinished 1990s megaliths. A man in a turquoise polyester security guard uniform is so drunk that he can barely see or stand. But he won't wait for the traffic lights, instead lurching and stumbling across four lanes of fast-moving traffic. It's utterly horrifying and I can't look. I hear horns and brakes but the expected crunch of metal on flesh never arrives. I open my eyes. Somehow he's made it. And now he stands on the other side, waiting quite patiently for his more safety-conscious friend to cross at the crossing when the light turns green. What was all the rush for?

From our vantage point above the forests outside the city, you can gaze across the centuries. The sky is a rumpled grey, the woods deep green with streaks of yellow from the turning larches, the wooded hills waving blue-grey into the far distance.

Katja and I are hiking in Stolby nature reserve, a few miles south of Krasnoyarsk. We're with Pavel, our guide for the afternoon, who picked us up from our hotel in his van a few hours earlier. If Aunty Lydia was a stereotypical babushka, Pavel is exactly what you might expect from a Russian former soldier, turned nature guide. He wears full camouflage and black wraparound shades. He is bald, bearded and built like a bear. He says barely a word until we're out of the city.

Stolby is famous for its rock formations: large piles thrusting up from the ground like thumbs. These dramatic shapes were formed from magma that remained un-erupted inside volcanoes, and which cooled and solidified into a durable mix of granite and basalt when they became extinct. Then the surrounding volcanoes, made from softer rock, gradually eroded away, to leave just these formations standing like pillars (*stolby*

in Russian means 'pillar'). They are quite extraordinary: pink
and grey and soaring above the height of the larches and pines.
The rocky ground is coated in just a thin layer of top soil and
the tree roots form an amazing sight: zig-zagging over and
across each other everywhere you walk. The occasional birch
has somehow found a footing high up in the rocks: one leans
out, bright and white, from a sheer crevice, its leaves green,
turning autumn yellow.

Pavel takes us to the top of one rock pillar. The climb is brief
but precipitous. As we head upwards, my foot slips on a glossy
tree root and I make the mistake of looking down. Shit. We
really are high above the forest: boulders and branches wait
far below should my other foot slip too. 'Don't look down,' I
whisper to Katja, unhelpfully. At the very top, the scale of the
view becomes apparent. 'Taiga,' announces Pavel, spreading
his arms out wide in a gesture of welcome and pride. For an
ex-soldier, Pavel is something of a showman. We gaze at the
view, take the appropriate photographs, and head back down.

Nature reserves can be strange places. Katja and I have come
here, fresh off the train, in part to escape the pattern that our
travels are already developing: train, city, museum, art gallery,
eat, drink, repeat. So, while the others go shopping, Katja and
I want to 'see Russia!' But Stolby is a carefully managed place –
at least in the areas that are open to the public. Designated as
a nature reserve since the 1920s, the entire park is now over
116,000 acres, of which just 3.5 per cent is open to visitors.
Elsewhere, there is an ecological research station and an education centre. Once upon a time they made nuclear weapons
here and the whole of the city was closed to foreigners. Today,
200,000 people come to Stolby every year.

Ahead of the 2018 football World Cup, new gravel paths and
wooden walkways were commissioned, but they were cheaply
installed and already look a little ragged. Along the walkways

at regular intervals are signs and information boards and mounted photographs telling visitors about the many different species of flora and fauna found within the reserve. A display of labelled tree trunks places *Betula pendula*, the silver birch (in Russian, *bereza borodavchataya*: warty birch), next to *Populus tremula*, the common aspen. Both are very white, the aspen smooth, the birch crackled like Raku.

As a dutiful guide, Pavel stops at every sign and tells us all about it. Even here in the forests of Siberia, the logic of the museum prevails. Later, Katja shows the rest of our group photographs on her phone, including photographs of the photographs of the animals we did not see. I can't quite get my head around it.

Stolby has not always been approached in this way. 'People have come here for centuries,' says Pavel as Katja translates for me. 'But it didn't used to be called "hiking".' Once out in the forest, Pavel becomes increasingly talkative. Lenin used to come here when he was exiled in Siberia, he tells us. Would-be revolutionaries would gather in the woods in spring, bringing food and drink so they could pretend they were simply meeting for a picnic should they be found by the Tsarist authorities. Forests have long been conceived as places of freedom, places where normal social mores do not apply. But forests are places of danger too, and the wrath of the authorities was not the only risk. 'OSTOROZHNO MEDVEDY!' reads a large yellow sign. 'Beware, bears!'

As we walk I ask Katja to ask Pavel about birch trees. 'You don't want to build your house out of birch,' he says after some thought, as if that were what I was planning. 'Your family won't feel well. They'll have headaches. Besides, birch doesn't grow straight enough to be used for houses. It's cold.'

It is only later that I'm prompted to consider the strangeness of Pavel's assertion that birch wood causes headaches. Where did he get this idea from? Looking online for possible answers, I come across the suggestion that birch can act as a diuretic. Maybe that's what he means.

Pavel sees every type of tree a little differently. 'You go into a birch forest to get married and have fun. You go into a spruce forest to hang yourself. Some trees give you energy; others take it away. If you hug a pine you can feel its energy.' As I'm told this, I can't help but wonder how much Katja is projecting her own views onto her translation. Surely big butch Pavel is not a tree-hugger?

At Pavel's suggestion, Katja embraces the nearest pine with visible delight. 'I can feel it!' Reluctantly I agree to do the same. I feel nothing.

From time to time, the conversation turns towards China. Russia has a sometimes uneasy relationship with its neighbour. There is occasionally a xenophobic tinge when Russians speak of environmental issues, as there is in many countries. When we're talking about the bears that inhabit Stolby, Pavel is quick to mention that, in certain parts of China, bear foot is regarded as a delicacy. 'Some poor locals hunt bears in Stolby to sell to China,' he tells us. He is clearly disgusted. A little later he tells us about a type of bark beetle that is devastating the evergreen forests of Siberia. According to one conspiracy, Pavel tells us, the beetle was deliberately introduced into Russia by Chinese forestry workers. China is one of the major export markets for Russian wood products ('Russia is an almost exclusive supplier of chop-sticks to China, with exports reaching almost $10 million a year,' boasts Made in Russia, that website with the birch-barcode logo) so it would certainly be in their interests to do so. There doesn't seem to be any evidence for this conspiracy theory, though, and it's unclear to what extent Pavel really buys into it.

Such species are not the only threat to the ecosystems of Siberia. In 2019, fires ravaged nearly 7.5 million acres of remote forest. Many were not far from where we are in Stolby. Satellite imagery from NASA showed smoke from the fires reaching as far as Alaska and down the west coast of Canada. The exact causes of the disaster have been disputed: regional authorities blamed a lightning strike after prolonged dry weather, while Greenpeace saw it as an effect of climate change. Russian Prime Minister Dmitry Medvedev speculated that they may have been deliberately started by illegal loggers. Thirty-three years on from Chernobyl and once again the playbook of the Russian authorities is to blame the saboteurs.

But 2019 was not the first year of such fires and the authorities could perhaps have been better prepared. The year before, over 740,000 acres of Siberian forest were on fire. That year, photographer Denis Sinyakov captured the dramatic effects in a panoramic photograph entitled *Landscape with Birches, Buryatia Oct 4 2018*. Blown up to life-size and lit from behind, so glowing brightly in Garage Museum of Contemporary Art in Moscow where I saw it exhibited, the composition is a dramatic contrast of white birch trees coated down one side in black soot. It is a timely reprisal of the nineteenth-century birch grove paintings of Isaac Levitan or Arkhip Kuindzhi. The difference is that Sinyakov's photograph is not self-consciously Russian; like Chernobyl, anthropogenic climate change and mass species loss are issues that cannot be contained within national borders. And this new image portrays not the timelessness of the natural world, but its fragility.

On the way back to the van, I remember the controversy around those Finnish hunters and I ask Katja to ask Pavel about wolves. Pavel thinks for a time before speaking: 'Out of a wolf litter of five or six, usually only two survive,' he says, 'but in a good year they all do. Then the population increases and more permits must be issued to keep the population in check.'

'Is it necessary to hunt wolves?' I ask, wondering to myself why killing wolves can be seen as a necessary duty while killing bears is simply an outrage.

Pavel tells a story about a woman being eaten by a wolf on the short walk home from her neighbour's house. I don't look convinced.

'Of course, it is interfering with the management of nature,' Pavel concedes. 'Nature would normally regulate these things without human intervention. But, on the other hand, it is survival of the fittest. Wolves have teeth and claws and we must protect ourselves. That is natural too.'

'In the UK we have no more wolves because we "protected" ourselves rather too well,' I say.

'Well, you're very welcome to collect some of ours,' he laughs, 'and take them home with you.'

Back in Krasnoyarsk, I read in the news about Pyotr Verzilov, the member of Pussy Riot whom I sat opposite at dinner in Moscow, who had previously invaded the pitch during the 2018 football World Cup final. The news is not good. Pyotr is in hospital in Berlin. He has almost certainly been poisoned and most reports assume that the Russian authorities are responsible. In addition to the World Cup protest, Pyotr had previously commissioned a report into the deaths of three Russian documentary film-makers in the Central African Republic in 2018. They had been investigating the operations of a Russian private military company but died in mysterious circumstances. Russia and the Central African Republic claim it was a roadside robbery gone wrong but there are many doubts surrounding this official version. Pyotr was due to receive the findings of the report when he was suddenly taken seriously ill.

Up to this point, the repressive violence of the Russian state apparatus has been for me an abstraction: something I read about while sitting at home in the UK, something I think about when Russians I meet avoid speaking of politics. Suddenly it is a real thing: nearby, breathing on the back of our necks or concealed around the next corner.

Before setting off on the Trans-Siberian I had written a feature for an online magazine about the art scene in Moscow. The article discussed the mayoral elections that had been taking place and their effects upon my experience of the city. Plants and trees had been installed as part of a city-wide garden festival, while battalions of orange-clad workmen kept the streets ruthlessly clean. Police and military were even more visible than usual. On the day of the election, streets were closed off and, without the appropriate ID, it was almost impossible to get back to central Moscow on foot. In the article, I tried to draw a contrast between the ultra cleanliness of this green-fingered authoritarianism and the altogether muddier and more complex aesthetic embraced by many of the artists I had seen in the city.

The article was due to be published while I was still travelling in Russia and I was starting to get nervous. What if I'd written the wrong thing? Who might read it? It was a very trivial piece of writing, certainly not exposing corruption or state-sponsored violence and cover-ups. But I am not a brave person. On the train from Krasnoyarsk my dreams are full of fear. Men in suits follow me at a distance. I'm given a cryptic warning by a stranger at a public fountain. Somebody hands me a bag of files. Paranoia ebbs and flows. The article, for reasons that remain unknown to me, was never published.

The hills outside Krasnoyarsk are patchy with birches scaling the slopes. In the foreground is a freight train transporting endless trucks of gas. Behind it the logo of the Russian state rail company, RZD, has been etched into the hillside.

On the train, I resume my position by the window and stare at the rural villages and small clusters of wooden houses trundling past. Most of the homes have satellite dishes. 'So the people know who to vote for,' somebody quips. Probably me.

We all gather in our cabin for lunch of cheese and bread and eggs. I chop plums with a pen-knife and leave them for a while in sugar and lemon juice.

Grey skies. Rain. Loosely wooded hills and fields. 'It's like England,' laughs Iona. 'Only we're in Asia.'

The fields are dotted with haystacks, hand-built, not the uniform oblong bales of mechanised modernity. We have travelled two thousand miles and we have not left the nineteenth century. The sky glows peachy behind blue clouds.

Outside a café in the Siberian city of Irkutsk, three teenagers are photographing their branded coffees and pre-packaged sandwiches, arranged into an Instagram-friendly still life on a pavement bench. Nearby I take my own photograph: the rusted peeling paint of an unloved nineteenth-century house.

In another café, that accursed 'No Roots' song is playing again. The voice of the singer, Alice Merton, is that of so many privileged itinerants aligning themselves with diverse nomadic traditions or the marginalised histories of the genuinely dispossessed:

> I build a home and wait for someone to tear it down.
> Then pack it up in boxes, head for the next town running.
> 'Cause I've got memories and travel like gypsies in the night.

Despite her claim to 'travel like gypsies in the night', Merton
is not of Roma heritage. Nobody has torn her home down;
her family moved around the world because her father was
a mining consultant. Has cultural appropriation ever been
so catchy?

Irkutsk Regional Museum of Local Lore is a treasure trove
of birch objects. There are bags for needlework and buckets
made from plaited strips of bark and some kind of scoop made
from birch wood. Many date from the nineteenth century, the
era in which Russians became obsessed with collecting such
things. To me they show the importance of birch, not simply
as a Russian symbol, but as a material with multiple functions
befitting the diverse lifestyles of a range of different people
living on the wide open lands of the Russian steppe.

As an institution, the museum pre-dates many of these
objects. It was founded in 1782 by Franz Klitschka, an officer in
the Russian army and later governor of the Irkutsk region. With a
particular focus on ethnographic objects, the museum provides a
partial overview of the material culture of the region's many peoples. Christianity did not arrive until the seventeenth century,
bringing bureaucracy and measurement, a written tradition and
gold. Already settled in the area long before were the Buryats,
represented in the museum by wooden toys and puzzles, fine
robes and an elaborate shamanic mask, and the Mongolians,
whose log yurts point to a semi-settled lifestyle. Collecting
objects from a culture, and oppression of that culture, frequently
go hand in hand and the museum also contains examples of the
multicoloured costumes of the Evenki and the Tofolars, nomadic
taiga peoples until they were resettled by the Soviets in 1932. In
1928, there were 2,828 Tofalars in Russia, according to the statistics I find online. By 1959, there were just 476. Today there are

perhaps a thousand, of whom fewer than a hundred still speak the Tofa language.

The birch played different roles for a number of cultures across this wide region. In strange corners of the internet I've read of Irkutsk deities climbing to earth down the trunks of young, ribbon-bedecked birches; or of ritual sacrifices enacted among groups of four sacred birches – one for each point of the compass – in worship of the steppe god Tengri.

If the birch offers one way to approach the relationship between Russian nature and identity, the steppe is quite another. From the nineteenth century onwards, the steppe has been a powerful factor in attempting to frame Russian identity: its vast flatness conducive to freedom and wildness, something expansive and uncontainable. For figures like nineteenth-century poet Alexei Koltsov, such wide open landscapes were emblematic of infinity. Just as their real freedoms were being forcibly curtailed, the region's nomadic peoples have become symbols of freedom, and of a way of living in the world that offers an alternative to the rigidities of urban, settled, European civilisation.

The lives of Russia's nomadic peoples were not just of interest for nineteenth-century ethnologists or the Russian state bureaucracy. In *Black Wind, White Snow*, journalist Charles Clover traces the history of Eurasianism, an ethno-nationalist ideology that sees Russia's origins and destiny as properly Asian and nomadic rather than settled and European. Clover tells the story of Lev Gumilev, son of Soviet poet Anna Akhmatova (writer of 'I, the Kitezh woman . . .'). Gumilev was frequently in and out of the gulag and, according to Clover, this experience of the camps strongly shaped his worldview. He studied the steppe people of inner Asia – the Huns, Turks, Mongols and Xiongnu – in order to, writes Clover, 'elevate the history of nomads and their culture'. In opposition to the dogma of the Soviet era Gumilev argued that 'history was driven not by classes, but by peoples, tribes and nations, whose complex interrelationship with the natural environment shaped their unique cultural identity'. According to Gumilev, it was not only natural environments that shaped the characteristics of different ethnic groups, but also radiation from outer space. As he grew older, Gumilev became increasingly antisemitic.

In the era of *perestroika*, as the USSR began to crumble and nationalism grew in power and confidence, Gumilev's theories were taken up once more. Clover quotes politician and Gumilev apologist Anatoly Lukyanov, Chairman of the Supreme Soviet from 1990 to 1991, on the effects of the steppe character upon the peoples that inhabit it: 'The climate is very severe, so the individual, the Western individualist, would find it impossible to live here.'

Under Putin, Gumilev has become relevant again. Influential fascist ideologue Aleksandr Dugin has championed Eurasianism for a new, autocratic era, finding in the theory useful justification for Russian supremacy. A mono-ethnic Russian nationalism has never really been tenable within such a diverse country, and Eurasianism is therefore a more politically expedient ideology. Where once the forest was seen as the locus of Russian identity, for Eurasianists it is the wide open landscapes of the steppe. As Clover puts it, 'Russians were encouraged to take pride and seek salvation in their enigmatic nation, the vast immortal landscapes of the hinterland'.

Eurasianism offers a new map of the world, one dominated by a Russia that transcends Europe and Asia while maintaining a moral and geopolitical superiority over both Islam and the capitalist West. Dugin himself would be closely involved in attempts to make this map a reality. No longer simply a fringe theorist, he is thought to have coordinated pro-Russian activists in Ukraine as a precursor to military action. In Clover's words:

It is hard to escape the idea that Putin's 'Eurasia' has become, in some sense, a geographical border around a separate truth. A century ago, the original Eurasianists gave birth to a new continent, a fictitious one, which over the decades has become more and more real; at the same time, Russia, a real entity, has become more and more fictional.

From Irkutsk we take an early morning bus that hurtles at breakneck speed past woodland cemeteries to our destination: Lake Baikal. On the map a vast crescent, Baikal is one of the natural wonders of the world, a place of superlatives. It is the largest freshwater lake in the world, containing more water than all of the North American Great Lakes combined – nearly a quarter of all the fresh surface water on the planet. With incredibly clear water that is rich in oxygen even in its depths, this unique ecosystem is home to thousands of species of plants, fish, animals and other organisms, many of which are endemic to Baikal. Baikal is also the deepest lake on earth and the oldest.

Baikal is an important place for birch trees too. *Betula fruticosa* (Japanese bog birch) and *Betula gmelinii*, a small shrubby birch, both thrive in the region, and it has been studied extensively by botanists from the nineteenth century onwards. Baikal is mentioned many times by Kenneth Ashburner and Hugh A. McAllister in *The Genus Betula*, both as a border and as a place of transition. In the 1830s, silver birches that had been brought back to Europe from Japan appeared so unfamiliar that it was thought they must be a separate species. It was only later, when botanists began to explore Siberia, that they realised the forests were full of 'intermediate-looking' birch trees. *Betula pendula* (silver birch) and *Betula japonica* were in fact regional variants of the same species.

By contrast, for other species of birch, Baikal denotes a limit. According to Ashburner and McAllister, 'the Lake Baikal region probably marks a relatively sharp transition' between *Betula pubescens* (white birch) to the west and *Betula ermanii* (stone birch) to the east. In the strictest botanical terms, therefore, for me this is the end of the white birch. Luckily, I'm not a botanist, and my white birch is not only *Betula pubescens* but any white birch. *Betula ermanii* is also white-barked and soon I hope to see it face-to-face for the first time.

Baikal is not simply beautiful or environmentally important or big. In his psychoanalytic reading of Russian national identity, Daniel Rancour-Laferriere cites scholar of Russian literature Kathleen Parthé in arguing that

> some localities – Moscow, Lake Baikal, Tolstoy's estate of Yasnaya Polyana, the Kulikovo battlefield, or just a typical peasant village (*'derevnia'*) – are sometimes understood by Russians to represent the larger Russia in some way. Rhetorically, this process is a synecdoche, while psychologically the process usually involves an intense idealization of some aspect of Russia.

What strikes me as odd about this is that some of these places – Tolstoy's estate, for example, or the 'typical' peasant village – are indeed relatively representative of certain aspects of Russian life. There are lots of country estates with orchards and birch avenues; there are lots of remote rural villages. But Moscow? Lake Baikal? These are extremes. There is no Russian city comparable to Moscow. There is nowhere quite like Baikal.

In the 1960s, Baikal became a focal point for a resurgent Russian environmental movement. Environmental policy expert Philip R. Pryde has described this as one of two 'environmental awakenings' in twentieth-century Russia (the other was Chernobyl). The catalyst was one of the Soviets' more outlandishly Promethean ideas: a scheme proposed in 1958 to increase production of hydroelectric power by setting off huge quantities of explosives at the source of one of the rivers that feeds into Baikal. Concerned in addition about overfishing, excessive tree felling and other sources of pollution, a loose group that included writers and scientists came together in defence of Baikal. In 1981, Valentin Rasputin, another writer associated with the 'village prose' movement, embraced the kinds of superlatives invariably associated with Baikal:

> Long ago [Baikal] became the symbol of our relationship to nature, and now too much depends on whether or not Baikal will remain pure and intact. This would have been not just one more boundary that the human race conquered and crossed but the final boundary: beyond Baikal there would be nothing that could stop people from going too far in their efforts to transform nature.

Here, Rasputin presents Baikal as the limit beyond which Soviet Prometheanism should not cross. When he writes of 'our relationship to nature', however, he writes not only of Russians or Soviets but of all humans. For Rasputin, there is still a 'pure nature' out there, but there must be a fight to protect it. This is not so much a battle between dissidents and the regime but of humanity against itself.

Although the hydroelectric scheme was eventually shelved, campaigners were unable to prevent the opening in 1961 of a paper mill on the southern tip of Baikal that would become a major source of water pollution. The mill was eventually closed in 2013 but the disposal of waste products is still an issue. Millions of tonnes of pollutants remain in the plant's tanks.

Other threats include the proposal to construct a bottled water plant near the shore. The plant, funded by a Chinese company, was widely opposed both on environmental and xenophobic grounds and was eventually ruled illegal by a Russian court in 2019. Russia looks to be quite capable of endangering Baikal without Chinese input, however: the government is currently discussing legal changes to allow forest clear-felling and other higher-impact activities previously restricted by law.

Over the decades, even though environmentalists have not often defeated the authorities, Baikal remains important for demonstrating that, even in the Soviet era, social groups could form based upon shared interests and values without the approval of the state. Baikal also demonstrated that, for many Russians, natural beauty is important – for scientific reasons, for nationalist reasons, for aesthetic reasons, for personal or emotional or spiritual reasons. In 2018, 1.6 million tourists visited Lake Baikal, most of them from within Russia. Tourism is the latest threat that needs to be managed.

Baikal is an important focal point in *Sea Buckthorn Summer*, the film about Soviet playwright Alexander Vampilov. For Vampilov, who was born in the town of Cheremkhovo near Irkutsk, and whose father was of Buryat ancestry, Baikal seems to provide succour, an escape from the Moscow literary scene, with its rigid censorship and closed hierarchies. In the end Baikal is also where Vampilov dies, lost overboard while fishing. In the film's final moments, he sees a vision of his father, whom he had never met (he had been shot by the Soviet authorities in 1938). Baikal becomes not only a place of escape but also an opportunity to realise the playwright's longing to meet his father. The whole scene is rather overcooked.

Before our journey I had suggested to Miina and Arttu that we try to visit Davsha, a little town on Baikal's eastern shore. Since 1916, Davsha had been home to rangers and field biologists studying the flora and fauna of the lake and its surrounding ecosystems. But in 2005, funding was cut, the occupants of the little wooden houses upped and left, and today Davsha is a ghost town. On the map, it's not more than an inch or so from the major cities on our route, Irkutsk and Ulan-Ude. An inch, it turns out, is a long way: 280 miles along overgrown roads that don't even show up on the map. We decide to give Davsha a miss.

Baikal reveals less to me than I expected. The town of Listvyanka, where the Angara River flows into the lake, is geared up for tourism. In the centre, boat trip providers and tour operators tout their wares from garish kiosks, blaring out music into the early morning sunshine. Around a school building are low white fences made from birch logs. At the edges of Listvyanka, all is crumbling, peeling. We take a boat out onto the lake and struggle to imagine the vastness all around us and deep below us. We have a hearty lunch: plate upon plate of barbecued fish, salted mushrooms with *smetana*, ceviche, potatoes, pickles . . .

And we roam along the rocky shore of Baikal to lie contentedly in the September sunshine. The variety of rocks is extraordinary. I pick up a lump of a soft iron-coloured stone that feels like it was released into the world unfinished. It flakes like buttery croissant in my hands. I gather pebbles, using one soft dark rock to draw patterns of spiralling circles on the others. Land art, of a sort. It's blissful here, but ultimately frustrating. Baikal! It should mean more than this.

All the while, for at least an hour, Arttu is lying face down on the shore. He does not say a word.

'What were you doing back there?' I ask as we eventually get up to leave.

'Just lying on the rocks, thinking about my loins.'

'I wish I'd known!' I laugh. 'I feel like I missed an opportunity there.'

'You should never miss an opportunity to think about the loins.'

We return to the train: one night from Irkutsk to Ulan-Ude travelling along the southern shore of Baikal. I take blurry photographs out of the window: little allotments separated by fences; polytunnels; piles of broken pallets for firewood. And is that what I think it is – *Betula ermanii*? An autumnal golden blaze amid the flat grey gloom. On the train a woman shuffles past our cabin, her walking stick tapping a slow rhythm against the metal of the corridor radiator.

Along Baikal are fishermen in camouflage, crows, gulls. The foreground is wet and loose, with broken trees edging into woodland, rivers crashing down into the great lake. Suddenly there are children at my knees: visitors from a neighbouring compartment. They soon tire of us and leave.

The sky is grey. A grey mist hangs over Baikal. A gully of water runs alongside the tracks. The paths are wet and muddy like rivers; rivers winding like paths. Dwarf birches form a carpet of fire.

The train's muttering temporarily turns rhythmic before phasing back out into clatter. My thoughts follow the same pattern: from moments of meaning to noise and back again. I see horses galloping through the wide expanse of steppe, muddy puddles, plastic bags, a burnt-out car, a pair of birch trees snapped in two. Birches! I'm half-sick of birches.

'The landscape feels so familiar,' says one of our group, I can't remember who. 'Like Finland. Timeless.'

I don't even bother to argue with them. Instead I play golf on my old Nokia telephone, hitting a white pixel through a neat green landscape.

On a low hill, a short but terrifying drive in a clapped-out Lada from the city of Ulan-Ude, the trees are tagged with a rainbow of dust-faded ribbons. The hill is home to Ivolginsky Datsan, a small complex of Buddhist temples that the Soviets permitted to be built in 1945 during a period in which restrictions on religious practices were temporarily relaxed. It seems to me that all the trees, including, I'm pleased to see, a dirty-looking birch, have been decorated regardless of their species. I later read that, in this region, where shamanic practices and Buddhist beliefs intertwine, birches decorated with ribbons represent wealth.

We're here at Katja's instigation to attend a morning ceremony. Inside, the temple is richly decorated. A square dais takes up most of the space around which pillars have been painted to look like fabric tassels. Monks in maroon robes seated in the centre perform a rhythmic, rousing kind of throat singing while one of their number beats a huge drum with a sickle-shaped drumstick. This is not only music that you hear but music that you feel reverberating within you. Worshippers in tracksuits and Nike trainers enter the building and circle the room clockwise before taking their seats. During one moment in the ceremony it becomes clear that we, the ignorant tourists, have got something wrong: we did not bring anything to cover our heads, so we leave, embarrassed. Outside, the ceremony continues with scattering of milk and water.

To Vladivostok! Our final journey. Each train we've taken since Moscow has been noticeably less luxurious than the one before: older, less comfortable, with fewer plug sockets and less and less reliable internet access. We play chess, read Chekhov to each other in the low evening light, prepare our meals and eat together. Apart from the landscapes sliding past the window, we have no knowledge of the world outside the train.

Beyond Ulan-Ude are low grey mountains, dark where they meet the pale grey sky. The foreground is a golden ruddy scrub. There are clusters of bare and bony birches. A heron flies low over a khaki river.

We stop somewhere at lunch-time and babushkas are selling homemade food and produce on the street. This kind of informal trade has been banned from Russian train stations in recent years. So everyone heads through the station to the street outside in order to stock up on delicious pierogies and fat little buns stuffed with cabbage.

A cat jumps up to the service hatch of a small kiosk and, unnoticed, heads inside, only to reappear a moment later. I grin to myself at this little moment. Iona, with the eye of a film-maker, has noticed it too.

At every significant stop are the men who come in pairs to tap out a happy, baffling rhythm with metal bars against the bellies of each carriage, tapping pipes and workings, checking the tanks and the couplings, perhaps also on the hunt for stowaways.

We set off again, past narrow rocky rivers and boggy fields, grass rippling in the wind. Bunches of orange-jacketed workmen sit and watch as our train jostles by. A wave of bare birches stands like fine hair on the skin of the steppe.

Notes:

- cows wandering a lane into a village
- dog kicking dirt over its faeces
- Soviet-era housing blocks; rusted cranes; a souped-up
  sports car
- a quarry, flooded and overgrown
- a concrete floor held in the air on concrete stilts, unfinished
  or unneeded

- a pair of brick chimneys splitting the horizon above a
   fine fuzz of birches

A long time passed – or maybe just a short time.

Tired of sitting, I take a walk along the train corridor. We've travelled nearly five thousand miles and are now just a couple of days from Vladivostok, but I'm struggling to work out what I've actually learned. I came here to find answers and now I can't even remember the question. All I've really seen from the train is a world passing by outside. This journey has simply revealed how much I do not know. On the one hand this stimulates a desire to know more, to travel further, deeper, to fill the gaps in my knowledge that I am all of a sudden so acutely aware of. I could spend a month living in some remote Russian village. Or longer: a year, ten years ... How long would be enough to really understand? Maybe I never will. Maybe I should accept the limits of knowledge, limits to the need to know. Is it really so important for me to impose myself upon some rural villagers in order to begin to understand some kind of 'authentic Russian experience'? Do I need to see *Betula fruticosa* for myself 'in the wild'? The belief in the need to see things first-hand is the self-justification of the colonial explorer and of the modern tourist. Maybe it's OK simply to imagine from afar. That's what books are for, and art, and the imagination. Maybe it's OK just to let people – and birches – be.

In the corridor I try to look outside but the light is wrong: bright inside, dark beyond. Instead of looking out of the window I can only look into the window, not through the glass but onto its surface. I see the reflection of my own face against the gloaming outside, top lit by the harsh glare of the corridor light. I notice the lines from the sides of my nose to the edges of my mouth are deeper than I recall. There are lines across my forehead that I had not seen before.

Behind this face, or rather through its transparent outline, move trees and trees: an endless dark flickering of birches, at once the backdrop and the subject. Reflected in this pane of glass, I've become indistinguishable from all these birch trees. We overlap, merge together. Neither is visible without the other. I am the frame and the lens; the incidental detail; an accidental centre. My mind is nothing but wood or pulp – what are these birches doing to me?

Thankfully, a freight train interrupts. It rattles past loaded with girders and concrete sleepers, timber, parts for a crane. I head back into our compartment.

A day out from Vladivostok and the temperature is rising. The sun glares in through the window and there is nowhere to hide from its surprising warmth. By the tracks pass traces of former industries, villages, homes, lives – gradually slipping back into the steppe or overtaken by the birches. There are posts and pillars, crumbling foundations, half a wall of broken bricks. How long before the rusted pylons fall?

A forest of bare white birches is like a fusillade of barbed arrows shot from distant bows and speared together in the earth.

A long time passed – or maybe just a short time.

And then, passing beach huts and Saturday barbecues and sunbathers on a slim stretch of pebbly beach, we arrive. Vladivostok.

'This is not Japan,' yells a teenage boy, panicking in dense forest. It's unclear who he's trying to convince: his small band of friends, himself, or maybe even the trees around him. What is clear, however, is the implication: demons may exist in the exotic nations of the East, but not here in modern, civilised Russia.

I'm watching *Bunige* (2017), a low-budget short film written and directed by Daniil Goncharov and shot on a shaky hand-held camera. Four students discover a corpse in the forest, which seems to have been subjected to an elaborate preservation technique. Somebody suggests it might be a demon. Cynicism gives way to belief, anxiety to outright panic. Spoiler alert: the demons are real. They emerge from the trees at the film's climax, their faces round and almost cute. But their skin reminds me of the bark of *Betula dahurica* in the way it peels like curling clumps of millefeuille. As tree bark, it is deemed rather desirable; as skin, not so much.

These trees are widespread in this part of Russia and Asia. The morning after watching *Bunige* I stumble across them, I think, on Russky Island, off mainland Vladivostok. Part of the Russian Empire since 1860, Russky Island has for the majority of that time been⁷ heavily militarised and inaccessible. In the last decade, however, it has begun to be opened up. A new university campus was inaugurated in 2012 and the world's longest cable-stayed bridge (over 3,600 feet!) now transports students, workers and tourists back and forth from mainland Vladivostok. In April 2019, the island played host to a summit between Putin and North Korea's Kim Jong-un.

These days, Russky Island may still be littered with overgrown fortress buildings but, past the university, it is predominantly a place where tourists go to take selfies on the beach and gaze out over Peter the Great Gulf in the Sea of Japan. Young South Korean couples in expensive casualwear fill the bus that crosses Vladivostok's great bridges on the way south to Russky: past the big and very ugly university campus, past the conference centre, past the aquarium. When the smart tarmac road comes to an end, they all get off the bus, and head off en masse down a signposted lane. I, an idiot, stay onboard.

The road now is a dusty rutted mess and the bus lurches from side to side. Around us is dense forest. I can't see anything other than trees and, besides, I don't really know what I'm doing or where I'm going. I'd been told by a woman in an art gallery that Russky Island was a beautiful place to visit. But she'd given only the haziest of instructions. The bus stops and an old woman disembarks. I panic and get off too. She looks like she knows what she's doing. Also, I really need the loo. I watch as she climbs out of view up slowly disintegrating concrete steps. I take a piss in the trees and then climb the same steps. At the top stands a broad white school building and a roofless structure of crumbling red brick, overgrown with greenery and litter.

It is here in this strange place that I come face to face with some of the most extraordinary birches I've yet seen. I think they are *Betula ermanii*, stone birch, but later when I look back at the photographs on my computer I wonder if they aren't perhaps *Betula platyphylla*, Japanese or Siberian silver birch, or in fact *Betula dahurica*, black birch. I don't know. These trees are so hard to identify, especially as I didn't measure the leaves or the stalks. It's the wrong time of year for catkins and I didn't look to see if the influorescences were pendulous, or whether the bracts were lanceolate. Was that a hairless nutlet or a long peduncle? Who knows. It is only much later that I find out Ashburner and McAllister reclassified *Betula platyphylla* as a subspecies of *Betula pendula*. Why did nobody tell me?

Instead, all I can do is look at images of the bark. *Ermanii* peels in a ragged way: white scraps leave a fleshy-pink undertone. *Platyphylla* is brighter and whiter. I think perhaps it is *dahurica* after all: that dark ash-grey and the most remarkable surface texture. I get right up close to one of them, its bark peeling from ashy grey to ochre, even pale pink. There is layer upon layer of bark, like the most delicate of sedimentary rock faces, or a book saved from the fire, just too late to be legible.

Here off the coast of Vladivostok, nearly six thousand miles from Moscow, this birch – whatever its species or scientific name – feels so completely different to all those I have encountered so far. It is not a lover or a mother or a nation. It is not slender and white and ethereal and timeless. It is not a symbol of suffering or survival or innocence or purity. It is, in every sense, a different species. To me this feels hugely significant; to anyone else, it's just another tree.

Crows are honking to each other overhead. The trees are full of life. A red-capped woodpecker has some kind of nut in its beak and is trying to tap it open on a tree trunk. Suddenly a bullfinch arrives and, all a-fluster, the woodpecker drops the nut to the ground. In the branches a little higher is a nuthatch. A pair of magpies chase each other through the canopy.

As I stare into the trees, a group of tartan-skirted school-girls emerge from the schoolhouse. I turn to leave, but a long piece of cassette tape gets caught on my boot. For a second it looks just like a snake and I nearly panic. Paranoia is creeping up again. I look back at the birch and I can't help thinking of the *Bunige* demon, its bark peeling like skin. The poisoning of Pyotr Verzilov returns to mind again too. I feel a shiver of something approaching fear. Last night, like a child, I dreamt of secret agents again – one of them tried to slip a jar of pills into my pocket. I think it was a warning or maybe a threat. Across the roofless red brick building somebody has graffitied a large white rabbit. Its face, if it ever had one, has faded to fearful anonymity.

I walk up the hill, past the school and down a little track. I think I'm going in the right direction, but I'm navigating from a

little city map, hardly better than an illustration. Russky Island,
I discover later, is not a small place; it's nearly forty square
miles, larger than the entire Vladivostok metropolitan region.
On my map it's the size of a coin. I'm starting to feel uneasy.

Down a narrow path are dilapidated houses and cars cut in
half. Somewhere just out of sight a dog hears my arrival and
starts to bark with rage. I retreat. Increasingly paranoid about
getting lost, I decide against venturing down any more wooded
paths; instead, I head back along the road where the bus has just
taken me. It proves to be a bad decision.

I walk for probably two hours. It's hot and dusty on this
ridged and pitted track and I have to hold my breath each
time a car or truck jolts past. Nobody is taking selfies here.
Everyone is in military clothing of some kind: the men in
the fire truck, the guys changing a tyre on their car. With my
(not entirely unjustified) fear of the Russian military, it gives
everything an intimidating edge. All of them look at me like
I shouldn't be here. They're probably right. I stop to look at
some crumbling buildings. There is a chain across the drive
as a signal to discourage entry. As I take out my camera, a
man (also in full military wear) emerges from a guard tower
to shout at me. I put the camera away and walk on. A little
further up the road, I pause and try again to take a photograph. But I'm not quite out of sight and the man shouts at me
again, bellowing this time. I raise my hand in apology and
walk away fast.

In the bushes to my left I catch sight of something glinting.
It's a bronze bust of an anonymous young man, stern-faced
with a neat side parting, perched atop a white-painted concrete plinth. A military hero, no doubt. I head off the road to
take a closer look when, suddenly, I hear an almighty crash in
the trees to my right. What the shit is that! I jump. It's a herd
of cows – big and white and just a few yards away from me. A

woman emerges behind them. She's wearing a white headscarf and a camouflage jacket. She too looks at me like I should not be here. I feel like I've accidentally entered an absurdist film shoot: a woman from the eighteenth century dressed for the twentieth; a town square statue in the middle of a forest. Everything here is wrong.

It has become clear to me by now that I don't like Russky Island. There is something amiss in the woods: all the leaves are covered in dark grey dust and the undergrowth is dense with rubbish. At a curve in the road dangles a two-litre plastic bottle from an overhanging tree branch. Somebody has carefully secured it there with a piece of string. What could it possibly mean?

I'm feeling distinctly paranoid again. A truck slows to a halt a few yards in front of me. The doors open. Two men get out. I panic: what do they want from me? Nothing. They don't even notice as I walk past them. Even so, every car that approaches fills me with simmering dread. Relief rises palpably each time they pass. I'm thinking all the time of Pyotr Verzilov from Pussy Riot. Or, I'm not really thinking; it's an unfocused sensation low in the stomach: fear. Maybe it's nothing to do with Pussy Riot. Maybe it's something more ancient than that. Am I afraid of the forest or of the people I might meet in the forest? And how can I really tell the one from the other? Twentieth-century Russian philosopher Vladimir Bibikhin feels this fear too:

The fear that grips us in the woods is not of the type that can be assuaged by technological means, because it is too intimately our own. It is as though the spirit of the woods is within ourselves; in their guise, we are afraid of ourselves, other to ourselves, altered.

Like Bibikhin, artist Ivan Novikov also argues that, instead of trying to reconnect with nature, we need to redraw a lost dividing line between nature and culture. He too advocates we rediscover our fear of the forest: 'Trying to find the Other in the world of plants is the only way to create a new form of art,' writes Novikov. Sat safely at home, I find these ideas alluring; in the strange forests of Russia's Far East, I'm not so sure. Russky Island is a dark mass of strange signs. Right now they're all simply telling me to leave. My only way off the island is to keep walking.

Eventually I get back to where I started, and against my better judgement I decide to explore a little in the direction I should have gone in the first place. I stroll up a steep path. Lilac flowers with yellow centres line the edges. A woman passes me walking her dogs. This is more like it. A little falcon peep-peep-peeps low in the sky above my head.

Before long, I come across a series of disused military buildings. Dark doorways in the concrete, half submerged in vigorous green. I start to lose my nerve again. What a coward I am. In theory I'm allowed to be here, but it doesn't feel like it. I head back to the roadside and wait for the bus home.

Later, I look up pictures of Russky Island on Google street view. It's a beautiful place with beaches and views across the sea. There are, it occurs to me, two possible morals to this story: one, buy a proper map; and two, when you see the Korean tourists getting off the bus, get off the bus.

On the roof of a former textile factory in the north of Vladivostok three Russian girls in brightly coloured trainers are laughing at a middle-aged Swedish man. The man, dressed all in black, is circling a heap of rubbish, chuntering nearly audible words that stutter from time to time into muttered song. He is surrounded by black plastic bin bags and a melee of bottles and cans, cartons and clothing, a synthetic bone-shaped dog chew, an empty packet of biscuits, a broken hubcap. The man wanders among this rubbish, tearing strips of fabric and stuffing white packing fluff into the black bin bags. His singing becomes gradually recognisable: 'Maybe This Time', famously performed by Liza Minelli in *Cabaret*. A distorted version blends with other droning noises emanating from a nearby speaker. Two crocheted lumps hang from the girders above. In the centre of the space is a totem-like form made from rubbish and part-suspended from the same girders. As the man tends to it, the form seems to be becoming some kind of figure.

This is not lunacy, but art. There's a bar in the corner.

We're at ZARYA, a contemporary art centre housed in a former Soviet textile factory, converted into offices and studios by a local alcohol magnate. We happen to be in Vladivostok during the annual film festival and the city is awash with film industry types: American directors in expensively scruffy clothes; excited film students with backpacks; vaguely recognisable actors looking bored in hotel lobbies; downtrodden journalists scribbling in their notebooks; and, for a brief moment, Steven Seagal. These days, the one-time straight-to-video action hero is an outspoken champion of Russia's war in Crimea. In 2018, Putin made him Russia's Special Envoy to the US. At the film festival, he's doing a Q&A and reminiscing about old times.

The black-clad performer is Swedish artist Leif Holmstrand. Watching on, impassive, is the Swedish ambassador, not a hair of his lawn-like beard out of place. He sticks it out dutifully before succumbing to the temptation to take out his phone. A man who looks exactly like Kevin Bacon, in black jeans, black blazer and orange festival wristband, sits in the corner whispering to his agent. The performance lasts four hours.

Outside, Miina and Arttu are chatting with another Swede. The night before had become a very boozy one. Katja and Iona were heading their separate ways, Iona back to Helsinki, Katja travelling on through China, while Miina, Arttu and I remained a little longer in Vladivostok. We drank beers on the harbour, stayed late in some basement bar. I can only marvel at Miina and Arttu's ability to nod at the appropriate juncture as the Swedish man name-drops curators nobody has heard of or lectures them on subjects about which they know far more than he does. I stand by in silence trying to decide if a plastic cup of free wine is a really good idea or a really bad one. Arttu is already getting stuck in; Miina holds hers only out of politeness.

As the rain arrives we're forced to head back under cover and watch some more of the performance. The singing has got louder, the totem is becoming more like a figure. The teenage girls are on their phones now too. The rain drums hard on the plastic corrugated roof. The wooded hills and city blocks gradually grey away. I'm increasingly certain that the man in the corner really is Kevin Bacon. It's not Kevin Bacon.

The performance, I later read, is 'based on local shamanistic tradition'. As Holmstrand himself puts it, in prose that mimics the nonsensical clutter of the performance itself:

> Local and foreign household waste and clothes, non-magic but effective rituals, mutating text-sound-composition version of Viking mythology-obsessed old national-romantic Swedish poetry as soundtrack and partly with live voice, neo-shamanistic construction of a body or a cocoon or an egg, non-worship of non-magic dolls/clothes/objects, an attempt to celebrate and grieve, an attempt to discover non-human layers in the human body and mind.

Way back in Stolby nature reserve outside Krasnoyarsk, our guide Pavel had warned us about the shamanists. He was referring to the temples on the border with Mongolia, but these days they flock also to Vladivostok to find ancient meanings in the landscape or to create them anew. One of their favourite destinations is Mount Pidan, the highest peak in the Livadi mountain ridge to the east of Vladivostok. The ridge is what is known as a horst – a raised slab of the earth's crust which has remained in place while the land around it has subsided. At the summit of Pidan is a formation of huge granite-like rocks called granodiorites that looks from certain angles like a wall or the remains of some ancient structure. The assumption is that these rocks are how Pidan got its name: in Chinese, *pi* means 'big' or 'great'; *dan* means 'rocks'. The internet is full of theories: 'Do these enigmatic megaliths offer evidence of an ancient, lost civilization that once lived in Russia?' asks one site. The answer, as you can probably guess, is no.

I get up at 5 a.m. to drive to Mount Pidan. It's just me and Oleg, a young man with strawberry blond hair and a big green truck. Oleg speaks very little English and I speak very little Russian, which means that, apart from when he occasionally fiddles around with a translation app on his phone, we have almost no means of communication. It feels really rather awkward for about ten minutes. After that, it's strangely relaxing.

I'd booked the tour only the day before, from a middle-aged woman in an office down an alleyway next to a sex shop. Her phone went off from time to time as we were negotiating prices. The ringtone rattled out from beside her computer: 'I've got memories and travel like gypsies in the night'. 'No Roots' yet again.

Oleg sets a relentless pace. It feels slow at first on the flat, but his rhythm never changes regardless of the increasing steepness of the climb, the rocks and roots underfoot. We criss-cross a river, haul ourselves on ropes up through the taiga, where trees grip the boulders with talon-like roots. Oleg is a solid presence: quietly spoken, quietly trod, with steps that melt into the ground. I stumble along behind.

Pidan may be the name that everybody uses, but that is not the mountain's official title. In the late 1960s, long-held suspicions between China and Russia erupted into a series of border clashes, despite the shared communist ideology. In 1969, the focus suddenly was on Damansky Island (or Zhenbao as the Chinese refer to it), a small shard of land, half a mile long, some three hundred miles north-east of Vladivostok. Damansky lies in the middle of the Ussuri River that has long marked the border between the two nations. Thankfully, war was averted, but suspicions lingered and skirmishes continued.

In 1972, the Soviet authorities did what they did best: they redrew the maps. Specifically, they renamed all Chinese place names in the Russian Far East, and Mount Pidan was among those that had to change. The name chosen, Livadiyskaya, is the adjectival form of the nearby village of Livadia (which itself had been named after a suburb of Yalta in Crimea, Ukraine).

As we move higher, the trees begin to change. Evergreens fade to birches. I grip them first for support, then for the joyful feel of another living being: hard and sleek or damp and spongy to the hand. The birches vary too: some dark red and polished to a high shine; some carved as if from bone; some half-wrapped in ill-fitting bandages like the limbs of a cartoon mummy. One is covered with eyes.

Pidan has its share of strangeness. We pass signs of camping: empty tents, black rings of fire. Painted white on a tree trunk is an Eye of Horus, an ancient Egyptian symbol of protection, a long way from home. There are shamanic symbols scrawled white and runes carved carefully into rocks. But, unlike my paranoid panic on Russky Island, here I feel no fear. Oleg's silent presence helps, as does the difficulty of the walk: this is an exhausting, relentless climb (I'm told many people don't finish it) and I simply don't have the energy for my thoughts to stray far beyond the next step. But I think it is also something about the nature of the place. Russky felt like a site of troubled histories, a place of aggression and suspicion that prickled at my presence. Pidan feels alive with ancient life.

We continue upwards through a cluster of birches, stunted and wiry and stripped white by the winds. These are not the slender, ethereal birches of Russian nineteenth-century landscape painting. Up close their bark is frayed and ragged: *Betula ermanii*, the stone birch, as botanist Hugh A. McAllister confirms to me by email later. Oleg and I climb higher and look down upon them, the tops yellow-ochre against the pines below. I've never seen anything like the birches here. They are gnarled and crooked and white and bony. There are hundreds of them twisting upwards together and the effect is extraordinary. Ancient woodlands always feel different but this is something else. The comparison between those nineteenth-century paintings is stark: nature here is not time-less or immortal; it is old. Not fixed in an ageless stasis but the product of time. It's almost as if the birches here might be older than symbolism, too remote for meaning. Right here, these are the birches I never knew I was looking for.

We reach the summit after several hours of climbing. Huge rocks form a wall-like ridge and I can begin to understand what the conspiracy theorists are on about. It really does look like the remains of some hill-top settlement.

Directly west is Bolshoy Kamen (Big Rock City), then Ussuri Bay, then Vladivostok. To the north is Lake Khanka, a fresh-water lake that spans the border between Russia and China. The Ussuri River, the location of those border skirmishes, flows through Khanka and down into Ussuri Bay, whose beaches, I see later online, are a glittering kaleidoscope of glass, washed up from nearby factories and pounded smooth by the waves. From the summit of Pidan, I look south across Peter the Great Gulf where dozens of container ships lie upon the sea. Oleg offers me sweet lemon tea from a flask, I hand him bread and cheese in return.

We drink and eat in satisfied silence. I take some photographs, make some notes.

Oleg ushers me towards a rocky promontory where he takes a photo of me. I turn away from his camera phone and gaze out across the hills, like Caspar David Friedrich in expensive walking boots. Behind me is Oleg; behind him a sinuous coastline and the Sea of Japan. 'The world is blue at its edges and in its depths,' wrote Rebecca Solnit. 'This blue is the light that got lost.'

I look out over the hills of Russia: fir trees, patches of yellow larch, and those spiny white birches, leafless in late September. Clouds leave map-like marks across the forests. The distance is a blue-grey far-away place. China lies beyond.

X.

HOME

'Sorrow conquers happiness.'

Ragnar Kjartansson, *God*, Moscow 2019

'Birches,' says one of the world's most famous architects, 'belong to this country, to Russia.' The octogenarian Renzo Piano is speaking at the Moscow headquarters of TASS, Russia's state-owned news agency. From within this distinctive example of 1970s architecture – a round-edged concrete grid with extensive marble panelling – the Soviet government controlled the dissemination of news throughout their vast territory. Under Putin, TASS has once again become an important locus of centralised power. For a foreign writer to be here is both exciting and a little unnerving.

Three other men sit alongside Piano, from left to right: Alexander Kibovsky, head of the Moscow Department of Culture; gas and chemicals magnate Leonid Mikhelson, the richest man in Russia; and Antonio Belvedere, a partner in Piano's architectural practice. Kibovsky and Mikhelson both wear blue suits and open-neck shirts. Piano, in a striped tie, grey cashmere v-neck and checked blazer, looks like a kindly old history teacher with a dashing past.

The four are presenting details to assembled media about a new contemporary art centre, commissioned by Mikhelson's V-A-C Foundation and being built inside a vast former power station on the banks of the Vodootvodny Canal in the centre of Moscow. Piano has been involved in some of the most expensive (and divisive) projects of the last three decades. His London work has been limited to the Lego-like Central Saint Giles, an acid-hued development near Tottenham Court Road, and the overbearing Shard. Moscow's new art centre, GES2, looks elegant by comparison, but this owes much to the strength of the existing building, a cathedral-like 1907 structure with tinges of Art Nouveau by Vasily Bashkirov. At the press conference, Piano's approach is clear: to draw some abstract form and have others impose it upon the world. There's something very childish, and very male, about it. His ability to ignore context is quite breathtaking: 'I've worked in many places in the world, but this,' he says, referring to Russia under Putin, 'is the most free.'

Kibovsky, with a bouncy bouffant of silver-grey hair, says that for Moscow to have a building designed by Renzo Piano will 'improve our ranking in the global space'. Mikhelson, who is paying for the entire project, is cagey when asked about the cost, which has been estimated at $300 million. It may be significantly more. Instead, jaw clenched in pugnacity or pride, he hopes that contemporary art will be as popular as the football World Cup and 'attract people from all over the world'. No mention, unsurprisingly, of that other great link between contemporary art and the World Cup: Pussy Riot.

While Mikhelson and Kibovsky speak blandly about economic growth and Belvedere goes into more design detail, Piano is more interested in waxing lyrical about birch trees. Outside the gallery the plans specify a forested area of 600 white birches designed not only to provide a pleasant environment for visitors to explore but also, as I found out on a hard-hat tour around the building site the year before, to conceal from view some of the surrounding buildings inconsiderate enough not to have been designed by Renzo Piano. If Piano is planting birches in the centre of Moscow, my instinct is to distrust them. Even though he declares birches to be characteristically Russian, they have in fact featured in his work before. In 1990, Piano completed a Paris housing complex, Square des Bouleaux, with an internal courtyard designed by French landscape architect Michael Desvignes. Exactly like Piano's proposal for Moscow, it is filled with white-barked birch trees.

At the press conference, Mikhelson admits to being initially unconvinced, but the venerable old architect won him over. 'They are beautiful in the summer when the leaves are green,' Piano elaborates, warming ever more to his love of white birches. 'And they are beautiful in winter when they are like lace.'

GES2 view from birch forest, rendering © RPBW

Around the corner from TASS is an exhibition of Russian protest art. It consists primarily of photography, film and other
documentation from a number of political art-actions carried
out by Russian artists since 2007. Protest art is often the only
type of Russian contemporary art covered by international
media, and a number of the works are familiar. A portrait
of Pyotr Pavlensky is instantly recognisable. It shows the
hollow-eyed artist (the one who once nailed his scrotum to Red
Square) with his mouth sewn shut in protest at the arrest of
Pussy Riot following their 2012 *Punk Prayer* protest in Moscow's
Cathedral of Christ the Saviour. Other well-known actions represented in the gallery include a 200-foot-high penis painted
on a Saint Petersburg drawbridge in 2010 by art collective
Voina (several members of which went on to form Pussy Riot).
When the bridge was raised the penis stood up tall and erect,
a provocative gesture directed at the city headquarters of the
FSB security services. The white emulsion paint was quickly
cleaned away but the photographs spread across the world.

A significant section of the gallery is dedicated to Pussy
Riot. There is video footage of numerous actions by the group,
including 'Putin Vassal', an anti-Putin protest song performed
in Red Square in 2012, and 'Putin Will Teach You to Love the
Motherland', which the group attempted to perform during
the 2014 Winter Olympics in Sochi. Before they could complete
the song they were violently attacked by uniformed Cossacks
wielding horsewhips and pepper spray. The Cossacks were
once an independent steppe people who resisted the imposition
of Russian authority, but by the eighteenth century they had
become a kind of paramilitary class, known for their ruthless
brutality and used by the Russian Tsars both in foreign wars
and against their own people. The violence of these Cossacks,
inflicted upon the unarmed members of Pussy Riot, was
never punished.

I've often heard it said that capitalism neuters art, that by exhibiting something in a cold, white art gallery, by making people cross a threshold that separates the gallery from the 'real world' outside, and by making the work available for sale, any political potential is automatically curtailed. I'm not so sure. When artists like Pussy Riot are covered in the international art press and news media, it can be difficult to separate the action itself from the agenda of the coverage. It's interesting to note, for example, how reporting on Pavlensky has become noticeably less enthusiastic since he moved to France and started stirring up trouble there: first setting fire to a Bank of France branch in Paris, then leaking sex messages and a video from Macron-endorsed Paris mayoral hopeful Benjamin Griveaux.

It is certainly true that no art gallery is free from institutional complexity or possible double standards. This particular exhibition is being shown in a place called Art4.Ru, which claims to be the first private museum in Russia and is today a strange mix of museum, commercial gallery and auction business. Owned by Igor Markin, Art4.Ru is housed inside an exuberant postmodern building whose upper storeys are ostensibly held up by copper-coloured herms at street level and whose interiors, according to photographs on some Moscow property websites, are amusingly lavish.

Nonetheless, I keep thinking of what Dmitry Vilensky of art collective Chto Delat said about protest in Russia: 'it's fucking winter outside'. Even artists need a place to come inside and keep warm. Standing here in this Moscow gallery, I realise I was wrong about Pussy Riot. Just because media coverage may be self-serving does not make their actions any less brave, inspiring or important. It may not fascinate me as art but as protest it is vital. What makes this kind of protest art so important is not just the action but the aftermath. This kind of bravery opens a window into the opaque and bureaucratic violence that the state is willing to inflict upon its citizens. Without such interventions, it is a violence that can often go unseen. The films on show in the gallery are so visceral and raw, the violence of the Cossacks is so immediate and shocking. But also the stakes are so much higher. To host some of these Pussy Riot films on a website is illegal in Russia and the gallery has only got round the ban through a legal loophole. I stand by the window and look out onto the street. TASS is just around the corner. The threshold that separates the world from the gallery doesn't seem so wide after all.

It is only later that I find out about Pussy Riot's long and active engagement with precisely the questions that I've been trying to explore. Maria Alyokhina, for example, was heavily involved with environmental activism before joining the group – she was also active in the 2011 anti-motorway protests in Khimki forest. As I look into this aspect of Pussy Riot's politics, it's not long before I discover – much to my surprise – a multiplicity of birches. These birches crystallise some of the many meanings that have clustered around this tree. In 2018, for example, the group released 'Unicorn Freedom', a song in support of Anya Pavlikova, imprisoned at seventeen because, as Pussy Riot put it, 'she chatted about politics, boys and exams'. The lyrics take satirical potshots at the police state's love of cutesy national clichés:

> a hedgehog's bearing an apple
> a cop's singin' Russian anthem
> hey my friend, take a flower
> a cop's gently huggin' a birch tree
> a squirrel crunches nuts
> it's not a sin to have fun
> Pikachu is our president
> i wanna be nice & friendly with a cop

Hedgehogs and apples, squirrels, flowers and birch trees: under the greetings card schmaltz of such innocent nature imagery is a regime that tries to control every aspect of contemporary life. Sing the national anthem – *and mean it* – or face the consequences of the Russian criminal legal system. I can't help but think back to Irina Ratushinskaya, whose poetry laid bare the discrepancy between the state's love of lyrical birches and the realities of life in the gulag. Pussy Riot's accompanying video features cartoon-like graphics of a rainbow-horned unicorn against a candy-pink background.

But this is not the only birch. In an article for *Critical Inquiry*, Harvard anthropologist Anya Bernstein describes the torrent of violent language that erupted in Russian public discourse following Pussy Riot's arrest:

> a well-known journalist and TV presenter, Maksim Shevchenko wrote: 'I think Orthodox women should catch and flog these little bitches with birch rods. Let them also have a "performance".'

And suddenly, as Bernstein herself notes, we're right back in a medieval era of witch hunts and public floggings, with the body once more part of a public spectacle of state control involving that 'most shameful symbol of serfdom', the birch rod. Bernstein continues:

> In the coming days and months, the blogosphere exploded with cruel fantasies, often of a sexual character, such as the calls 'to strip them naked,' 'to have them tarred and feathered,' 'to strip them naked and tie them to the whipping post,' to 'spank' (*otshlepat'*), 'flog' (*vyporot'*), 'whip' (*vysech'*), and 'birch' them (otkhlestat' rozgami), or to 'give them "a fatherly spanking"' (*otecheski otshlepat'*).

The birch meets Pussy Riot from two apparently opposite, but in fact inseparable, semiotic directions: first, the living tree that is in fact an old, overloaded and easily co-optable symbol of feminine purity; and second, the flail of birch twigs, an instrument of biopolitical control from the feudal era right through to the twentieth century. Assailed by all these birches, Pussy Riot's actions reveal the ways in which the Putin regime exerts control not only like the Tsars, through the public spectacle of violence, but also, as under communism, through the far less visible apparatus of the police, judiciary and jails.

At Art4.Ru, we're given a tour by the exhibition's curator, Marat Guelman, a charismatic, if complicated figure. He speaks sweepingly about art history and about its future. 'In Russia, art must be in the avant-garde,' he says. A prominent face in the Moscow art scene, who ran a series of galleries in the capital throughout the 1990s and 2000s, Guelman now lives in Montenegro. As director of PERMM contemporary art museum from 2008, he had been leading a small cultural renaissance in the city of Perm close to the Ural Mountains. (We stopped there on the Trans-Siberian for no more than a few short minutes.) But an exhibition critical of the Sochi Winter Olympics was closed down by the local authorities, Guelman was dismissed, and he decided to leave the country.

If Guelman has suffered for the repressive turn that Russia has taken, he also bears some responsibility for enabling it to happen. In the early years of Putin's presidency, Guelman was deputy director of state-owned television station Channel One. During this time he helped shift the channel away from the independent editorial position it had enjoyed under Yeltsin towards a far more Kremlin-friendly line. In 1995, Guelman established the Foundation for Effective Politics (FEP) along with Maxim Meyer and Gleb Pavlovsky. The FEP was a political think tank responsible for a number of election campaigns, including Putin's presidential campaign in 2000.

In his analysis of Russia's new nationalism, Charles Clover describes Guelman as 'a gallery owner with an almost endless supply of aerodynamic-looking designer spectacles which framed his chubby, cherubic face and permanently scraggly beard'. Clover notes how Guelman promoted the career of, among others, Aleksandr Dugin, whose fascist philosophy has been adopted by Putin to the extent that, according to Masha Gessen, it has now 'attained the status of a national project'. In his book, Clover recalls a conversation with Guelman in 2004: 'Guelman looked back on the system he had helped to create with some misgivings. "In 1996, we beat the Communists, but in so doing, we gave the regime a tool for staying in power until the end of time."'

I was introduced to Guelman by chance a few nights before visiting his exhibition. At a gallery opening I ran into Sergey Kishchenko, a year on from our hung-over interview in a Moscow art fair. This time, he revelled in the role of master of ceremonies, whisking me across town with an Austrian curator (dressed for the Resistance in beige raincoat and red beret), pausing to point out details of architectural history, and on to another opening: a new restaurant-bar-club taking over three floors of a grand old mansion.

On opening night, the new venue is set up like a communal apartment, but with video art on the stairs and a neon installation in the courtyard. There's a wine tasting in one corner, and a military brass band outside. The place is packed with beautiful people. I'm listening to a pair of black-clad artists discussing the difficulties of making art in contemporary Moscow when we're joined unexpectedly by a jovial newcomer in brightly coloured anorak. From time to time he reaches into his rucksack, has a momentary rummage, and pulls out, first a bottle of wine, then a sachet of cat food, then a yo-yo. 'Is that the art?' says someone behind us.

Sergey drags me over to meet Guelman in the dining area, where starched white tablecloths and low red banquettes give an air of fin-de-siècle Vienna. Guelman, recognisable from Clover's description with sleek glasses and stubbly beard, is wearing a t-shirt that bears a slogan in Russian. Sergey translates for my benefit: 'You too could be Pussy Riot,' it reads. Sergey points at me and laughs uproariously: 'Even you!'

On one of those cold autumn mornings when winter approaches and the world grows grey, I walk across Red Square in a heavy overcoat. Stuffed with fried, quark-filled pancakes called *syrniki*, I make my way slowly past a bedraggled Swedish birch (*Betula pendula* 'Dalecarlica'), all jaundiced by fumes and autumn, and onwards to Zaryadye Park.

Zaryadye was unveiled in 2017 by Vladimir Putin and Moscow mayor Sergey Sobyanin, ostensibly as a gift of green space right in the heart of the city. Moscow is rarely celebrated for its greenery and Zaryadye is the first major new park in fifty years. If Zaryadye is a gift, then at 840,000 square feet it is a generous one. Once a medieval trading settlement, Zaryadye was by the late nineteenth century home to over half of the 35,000 Jews living in Moscow. In the 1930s and '40s the Soviets demolished the entire district. There were plans for an 'eighth sister' to join the seven other post-war Stalinist skyscrapers but it never materialised. Instead, the vast rectangular Rossiya Hotel was built here in the 1960s. For a time it was the largest hotel in the world, but it was demolished in 2006 and the site has lain empty ever since. A Norman Foster-designed entertainment complex was in the pipeline for a while, but it too never materialised. The lead architects of the new Zaryadye Park, US studio Diller Scofidio + Renfro, best known for their work on New York's High Line, describe the location as 'historically charged' and 'saturated by Russia's collective past and evolving aspirations'. If that is so, then what does Zaryadye say about Russia's hopes today?

The park has been organised into several climatic regions – from meadow and forest to steppe and tundra – and there is also an exhibition centre, concert hall, domed amphitheatre and underground ice cave. Most popular of all is a cantilevered viewing platform or 'floating bridge'. It leans out over the Moskva River and the six-lane motorway that runs alongside it and provides photogenic views back to the Kremlin. Within less than a month of opening, a million people had visited the park. On that metric alone, Zaryadye has been a success.

But few gifts come without strings attached. Since becoming mayor of Moscow in 2010, Sergey Sobyanin has embarked on a lavish programme of public prettification. He has repaved the streets multiple times and in 2013 launched the 'million trees' campaign, which saw more than forty thousand trees and nearly a million shrubs planted across the city within two years. Some 300 million roubles have been spent planting trees on Tsverskaya Street alone. At the same time, Putin's regime has grown ever more repressive, especially against homosexuality. There has been a huge rise in state-stirred hate crime, often carried out in the name of patriotism. 'Glory to Russia,' is the cry of Kremlin-backed thugs. Mayor Sobyanin has toed the line, banning LGBTQI+ parades and ramping up anti-immigration rhetoric. As Moscow embraces the aesthetics of the green city, the torture and imprisonment of a group of young eco-activists in February 2020 makes quite clear that the regime is no friend of environmentalists. Moscow remains choked with traffic.

Zaryadye is a difficult place to love. Diller Scofidio + Renfro certainly talk a good game, but in a project of this scale, prominence and political complexity, it's hard to know how much input they really had. The website is full of paragraphs like this:

> Zaryadye provides a public space that resists easy categorization. It is at once park, urban plaza, social space, cultural amenity, and recreational armature. To achieve this simultaneity, natural landscapes are overlaid on top of constructed environments, creating a series of elemental face-offs between the natural and the artificial, urban and rural, interior and exterior.

'Recreational armature'! 'Elemental face-offs'! It's baffling but undeniably exciting. If this were the press release for a contemporary art exhibition I would be fascinated. But art and design do not share the same aims, nor should they. A garden is not a thesis. A park is not just a critique of past parks. As I have learned, Russia's landscaped estates were initially influenced by formal French classicism until the fashion for picturesque English naturalism took over. Both the French and English styles sought resolution: first of human reason over wild nature, then of timeless nature over human mortality. Such approaches may be politically suspect but they make for beautiful gardens. Zaryadye apparently resists resolution. Instead, as a constructed park that self-consciously lays bare (some of) its own construction processes, it revels in the juxtaposition of opposites. This is landscape design after postmodernism, and it doesn't work. The beauty of great parks and gardens is their ability both to imagine a dream world and at the same time to make it real. Zaryadye is neither dream nor reality.

As I wander through the park, I notice benches made to look like casually arranged stacks of timber. Concrete paths lead to wood chips among planted areas of birch or spruce. It's clever but superficial. The landscape never takes you on a journey. There are knee-high information plaques explaining, as if in an art gallery, the difference between downy birch and silver birch. This is public park as museum exhibit.

Nonetheless, Zaryadye's website acknowledges the importance of creating picturesque lines of sight.

> At the entrance to the Park from the side of the Red Square is a birch grove. Its ground cover is made up of wild thyme, northern hawkweed and other herbs. Through the birches (one of the symbols of Russia), you can see the Red Square, St. Basil's Cathedral, and the Kremlin.

It is certainly true that the views across to the great icons of Russian power are impressive. Birches divide the vista in exactly the same way as in so many of the paintings and photographs I have been looking at. But so do the lamp-posts and the countless signs explaining what is permitted and what is not. Music and tinny announcements from overhead speakers are a constant reminder of control. If parks often offer the possibility – or at least the illusion – of escape, no such illusion exists in Zaryadye.

The giveaway, as I think back on it, is that there are no animals in the park. I don't spot a single squirrel darting among the tree trunks, no birds in the branches, no insects. Like a gallery or a hospital, this is a sterile space. The rhythmic tapping I can hear is not woodpeckers but builders. I was told by a Moscow curator that during the first few weeks, young couples would meet in Zaryadye to have sex in green corners. Security cameras are in place to curb such licentious behaviour. The people must be as stainless as the world they are given to live in. Everywhere are cleaners and workmen. Uniformed soldiers stand around, idle and suspicious. The large dome smells strongly of shit.

That same Moscow curator compares Zaryadye to the French parks built under Louis XIV. Versailles was the model for Peterhof and Gatchina and many other Russian estates. 'The need to express yourself through parks is characteristic of absolutism,' he tells me, sitting on a bench in Gorky Park (itself the subject of major, ongoing, transformation) and smoking a cigarette in the sunshine.

I turn again to the Zaryadye website:

> In nature, birch forest is an intermediate type of forest, under its canopy of broad leaves spruce trees develop, and in the long run the birch forest always turns into a spruce one. Therefore, in 'Zaryadye' the birch grove borders with the coniferous forest, which reproduces the natural order of things. The change of one type of vegetation to another in botany is called 'succession'; this phenomenon is clearly represented on the boundary of the birch grove and the Great meadow.

There are at least three problems in this short paragraph. First, as I saw when I visited the artist colony at Abramtsevo and discovered the antisemitism of Russian landscape painters like Mikhail Nesterov and Viktor Vasnetsov, appeals to 'the natural order of things' are rarely a good sign. Second, to represent is not to embody: Zaryadye may *represent* succession, but no succession will actually take place in what is essentially a static landscape. And third, the facts here are scientifically disputed. The idea that 'in the long run' birch forests 'always' turn into spruce forests is a reference to what was once known in ecology as a climax community: the stable end point towards which all environments inevitably tend. But the world rarely corresponds to neat models of linear progress. The birch forests atop Mount Pidan were not merely 'intermediate', nor is it productive to think of them as such. Ends, like beginnings, rely on the imposition of a narrative and birch forests do not 'always' turn into spruce forests. Fire and humans are just two of the possible factors that might prevent this succession, and to exclude those from the reckoning is to suggest that neither is quite natural. In reality, as French gardener and writer Gilles Clément has argued, 'fire has been appearing naturally for thousands of years'. (Pyrophytes is the name for plants evolutionarily adapted to tolerate fire; indeed, some cannot survive without it.) That is why this view of ecosystem succession – like liberal democracy as the logical endpoint of all political systems (expounded famously in Francis Fukuyama's post-Cold War analysis *The End of History and the Last Man*) – is now considered outdated and simplistic. Humans are animals too.

Parks like Zaryadye are always political, which is not to say that everyone involved knows what is going on. To offer visitors a wide range of ecosystems to walk through is to offer a pleasant experience. But it is more than that. Like those botanical gardens whose array of global species was often a tribute to colonial violence and extraction, Zaryadye is also a display of power. To present a wide range of Russia's different environments all together here in the centre of Moscow is to suggest the control of the centre over the full diversity of Russia's peripheries. Architecture journalist Alex Ulam called Zaryadye an example of Eco Nationalism. To claim that the park merely 'reinforces the prevailing order' – rather than, say, 'asserts a new kind of order' – is not only to deny agency and therefore responsibility but also to attempt to fix the political status quo as itself natural. Aesthetically, Zaryadye may present itself as cutting-edge, but politically it is not so far from the aristocratic estates of the eighteenth and nineteenth centuries.

It is interesting briefly to compare Zaryadye with another great exercise in the public display of power. Six miles to the north lies VDNKh, or the Exhibition of Achievements of the National Economy, a huge outdoor park with pavilions and exhibition centres. Begun in the 1930s as a way of celebrating Soviet agricultural productivity, VDNKh expanded to become a wide-ranging statement of progress under the Soviets. But it has always had a problem: all of its signifiers are so specific that, when history changes, they must change too. The pavilion of camel farming is now a Georgian restaurant. The Latvian pavilion is now a physics pavilion. A painted depiction of Stalin was once blurred out; now it has been restored. Events, it turns out, frequently move faster than their immortalisation in stone.

This can lead to moments of inadvertent symbolism. On my visit to VDNKh, I'm shown an enormous fountain constructed in 1956 which includes references to Belarus, Russia and Ukraine. It's called *The Friendship of Nations*. Given the war in Crimea this now seems bitterly ironic. 'The fountain is not as powerful now,' says our guide sadly. 'It doesn't pump as much water as it used to.'

By contrast, Zaryadye offers a much more stable vehicle for the universalisation of power. By eschewing the specifics of history or geography, in favour of climatic regions, Zaryadye's vagueness offers a glimpse of eternity. In that way, it really does mark a return to the kinds of landscapes commissioned under the Tsars. The difference is that Zaryadye is not a rural retreat but a park in the very heart of the city. And Zaryadye is not reserved for the aristocracy; millions of people are encouraged to visit.

At the same time that Zaryadye professes to follow natural order, it also makes big claims for human agency. Even the climate seems to be controllable. The website waxes lyrical about 'augmented microclimates', 'climate-control strategies', 'calibrating ... topography', and 'leveraging ... warm air'. It's all rather redolent of Soviet Prometheanism. But other than simply exercising control for its own sake, there is an apparent purpose to all this complex, jargon-heavy engineering:

> These natural zones provide places of gathering, repose and observation, in concert with performance spaces and enclosed cultural pavilions. In addition to these programmed destinations, a series of vista points provide a frame for the cityscape to rediscover it anew. Each visitor's experience is tailor made for them, by them.

Here, Zaryadye pitches itself as a place of leisure but within prescribed parameters: 'gathering' (not protest!); 'repose' (not sex!); 'observation' by visitors of the carefully designed 'vista points' and 'programmed destinations'. This is perhaps the ultimate irony. It is too easy to mock adolescent attempts to assert individuality through copying the behaviour of others, in this case making the same Instagram posts as everybody else. But under Putin the crushing of individuality has become state policy once again. For some, the communist 'we' never quite did transition into the 'I' of liberal democracy. In *The Future is History* Masha Gessen quotes one of Dugin's acolytes:

> Individualism and the independence of opinion are traits characteristic of Europe, where we don't belong. Obedience and love for one's leader are the traits of the Russian people.

There are many valid criticisms to be levelled at the Western individualist 'I', but imposing obedience in the name of a collective 'we' is not only cruelly authoritarian; it is also hypocritical and philosophically inconsistent. Such an imposition relies upon the exceptionalism of a ruler (or, in reality, a ruling class) who are not bound by 'obedience and love' and are therefore, by the logic of these nationalists, not really Russian at all.

In Zaryadye, there is another direction of observation taking place: the observation of visitors by the state. It strikes me as surprisingly appropriate that so many CCTV cameras are positioned on lamp-posts among the birch trees. The birch, with its eye-shaped lenticels, has long been known in different folk traditions as the 'watchful tree'. Here, the lenticel is a camera lens. 'Big smile for the camera, it's always on,' sang Pussy Riot in 'Police State'. You may think you are looking at Russia, but in fact, in Zaryadye, Russia is watching you.

As I comb the internet, I find many photographs of a Russian artist called Ilya Glazunov alongside Vladimir Putin. In almost all of them it is Glazunov doing the talking. He presents his exhibition with arms open wide, points out a detail in a painting, or whispers into the president's ear, with his hand lightly on his shoulder. When Glazunov died in 2017 at the age of eighty-seven a Putin spokesperson was quoted as saying that 'the president has always considered Glazunov an outstanding artist of our time'.

There is an amusing anecdote involving Glazunov and the Russian president. Apparently Putin was critical of the size of the sword wielded by the medieval Prince Oleg of Novgorod in one of Glazunov's paintings. 'The sword is a bit too short, it looks like a pocket knife in his hands,' Putin was quoted as telling the artist. 'It looks like it is only good for slicing sausage.' The artist promised to rectify the error. Cue sniggering articles from the international press.

Glazunov is a controversial figure. During the Soviet era, his deeply conservative, pro-Tsarist paintings, saturated with Orthodox imagery, were the antithesis of state-approved Socialist Realism and he was shunned by the artists' union and ignored in the media. At the same time his work was admired and collected by high-ranking officials. Following Gorbachev's policy of *glasnost* in the late 1980s and the subsequent end of the USSR in 1991 Glazunov came to be embraced by Russia's newly emboldened nationalists. Not only was Glazunov feted by Putin but also by Patriarch Kirill, the fiercely pro-Putin head of the Russian Orthodox Church who has been a vocal supporter of the annexation of Crimea.

Glazunov's best-known paintings are large-scale dioramas packed with prominent figures from Russian history and contemporary political and cultural life – saints, Tsars, writers and politicians – alongside anonymous soldiers and workers, men, women and children. Glazunov presents a synchronic view of the nation, in which all of history happens at once in the fixed present tense of the painting. They are impressively complex compositions, spectacular in scale and full of details that reward prolonged viewing. They speak to an audience already familiar with the world of references that Glazunov draws upon. To anyone who hopes that art might resist rather than celebrate authoritarianism, they are not only kitsch but politically repellent.

As a lover of timeless Russian clichés, Glazunov was also a great lover of birches. There are numerous photos of the artist among birch trees, looking something of a dandy in flared trousers and luxuriant sideburns. In his painting *Dispossession of the Kulaks* (2010), at 26 feet across a typically grandstanding work, a crowd has gathered outside a church to bear witness as Soviet troops set fire to a pile of icon paintings. In the centre a nun beseeches a stony-faced commissar for mercy. Next to them, a pair of white birches divide the composition, just like countless other paintings I have been looking at: from the famous landscapes of the nineteenth century to the churned-out souvenirs in today's tourist shops. A boy sits in the branches among the yellow leaves while a soldier below threatens to shoot him down. In the snowy autumn background, a medieval walled town is on fire and the sky is filled with dark smoke.

Glazunov also painted a number of portraits, of which three in particular catch my eye. They also feature birches. The first, from 1984, is a portrait of Vladimir Soloukhin, the village prose writer whose *A Walk in Rural Russia* describes the countryside I travelled through on the Trans-Siberian. Glazunov depicts Soloukhin looking serene in a landscape of snow and birches. Blond-haired and blue-eyed, he wears a long coat with a fur collar. He is framed by two white birches, while four more are visible behind his right shoulder. The meandering river is frozen with white ice and the same bright blue as the sky and the eyes of the sitter.

The second portrait, from 1988, is quite different. The composition is sparse, the painting much flatter and altogether the effect is less naturalistic than the portrait of Soloukhin. *Glasnost* had begun and this is more icon-like in style. A woman is shown right up close in profile, wearing a black headscarf with a floral pattern. She looks blankly towards a birch tree that curves from the bottom-right corner of the painting up to the top. A little bird sits in its bare branches, a monastery is visible between the snowy ground and the grey-blue sky. There is a suggestion of a wooden house, covered in snow, to the left of the painting. Femininity, religion, nature, home: this painting crystallises so many of the tired-out clichés of Russianness that made Glazunov the darling of a regime intent on turning such old images into a new reality.

The third portrait combines elements of these first two, fusing naturalism with something more archetypal or symbolic. Dating from 1999, the last year of Yeltsin's presidency, the work is a self-portrait that shows the artist, sixty-nine years old and resplendent in embroidered scarf and the lush grey bouffant of an ageing matinee idol. Glazunov occupies the right third of the painting. Behind him is, once again, a bright blue sky and river curving towards the distance. Separating subject from backdrop is a line of birches, the largest and oldest of which are directly behind the artist's head. This is Glazunov as he wished the world to see him: handsome and confident in a timeless Russia of rivers and birches. Glazunov does not seem like an artist troubled by such a thing as self-doubt.

As I enter the Gogol Centre in the east of Moscow – an internationally renowned venue for theatre and the performing arts – and walk up the steps inside, I'm confronted by a strange sight: a large, bright red horse stares down at me, its big red face blank and inscrutable. By its side a wolf lopes forwards. This unlikely pair is flanked by two men, one in trainers and blue beanie, carrying a Kalashnikov; the other wearing an Adidas tracksuit and a jewelled crown. Pristine white birches separate the foreground figures from a background of housing blocks and a blue colour-gradient sky.

On the evening of my visit, the Gogol Centre is packed with people. There is concern in the air: the centre's artistic director, Kirill Serebrennikov, has been accused of embezzlement by the Russian authorities. Most assume the charges are politically motivated and the Moscow art scene is vocal in support (in June 2020, he was convicted and sentenced to a huge fine; in 2021, he was fired). We're all here for the opening of an exhibition of new work by artist Pasmur Rachuiko. The red horse is the first of many strange, but ever so familiar sights throughout the exhibition. Rachuiko is an artist who revels in the visual clichés of Russian culture: not only wolves and birches and Kalashnikovs but also Orthodox cathedrals, the Kremlin, fur coats and uniformed policemen. I'm reminded of those Pussy Riot lyrics about hedgehogs and cops. The red horse, made famous by Kuzma Petrov-Vodkin in his 1925 painting *Fantasy*, is one of the most recognisable images in Russian art history.

I think there is a comparison to be made between Rachuiko's work and that of Ilya Glazunov. Both make use of conventional compositional approaches and a shared vocabulary of familiar Russian visual tropes. But where Glazunov is very clear about where his allegiances lie, Rachuiko is both confrontational and tricksy. For one thing, the subjects of his paintings are almost always portraits of Rachuiko himself, playing many different roles, but always staring directly at the viewer as if challenging you to laugh or to take offence. In addition, alongside the clichés of Russianness are other familiar images associated with non-Russian identities: Nike and Adidas sportswear, women in burqas, koalas, parrots and Native American headwear.

Where Glazunov is in no doubt which subjects are to be celebrated and which to be denounced (there is no ambiguity between 'us' and 'them'), Rachuiko is equivocal. As in Chekhov's plays, it is never quite clear which characters or images are being endorsed and which critiqued. By bringing all these characters together, and by playing them all himself, Rachuiko draws attention to the idea of identity as a performance that must be repeated in public again and again. It is precisely this repetition compunction that I encountered in the 'mail-order bride' photographs in Maria Kapajeva's film. But while those images understood repetition as essential for continuity, Rachuiko sees repetition as an opportunity for change.

For an artist like Glazunov, the repetition of old identities is a very serious business. But for Rachuiko, repetition also creates the possibility of something more ironic, playful, queer. Rachuiko paints with a wry smile, a raised eyebrow, but his game-playing is not simply fun. To play games under totalitarian rule is to take serious risks. His paintings force you to ask: how much of modern Russia is in quotation marks? No wonder Rachuiko now lives in Georgia.

There is another difference between Glazunov and Rachuiko and it has to do with the locus of power in Russia. In an exquisite text written to accompany Rachuiko's exhibition, and thankfully translated into English, artist and curator Anastasia Vepreva writes of the relationship between the centre and the periphery. She argues that Rachuiko's work constitutes a view of the periphery from the periphery, and that therefore it is full of subversive possibilities. By contrast, an artist like Glazunov occupies the centre. Perhaps he didn't always. During the Soviet era his outspoken opposition to various government policies was potentially risky. But since 1991 he has been exactly what the establishment required. Glazunov stands at the centre – or at least one centre – of a cultural milieu that speaks from and on behalf of those with power, influence and security. Rachuiko, by contrast, speaks from the margins.

'The "periphery" is silent as long as there is a kingdom of the center,' writes Vepreva, 'and art is silent as long as there are words.' It is a powerful conclusion to a bewitching text that I find more and more to love each time I read it:

> In the large and fabulous country of Russia there is one main central kingdom and many small peripheral districts. All of these have lost their particularities and merged into one huge periphery, squeezed out of the orbit of the wonderful, successful center. The borders between these districts cannot be marked on a map, they occur in time or space and in the most unexpected way. From time to time, the periphery breaks through into the real world in alarming flashes, as demons break through in spots of weak energy, bringing chaos as they rebel against the ruling kingdom.

> 'Sad Boy' Pasmur Rachuyko becomes the arbiter of this dark revolt, showing us things we are not always ready to see – a whole array of disturbing beings penetrate our reality.

They are fairy-tale characters frozen inside their story, half-way through an unknown initiation in an unknown time, but in a familiar space. Just as fairy tales grow as a profana-tion of the sacred world of myth, Rachuyko's 'spirits' become the carriers of a new folklore and at the same time, of a decol-onialised poignancy. Those who have been ousted (from the center) are shown here, shorn of the forced civility of everyday life in the 'periphery', as a political gesture herald-ing the transfer of power through art. The heroes of Pasmur Rachuiko's 'fairy tales' look down at us like saints in icons, their poses reminiscent of both the Renaissance great mas-ters of the past and social media photos from Odnoklassniki or Vkontakte. With his arrogant claim to high art, his incred-ible impudence in equating the 'base' with the 'eternal', this phony artist can't fail to contaminate us with his intensity.

This transfer of power reaches its height as the artist includes his own self-portraits as a series of different dom-ineering characters, ranging from a member of Rosgvardia (Russian National Guard) to a *gopnik* (petty criminal) from out of town, literally assuming their power and so neutral-ising the nightmare of life in the notorious 'periphery'. Now figures of authority look at us from familiar landscapes, from the kind of interiors we know well and we see that they are the same as us, that we too have power, albeit only in a fictional space up to now. The 'periphery' is silent as long as there is a kingdom at the center – and art is silent as long as there are words. So it's now high time for me to bring my own reign to an end, by ending this text.

A sunny summer day back home in Edinburgh. Mid-August, pre-Covid. I make my way through the festival crowds to the peace and quiet of the botanical gardens. A new tree has been

planted just a few days before: a small *Betula schmidtii* Regel.
Mostly found in Japan, Korea and parts of East Asia, Schmidt's
birch also thrives in the area around Vladivostok. I think I
would have walked among these trees on the approach to
Mount Pidan, but I can't be sure. It is a fast-growing species
and can reach up to a hundred feet tall. But the freshly planted
specimen in Edinburgh is waist-high and still slight.

The tree has been planted as a symbol shared by people
in both Scotland and Russia. It is also, in part, a piece of
publicity. It was planted by Russophile actor Brian Cox, who
has supported a festival production by graduates of Moscow
Art Theatre (founded in 1898 by the legendary Konstantin
Stanislavski). Entitled simply *LES* ('The Forest'), it is a piece of
dance-led physical theatre that draws upon the philosophies
of Vladimir Bibikhin in order to present a return to a primal,
pre-modern relationship between humans and the natural
world. Combining theatre and dance with film and song,
LES is in many ways a triumph: beautiful, tender, emotionally intense, and never less than thrilling. So much so that I
see it twice.

What interests me, however, are its failures. Despite an
attempt to reach back to a time before society, it seems that such
a thing is ultimately impossible. Residues of social convention
remain, most obviously in the form of restrictive gender roles.
This is perhaps a legacy from Bibikhin, who dwells upon hair
as an important sign of essentialist gender difference. Or perhaps it's a sign of how Russian society conceives of gender roles
today. In the production there are seven teenage boys and seven
teenage girls and the performance divides frequently along
these lines (the boys fight while the girls cower) or they are
paired together, in which case they invariably form heteronor-
mative couples: male, female, male, female ... The girls sing folk
songs in Old Slavonic, Ukrainian, Russian and Bulgarian while

cradling babe-like logs. The air is full of the sounds of falling trees and the clunking whir of mechanised forestry.

This is not a deliberately conservative work, but that makes it all the more interesting. To not even realise that the work presents prescriptive gender roles as if they were outside of culture or history or geography is to suggest – quite unwittingly – that they cannot be changed. That they are natural. But this is a very narrow view – both of human behaviour and of animal behaviour. Countless species do not behave like this. There is no essential reason why humans have to either. I mention this to one of the producers afterwards. 'But several of the cast are gay,' she says, which rather misses the point.

After the performance I sit down with the director in the corner of an adjacent café. Black-clad with a black circular ear stud, Dmitry Melkin speaks in that bold, thrilling way of many Russian artists I have met. He says things like:

'The Eastern way is to magnetise things back, to make them transcendent again. It's probably a very Romantic idea.'

and

'Beauty will save us – from art.'

and

'We cut the forest to know the trail.'

and

'Culture starts somewhere there where you cut.'

I nod and scribble things down in my notebook while Dmitry's girlfriend scrolls through her phone.

There is one moment in the performance that I find quite devastating. Towards the end, all seven women, clad in long white cotton tunics, stand in a line atop plinth-like trunks of varying heights. One by one, they are felled: falling backwards to be caught in the arms of the men. The gentle folk singing fades and the only sound is the crackle of fire from the film behind them. It grows to a roar as they fall. White-clad Russian women standing in for trees: to me, now so acutely aware of the many layers of history and meaning that have accrued around this image, they are inescapably birches.

This sight takes me right back to the beginning: to the 'mail-order brides' in Maria Kapajeva's *Birch Trees of Russia*, to the birch forest as a realm of sexual possibility in Tarkovsky's war-time film *Ivan's Childhood*, and to the photograph of two Russian policemen kissing by Vyacheslav Mizin and Alexander Shaburov. The felling of birches speaks to me now of all those trees cut down for a motorway through Khimki forest, of the Lubyanka executioner who saw human corpses as 'white-trunked birch trees', and of those nineteenth-century fears that Russia was running out of woods. And it speaks of a new fear, that despite the birch-led rewilding that has taken place in the aftermath of Chernobyl, perhaps there is no such thing as natural any more. Perhaps there never really was. 'Culture starts somewhere there where you cut,' says Melkin and perhaps he's right: no culture without cultivation; no civilisation where the forest still remains.

The birch is a tired old symbol of Russianness and suffering, of beauty and femininity. It is a symbol that has been particularly potent, but also particularly narrow, during charged times: the early 1900s, World War II, and once again today. In this time of resurgent totalitarianism, the birch is a symbol that many would rather simply forget about. But, as I have slowly begun to learn, the birch is also far more complex than that. Birches have proved to be a vital material resource employed in myriad ways by diverse peoples who have lived and continue to live throughout Russia. Birches have provided food and drink, material for furniture and objects and communication, and, it should not be forgotten, a feared means of punishment in the form of the birch rod, both in the feudal age and, in the minds of some, once again today. Birches are themselves far more varied than I had realised, than the old cliché of the slender white tree allows. From the dwarf birches lining the route of the Trans-Siberian railway to the peeling grey birches on Russky Island, or the ancient crooked birches of Mount Pidan, the genus *Betula* is dizzyingly diverse. As hermaphrodites, birches resist the multiple layers of gendered meaning that have been attached to them. As hybridising wind-pollinators, they undermine images of purity. As edgeland species, they breach the borders between culture and the wild.

I would add also that, in the richly ironic or subversively questioning contemporary art produced by the likes of Irina Korina or Nikola Ovchinnikov or Pasmur Rachuiko, lie the possibilities for self-reflexive re-appropriations of the birch, not repeated over and over from the centre but sprouting anew from the peripheries. In the process, the symbolism of the birch, a colonising species, might itself be decolonised. The finest Russian birches, after all, were painted by Jewish artists.

Much of what I have been examining is specifically Russian, but there are wider resonances too. Philosopher Michael Marder has long argued that we need to recalibrate our relationship with the nonhuman world, not only animals but also plants. In a 2012 article for the *New York Times* that proved surprisingly controversial, Marder argued that we ought to pay more attention to the possibilities of plant subjectivities, not by imposing our own thoughts and feelings upon plants but by recognising that they may have their own subjective relationships with the worlds they live in. For Marder, the stakes of his philosophical project are high: 'Nothing less will do,' he writes, 'than reversing the direction of culture and reconceiving it as a loving cultivation of the vegetal world and of the living.'

In *Through Vegetal Being* (2016), an epistolary conversation between Marder and fellow philosopher Luce Irigaray, Marder writes:

The plants' rootedness in a place, their fidelity to the soil, is something we can only admire, especially because our condition is that of an increasing and merciless uprooting.

Marder's contribution to *Through Vegetal Being* concerns the place of the human in the world and the place of the plant. He too cites Vladimir Bibikhin, who so influenced theatre director Dmitry Melkin and whose writings Marder has translated from Russian to English. In particular, Marder dwells upon Bibikhin's use of the Russian word *neumestnyi* to describe human beings. The word means 'unsuitable', 'strange' or 'uncanny', but also etymologically, Marder notes, 'the one who is out of place'. He writes:

> The lack of human place in the living whole puts us at the greatest remove from the world of plants that are rooted in the earth ... But the etymological intuition in Russian goes further than that: without their place, human beings are no longer suited to their environment, to the world that they physically inhabit and that they, in turn, make less and less suitable for life.

Marder's own life has been one marked by frequent uprootings. He was born in Moscow in 1980, where he 'felt an acute sense of nonbelonging and displacement as a Jewish child growing up in the capital of Russia'. At the age of thirteen, Marder emigrated with his family to Israel/Palestine ('the land that, more so than all the others, will have never been nor become "mine"'), then Canada, the US, Portugal, and the Basque Country in northern Spain where he is now a research professor.

'In each of these places,' he writes, 'plants have become the keepsakes of my memories': a palm tree and overgrown cactus in Israel/Palestine; strawberry bushes and tulips in Canada; an olive tree in Portugal. But before all of those, Marder names the birch: 'A tall birch tree that was planted by my grandfather and grew opposite the window of my room in Moscow'.

It is perhaps unsurprising that during periods of upheaval people reach for symbols of familiarity. My research suggests that it has been precisely during such moments – the early years of the twentieth century, World War II, the end of the Soviet Union – that Russians have looked to the birch as an image of continuity. At the same time, a paradox has emerged: that it is often those doing the uprooting who are most eager to exploit easy images of rootedness.

Seventeen years after leaving Moscow, Marder returns to the city of his birth and revisits his childhood home. The birch tree is still standing, but something seems to have changed:

> I was struck by the relative smallness of the birch tree grow-ing opposite the window I could now observe only from the outside. What for a child seemed like a gigantic tree was a common birch, though still clothed in layers of personal and cultural significance that made it much more than a tree. (I cannot help but think of Sergey Yesenin's poem, 'The White Birch Underneath My Window', which we had to learn at school.)

For me, Marder's recollection of the Moscow birch is vital. In recalling the disconnect between memory and the world itself, Marder is able to cherish continuity without fixating upon eternity. He recognises change without a blind celebration of upheaval. And he offers a way to consider rootedness that is not linked to nationalism, that recognises deep connections between people and place without excluding the arrival of others: an 'us' that does not define itself by excluding or repressing 'them'.

Throughout, I have thought of this book as an extended

exploration of what Marder terms those 'layers of personal and cultural significance' that clothe the birch in Russia. In so doing, my aim has not been to strip them away and discard them, but to try to see them better, and maybe even add to them. At times the birch has nearly disappeared completely, lost in a fog of contested human symbolism. But it has always returned – not simply an idea but a real tree, its branches crawling with ants, its roots nourishing the soil. The birch speaks to me now in a way that it did not before. It speaks of the perennially tangled relationships between different forms of knowledge and under-standing, between image and reality, and between nature and culture. And, as a common, familiar tree, it speaks of a value – material, emotional – that is not dependent on scarcity. By now, I hope, the birch emerges a little more fully, if no less complex than before.

Back home in Edinburgh, with my journeys of research loop-ing back on themselves and drawing towards a close, it feels as if what began as simply a personal obsession might, in the end, prove to have a wider resonance than I anticipated. Yes, in Russia, the white birch is a cliché, saturated with outdated gender stereotypes and exploited by nationalists with little meaningful interest in the place they claim to love so deeply. But the birch is nonetheless beloved – not only as a symbol, but as a living being. And that is important, maybe now more than ever.

The birch, as a species that thrives on disturbed ground, is always with us. Birches are not confined to the backwoods, they do not insist on a pure, untouched wildness far away. When we stay put the birch is here with us: at home on a housing estate or at the edges where field meets forest. When we travel the birch is there too: lining footpaths and trainlines, roads and rivers. This proximity is vital, more vital than any symbolism.

Humans have laid waste to the planet. The climate is in crisis; we are living through another mass species extinction that we ourselves have caused. But humans are animals too. We are also natural, and it will not help to flee further from the world, to wall ourselves off, or believe that nature can only thrive when humanity vacates. If rewilding must rely on the exclusion of all humans, it cannot, by definition, offer us a model for living better. For the wild is not only far away. It has always been right here with us. Birches are part of our world and we are part of theirs. This should not be forgotten.

As the concrete crumbles and the birches return to even the most ravaged of landscapes, they offer us hope for a more sensitive human understanding of nonhuman worlds. They also offer a warning: life will do just fine without us. Birches colonise and birches move on. But when they do so they leave behind a soil that is more conducive to the growth of others than when they arrived. Birches are not managers or stewards or capitalists or conservationists. They take what they need and they give more back. In life and in death they change the world just a little, and they do so for the better. If dwelling in the ruins is our present and our future, then let us watch what the birch does and see if maybe we can do likewise. Or maybe I just need to stop moralising?

In Edinburgh's botanical gardens I seek out this new Siberian birch, planted among dozens of other *Betula* species in the woodland garden. I kneel down to take a look – a Russian birch in some ways so emblematic of everything I have been trying to examine, and in other ways so completely different. It is not in Russia, but Scotland, it is not white, but pale brown, with touches of reddish purple in the smaller twigs and branches. It's not a painting or a poem or a photograph. Still it can't help becoming a symbol. Its leaves are yellowing, just beginning to catch brown along serrated edges.

Among my most treasured encounters throughout these journeys of research have been not only the people and paintings and poems but the birches themselves. The birch I began with, the birch of Russian cliché, is invariably slender and white. But there are so many birches in Russia. Around this particular birch in the botanical gardens are all the others, each designated in white writing on little black hanging labels: *Betula pendula*, the silver birch; *Betula medwediewii* from Eastern Turkey, Northern Iran and the Caucasus; *Betula x borggreveana*, a hybrid cultivated in Germany; and many more. I take photographs of bark and leaves, wander among a carpet of catkins.

On the grass a few yards away is a dark purple scroll of bark, big, perhaps a foot long, perfectly peeled from the trunk of a nearby Himalayan birch (*Betula utilis*) and lying, useless, upon the ground. I have it now on my shelf at home, an extra piece added to my little collection. To me this page of bark is etched with all the memories of writing this book. It has sat on the shelf and watched almost everything through those thousand pale eyes, lenses, lenticels. Found in Edinburgh, fallen from a species growing in the mountains of Asia, this birch-bark page has nearly nothing to do with Russia, even though for me, an association has formed that I cannot shake. It is a dark leathery brown, fading towards tan in the centre where it has flattened out, darker and redder at the edges where it scrolls upwards. The top-left is a little tatty, layers peeling back, glowing like shards of caramel when I hold it to the sun. The front, which would have been the exterior layer, appears shiny as if laminated; the rear or interior is matt red. The white dashes of the lenticels form musical notation or an indecipherable code. With my eyes closed, I run a finger across the smooth surface of the bark, feeling for the raised lines of the lenticels, like the half-concealed language of the birches or the still tangible traces of a thousand healed scars.

FURTHER READING AND VIEWING

INTRODUCTION

Anne O. Fisher, Derek Mong, 'Resisting the art of entropy triumphant: an interview with Maxim Amelin', *Jacket2.org*, 6 August 2014

Tom Jeffreys, '*Oikeusjuttu* (The Trial): an interview with Terike Haapoja and Laura Gustafsson', *The Learned Pig*, 15 October 2014

Kirill Medvedev, *It's No Good* (translated by Keith Gessen), Fitzcarraldo Editions, 2015

I. POSING

Brian James Baer, *Other Russias*, Palgrave Macmillan, 2009

Ivan Bunin, *Dark Avenues* (translated by Hugh Aplin), Alma Classics, 2008

Doctor Zhivago opening credits, 1965: www.youtube.com/watch?v=HRU5cM-5jlw

Masha Gessen, *The Future is History*, Granta, 2017

Wassily Kandinsky, *Russian Beauty in a Landscape*, 1903: www.lenbachhaus.de/en/discover/collection-online/detail/die-braut-30003728

Maria Kapajeva, *Birch Trees of Russia*, 2012: www.mariakapajeva.com/birch-trees-of-russia/

Maria Kapajeva, *Dream is Wonderful, Yet Unclear*, Milda Books, 2020

Maria Kapajeva, *You can call him another man*, Kaunas Photography Gallery, 2018

Philippa Lewis, 'Peasant Nostalgia in Contemporary Russian
    Literature', *Soviet Studies*, Vol. 28, No. 4 (October 1976)

Boris Pasternak, *Doctor Zhivago*, 1957: www.archive.org/stream/
    DoctorZhivago_201511/Doctor%20Zhivago_djvu.txt

Daniel Rancour-Laferriere, *Russian Nationalism from an Interdisciplinary
    Perspective*, The Edwin Mellen Press, 2000

Daniel Rancour-Laferriere, *The Slave Soul of Russia*, New York
    University Press, 1995

Ellen Rutten, 'Mikhail Nesterov and Aleksandr Blok: Feminizing
    Russian Landscape around 1900', *The Slavonic and East European
    Review*, Vol. 84, No. 2 (April 2006)

Andrei Tarkovsky (director), *Ivan's Childhood*, 1962

II. PLANTING IDEAS

Kenneth Ashburner and Hugh A. McAllister, *The Genus Betula: A
    Taxonomic Revision of Birches*, Royal Botanic Gardens, Kew, 2013

Rik Van Bogaert, 'The oldest scientifically dated living birch tree in the
    world (outside Kamchatka)', PhD thesis, 2010

Charles Clover, *Black Wind, White Snow*, Yale University Press, 2016

James Cracraft and Daniel Rowland (eds), *Architectures of Russian
    Identity: 1500 to the Present*, Cornell University Press, 2003

Masha Gessen, *The Future is History*, Granta, 2017

Peter Hayden, *Russian Parks and Gardens*, Frances Lincoln, 2005

Vera Inber, *Leningrad Diary* (translated by Rachel Grieve and Serge
    M. Wolff), Hutchinson, 1971

Alexander Kudriavtsev, *Uses of Tradition in Russian and Soviet Architecture*
    (translated by Catherine Cooke), Architectural Digest, 1987

Osip Mandelstam, *Voronezh Notebooks* (translated by Andrew Davis),
    NYRB Poets, 2016

Serhii Plokhy, *Lost Kingdom*, Penguin, 2017

Semyon Shchedrin, *The Stone Bridge at Gatchina*, oil on canvas, 1799–
    1801, Tretyakov Gallery: www.tretyakovgallery.ru/en/collection/
    kamennyy-most-v-gatchine-u-ploshchadi-konetablya/

Maria Shlikevich, 'Carl von Kügelgen: A German Landscape Artist
    in Russia', in Vincent Boele and Femke Foppema (eds), *Caspar
    David Friedrich and The German Romantic Landscape*, Hermitage
    Amsterdam, 2008

Dimitri Shvidkovsky, *The Empress and the Architect: British Architecture and
    Gardens at the Court of Catherine the Great*, Yale University Press, 1996

Peter Wohlleben, *The Hidden Life of Trees* (translated by Jane
    Billinghurst), William Collins, 2017

III. PROTEST (ART)

Eric Ashby, *Scientist in Russia*, Penguin, 1947

'Russian Khimki forest journalist Mikhail Beketov dies', 9 April 2013:
    www.bbc.co.uk/news/world-europe-22078842

Daniel Beilinson, Khimki Forest, 4 May, 2011: www.flickr.com/photos/
    beilinson/5688252760/

Stephen Brain, *Song of the Forest: Russian Forestry and Stalinist
    Environmentalism, 1905–1953*, University of Pittsburgh Press, 2011

Terry Eagleton, *Why Marx Was Right*, Yale University Press, 2011

Alexey Eremenko, 'Russia Is Running Out of Forest', *Moscow Times*, 30
    September 2014

John Bellamy Foster, 'The Communist Manifesto and the Environment',
    The Socialist Register, 1998

Keith Gessen, *A Terrible Country*, Fitzcarraldo Editions, 2018

Tom Jeffreys, 'Violence to Endurance: Extreme Curating
    at the ICA', *Spoonfed*, 2008: www.tom-jeffreys.co.uk/
    violence-to-endurance-extreme-curating-at-the-ica/374

Sergey Kishchenko, *Observation Journal*, 2016: https://yadi.sk/i/
    dXTFTcHvxdmv4

Irina Korina, *Yesterday's Snow*, 2018: www.irinakorina.
    com/2018-yesterdays-snow/

Kirill Medvedev, *It's No Good* (translated by Keith Gessen), Fitzcarraldo
    Editions, 2015

Nikola Ovchinnikov, 'They come back', 5 March 2010: www.
    artinvestment.ru/en/news/exhibitions/20100305_aidan_
    ovchinnikov.html

Anita Pisch, *The Personality Cult of Stalin in Soviet Posters 1929–1953*,
    ANU Press, 2016

Tena Prelec, 'Something has changed – The story of Khimki
    Forest', *Cartografare Il Presente*, 16 February 2012: https://
    cartografareilpresente.org/en/article745

'France looks into bribery allegations against Vinci Russian unit',
    Reuters.com, 3 October 2013

Ellen Rutten, 'Mikhail Nesterov and Aleksandr Blok: Feminizing
    Russian Landscape around 1900', *The Slavonic and East European
    Review*, Vol. 84, No. 2 (April, 2006)

Maria Semendyaeva, 'Irina Korina: I feel like a balcony', *The Art
    Newspaper Russia*, No. 53, May 2017: http://www.theartnewspaper.
    ru/posts/4457/

Anya Smirnova, 'What Is To Be Done? On Excavating Utopias and the
    Difficulties of Making Art Politically in Russia', *Kajet Journal*, 2018

Oxana Timofeeva, *History of Animals: A Philosophy*, Bloomsbury, 2018

IV. MYTHS AND MATERIALS

Gillian Avery, *Russian Fairy Tales*, Everyman's Library, 1995

Robert Chandler (ed.), *Russian Magic Tales from Pushkin to Platonov*,
        Penguin, 2012

www.georgecleverley.com/store/passport-holder/

Jane T. Costlow, *Heart-Pine Russia: Walking and Writing the Nineteenth-
        Century Forest*, Cornell University Press, 2013

Ekaterina Drobinina, 'The Russian Online Art Market', Arterritory.
        com, 2015: https://arterritory.com/en/visual_arts/
        articles/13183-the_russian_online_art_market_when_birch_
        trees_are_not_in_demand/

Stephen P. Frank, 'Emancipation and the Birch: The Perpetuation of
        Corporal Punishment in Rural Russia, 1861–1907', *Jahrbücher für
        Geschichte Osteuropas*, Neue Folge, Bd. 45, H. 3 (1997)

Simon Franklin and Jonathan Shepard, *The Emergence of Rus 750–1200*,
        Routledge, 1996

Sasha Galitzine, 'Going public: suburbanites become situationists in St
        Petersburg art project Critical Mass', *The Calvert Journal*, 18 June
        2013

www.gramoty.ru/birchbark/

Viktor Ivanov and Olga Burova, *All Hope Lies with You,
        Red Soldier!*, 1943: www.tate.org.uk/art/artworks/
        ivanov-burova-all-hope-lies-with-you-red-soldier-p81662

www.olgakoroleva.com/

Andrew Lang, *The Red Fairy Book*, 1890: www.sacred-texts.com/neu/
        lfb/re/refb13.htm

Anna Lewington, *Birch*, Reaktion Books, 2018

Fiona MacDonald: Feral Practice, 'Interspecies Art with Ants: An
        Experiential Exploration of the Ethics of Co-production', *Ethical
        Materialities in Art and Moving Images*, Bloomsbury, 2021

MagPie's Corner – East Slavic Rituals, Witchcraft And Culture:
        www.facebook.com/slavicmagpie

Georgy Manaev, 'Why lapti are the most Russian of all shoes',
        Russia Beyond the Headlines, 11 January 2019: www.rbth.com/
        lifestyle/329839-why-lapti-is-most-russian-shoes

moya-birchbark.com

W. R. S. Ralston, 'The Fool and the Birch Tree': www.fairytalenight.com/
        2017/10/11/the-fool-and-the-birch-tree-russian-fairy-tales-by-w-r-s-
        ralston/

Daniel Rancour-Laferriere, *Russian Nationalism from an Interdisciplinary
        Perspective*, The Edwin Mellen Press, 2000

George Ryley Scott, *The History of Corporal Punishment*, T. Werner Laurie
        Ltd., 1938: archive.org/details/in.ernet.dli.2015.173632

Unesco, Historic Monuments of Novgorod and Surroundings: whc.
    unesco.org/en/list/604/
Elizabeth A. Warner, 'Russian Peasant Beliefs Concerning the Unclean
    Dead and Drought, Within the Context of the Agricultural Year',
    Folklore, Vol. 122, No. 2 (August 2011)
West Highland Museum, Fort William: www.westhighlandmuseum.
    org.uk
www.visitnovgorod.com
Annemiek Wintraecken, '1917 Birch Egg': www.wintraecken.nl/mieks/
    faberge/eggs/1917-Birch-Egg.htm
Verra Xenophontovna, Kalamatiano De Blumenthal, *Folk
    Tales from the Russian*, 1903: www.gutenberg.org/
    files/12851/12851-h/12851-h.htm#BABA%20YAGA
zvetenze, Tumblr: zvetenze.tumblr.com/post/168574470420/
    kumlenie-is-an-east-slavic-most-of-european
Irina Zheleznova (ed.), *Russian Fairy Tales*, Progress Publishers, 1966:
    www.arvindguptatoys.com/arvindgupta/65r.pdf

V. PAINTING RUSSIA

J. Beavington Atkinson, *An Art Tour to Russia* (1873), Waterstone & Co., 1986
Joseph Backstein, 'History of Angels', in *Cosmic Shift: Russian
    Contemporary Art Writing*, Zed Books, 2017
Walter Benjamin, 'The Work of Art in the Age of Mechanical
    Reproduction' (1935), in Hannah Arendt (ed.), *Illuminations*,
    translated by Harry Zohn, Schocken Books, 1969: web.mit.edu/
    allanmc/www/benjamin.pdf
Stephen Brain, *Song of the Forest: Russian Forestry and Stalinist
    Environmentalism, 1905–1953*, University of Pittsburgh Press, 2011
John Croumbie Brown, *Forests and Forestry of Northern Russia and Lands
    Beyond*, Oliver and Boyd, 1884
Anton Chekhov, *Five Plays* (translated by Ronald Hingley), Oxford
    University Press, 1977
Jane T. Costlow, *Heart-Pine Russia: Walking and Writing the Nineteenth-
    Century Forest*, Cornell University Press, 2013
Józef Czapski, *Inhuman Land* (translated by Antonia Lloyd-Jones),
    NYRB, 2018
Christopher Ely, *This Meager Nature*, Northern Illinois University Press,
    2002
Nikolai Gogol, 'Nevsky Prospekt', *The Diary of a Madman, The
    Government Inspector and Selected Stories* (translated by Robert
    Wilks), Penguin, 2005

Boris Groys, 'Russia and the West: the quest for Russian national identity', *East European Thought*, Vol. 43, No. 3 (May 1992)

Boris Groys, 'The Truth of Art', *e-flux journal*, #71 March 2016: www.e-flux.com/journal/71/60513/the-truth-of-art/

David Jackson, *The Wanderers and Critical Realism in Nineteenth-Century Russian Painting*, Manchester University Press, 2006

Averil King, 'Levitan and the Silver Birch', *Apollo*, Vol. 159, No. 509 (July 2004)

Rena Lavery and Ivan Lindsay, *Art of the Soviet Union: Landscapes*, Unicorn, 2018

Rena Lavery and Ivan Lindsay, *Soviet Women and Their Art*, Unicorn, 2019

Vladimir Lenyashin, 'Everything Gravitates Towards the Landscape', in David Jackson and Patty Wageman (eds), *Russian Landscape*, Groninger Museum, The National Gallery, 2003–4

www.moorhen.me.uk/iodsubject/birds_-_rook_04.htm

Serhii Plokhy, *Lost Kingdom*, Penguin, 2017

Richard Hook Richens, *Elm*, Cambridge University Press, 2012

www.tretyakovgallery.ru/en

VI. ABRAMTSEVO

Viktor Alfyorov (director), *Sea Buckthorn Summer* (2018): www.youtube.com/watch?v=7jgxdvPl92g

Kenneth Ashburner and Hugh A. McAllister, *The Genus Betula: A Taxonomic Revision of Birches*, Royal Botanic Gardens, Kew, 2013

Jane T. Costlow, *Heart-Pine Russia: Walking and Writing the Nineteenth-Century Forest*, Cornell University Press, 2013

Fyodor Dostoyevsky, *The Russian Soul* (translated by Kenneth Lantz), Evanston: Northwestern University Press, 1994

Musya Glants, 'Jewish Artists in Russian Art', in *Jewish Life after the USSR*, Indiana University Press, 2003

Alexander Gronsky, *Pastoral* and *Pastoral Revisited*: www.alexandergronsky.com/pastoral

Evgenia Kirichenko, 'The Historical Museum', *Uses of Tradition in Russian and Soviet Architecture*, Architectural Digest, 1987

Anna Lewington, *Birch*, Reaktion Books, 2018

Nicolette Misler, 'Mikhail Nesterov and Russian Religious Philosophers', *Tretyakov Gallery Magazine*, #2 2007 (15): www.tretyakovgallerymagazine.com/articles/2-2007-15/mikhail-nesterov-and-russian-religious-philosophers

Georgy Nikich, 'Materials for the History of Modern Art of "Rural" Russia', in Myvillages (eds), *Documents of Contemporary Art: The Rural*, Whitechapel Gallery/The MIT Press, 2019

Dominic Rubin, *Holy Russia, Sacred Israel*, Academic Studies Press, 2010

Ellen Rutten, 'Mikhail Nesterov and Aleksandr Blok: Feminizing Russian Landscape around 1900', *The Slavonic and East European Review*, Vol. 84, No. 2 (April 2006)

Ilona Svetlikova, *The Moscow Pythagoreans*, Palgrave Macmillan, 2013

Tatyana Tolstaya, *The Slynx* (translated by Jamey Gambrell), NYRB, 2003

VII. BORDERS, BIRCHES, WAR

Anna Akhmatova, *Selected Poems* (translated by Richard McKane), Bloodaxe Books, 1989

Svetlana Alexievich, *Boys in Zinc* (translated by Andrew Bromfield), Penguin, 2017

Svetlana Alexievich, *Second-Hand Time* (translated by Bela Shayevich), Fitzcarraldo Editions, 2016

Svetlana Alexievich, *The Unwomanly Face of War* (translated by Richard Pevear and Larissa Volokhonsky), Penguin, 2017

Mikhail Bubennov, *The White Birch I and II*, Foreign Languages Publishing House, 1954

On Mikhail Bubennov's antisemitism and drunken brawls: https://ygashae-zvezdu.livejournal.com/26277.html and https://litrossia.ru/item/4268-oldarchive/

Oleg Chukhontsev (ed.), *Dissonant Voices: The New Russian Fiction*, Harvill, 1991

Robert Conquest, *The Nation Killers*, Macmillan, 1970

Gilles Deleuze and Félix Guattari, *What is Philosophy?*, Columbia University Press, 1996

Orlando Figes, *The Whisperers*, Penguin, 2007

Moshe Gammer, *The Lone Wolf and the Bear: Three Centuries of Chechen Defiance of Russian Rule*, Hurst and Company, 2005

Masha Gessen, *The Future is History*, Granta, 2017

Nikolai Gogol, 'The Overcoat', *The Diary of a Madman, The Government Inspector and Selected Stories* (translated by Robert Wilks), Penguin, 2005

Nora Ikstena, *Soviet Milk* (translated by Margita Gailitis), Peirene, 2018

Vera Inber, *Leningrad Diary* (translated by Rachel Grieve and Serge M. Wolff), Hutchinson, 1971

Mikhail Kalatozov (director), *The Cranes Are Flying*, 1957 (with English subtitles): www.sovietmoviesonline.com/melodrama/27-letyat-zhuravli.html

landart-mogritsa.org.ua

Thomas Meaney, 'The Idea of a Nation', *The Point*, Summer 2020

Elena Melnikova, *Best friend of children. Glory to great Stalin!*,
    1951: properganderpressblog.wordpress.com/2017/10/10/
    stalin-poster-of-the-week-48-elena-melnikova-best-friend-of-
    children-glory-to-great-stalin-1951/
Gretta Palmer, *Through God's Underground: The Adventures of 'Father
    George' Among the People Under Soviet Rule as told to Gretta Palmer*,
    Garden City Press, 1949
Serhii Plokhy, *Lost Kingdom*, Penguin, 2017
Daniel Rancour-Laferriere, *Russian Nationalism from an Interdisciplinary
    Perspective*, The Edwin Mellen Press, 2000
Mikhail Sholokhov, *One Man's Destiny*, Abacus Books, 1984
stedleyart.com/pervyj-v-ukraine-lend-art-park.html?sl=EN
Jonathan Steele, *Eternal Russia*, Faber and Faber, 1994
John Steinbeck, *A Russian Journal, with photographs by Robert Capa* (1948),
    Penguin, 1999
Mikhail Tolmachev, *Line of Site*, 2015: mikhailtolmachev.net/
    Line-of-site-2015
Leo Tolstoy, *How Much Land Does a Man Need?* (1886), Penguin, 2015
Ivan Turgenev, *Hunter's Sketches* (translated by Constance Garnett),
    Heinemann, 1897: ibiblio.org/eldritch/ist/hunt.htm

VIII. CHERNOBYL

Svetlana Alexievich, *Chernobyl Prayer* (translated by Anna Gunin and
    Arch Tait), Penguin, 2016
Anne Applebaum, *Gulag*, BCA, 2003
Kenneth Ashburner, 'Birches in the wild, their habitats and ecology',
    in *Proceedings of the IDS Betula Symposium, 2–4 October 1992*,
    International Dendrology Society, 1993
Graeme Gill and Roger D. Markwich, *Russia's Stillborn Democracy?*,
    Oxford University Press, 2000
Bruno Latour, Isabelle Stengers, Anna Tsing and Nils Bubandt,
    'Anthropologists Are Talking – About Capitalism, Ecology, and
    Apocalypse', *Ethnos Journal of Anthropology*, Vol. 83 Issue 3 (2018)
David McMillan, *Growth and Decay*, Steidl, 2019
Metasitu, *14th District*, 2016–17: metasitu.com/14th-district.html
Alice Miceli, *Projeto Chernobyl* on e-flux.com: www.as-coa.org/
    alice-miceli-projeto-chernobyl
Mary Mycio, *Wormwood Forest*, National Academies Press, 2005
Megan Nolan, 'An Art Opening at Chernobyl', *The Outline*,
    28 January 2019: www.theoutline.com/post/7017/
    an-art-opening-in-chernobyl-artefact

Tony Parker, *Russian Voices*, Jonathan Cape, 1991

Irina Ratushinskaya, *Pencil Letter*, Bloodaxe Books, 1988

Jonathan Steele, *Eternal Russia*, Faber and Faber, 1994

Anaïs Tondeur and Michael Marder, *The Chernobyl Herbarium*, 2016

Kathryn Yusoff, *A Billion Black Anthropocenes or None*, University of Minnesota Press, 2018

IX. MOSCOW TO VLADIVOSTOK

Kenneth Ashburner and Hugh A. McAllister, *The Genus Betula: A Taxonomic Revision of Birches*, Royal Botanic Gardens, Kew, 2013

Vladimir Bibikhin, 'The Wood(s)' (translated by Michael Marder), in *Stasis*, Vol. 3 No. 1, 2015: www.stasisjournal.net/index.php/journal/article/view/124/200

Robert Chandler (ed.), *Russian Magic Tales from Pushkin to Platonov*, Penguin, 2012

Charles Clover, *Black Wind, White Snow*, Yale University Press, 2016

Józef Czapski, *Inhuman Land* (translated by Antonia Lloyd-Jones), NYRB, 2018

Daniil Goncharov (director), *Bunige*, 2017: www.youtube.com/watch?v=P0-Rnuv1Lc8

J. L., Luandi Huns: sites.google.com/site/luandihuns/home/the-huns-2/the-huns-3/the-huns-4/the-huns-5/the-huns-6/ashina/the-ashina-2/shamanism

Holy Nose Shaman Centre, Baikal: www.samanhn.com/en/novosti/70-svyashhennaya-roshha

Lynn Jenner (ed.), 'Siberian Smoke Reaches U.S., Canada', 31 July 2019: www.nasa.gov/image-feature/goddard/2019/siberian-smoke-reaches-us-canada

Tony Judt, 'The Glory of the Rails', *New York Review of Books*, 23 December 2010: www.nybooks.com/articles/2010/12/23/glory-rails/

madeinrussia.ru/en

Allison C. Meier, 'Davsha', *Atlas Obscura*: www.atlasobscura.com/places/davsha

Ivan Novikov, 'I want to be afraid of the forest', in *Cosmic Shift: Russian Contemporary Art Writing*, Zed Books, 2017

Lyudmila Parts, *In Search of the True Russia*, University of Wisconsin Press, 2018

Philip R. Pryde, *Environmental Management in the Soviet Union*, Cambridge University Press, 2009

Daniel Rancour-Laferriere, *Russian Nationalism from an Interdisciplinary Perspective*, The Edwin Mellen Press, 2000

Nicole Segre, *Trans-Siberian: A Short History of the Longest Railway*, Elaro Press, 2017

'Concern over raging wildfires as smoke from Siberia crosses Alaska and Canada, reaching New England', *The Siberian Times*, 13 July 2018: www.siberiantimes.com/ecology/others/news/concern-over-raging-wildfires-as-smoke-from-siberia-crosses-alaska-and-canada-reaching-new-england/

Rebecca Solnit, *A Field Guide to Getting Lost*, Canongate, 2006

Vladimir Soloukhin, *A Walk in Rural Russia* (translated by Stella Miskin), Hodder & Stoughton, 1967

Colin Thubron, *In Siberia*, Vintage Books, 2008

Ivan Turgenev, *Kasyan from the Beautiful Lands* (1851) (translated by Richard Freeborn), Penguin, 2015

Douglas R. Weiner, *A Little Corner of Freedom: Russian Nature Protection from Stalin to Gorbachev*, University of California Press, 1999

www.zaryavladivostok.ru

X. HOME

Art4.ru, archival history of the Voina group: art4.ru/show/arkhivnaya-istoriya-gruppy-voyna-pamyati-l-l-nikolaeva/

Art4.ru, Pussy Riot archive (to be continued): art4.ru/show/arkhiv-pussy-riot-prodolzhenie-sleduet/

Anya Bernstein, 'An Inadvertent Sacrifice: Body Politics and Sovereign Power in the Pussy Riot Affair' in *Critical Inquiry*: criticalinquiry.uchicago.edu/an_inadvertent_sacrifice_body_politics_and_sovereign_power_in_the_pussy_rio/

Gilles Clément, '*The Planetary Garden' and Other Writings* (translated by Sandra Morris), University of Pennsylvania Press, 2015

Charles Clover, *Black Wind, White Snow*, Yale University Press, 2016

Diller Scofidio + Renfro, Zaryadye Park: www.dsrny.com/project/zaryadye-park

Masha Gessen, *The Future is History*, Granta, 2017

Luce Irigaray and Michael Marder, *Through Vegetal Being*, Columbia University Press, 2016

Michael Marder, 'If Peas Can Talk, Should We Eat Them?', *New York Times*, 28 April 2012: opinionator.blogs.nytimes.com/2012/04/28/if-peas-can-talk-should-we-eat-them/

Moscow Art Theatre, *LES*, 2018: www.youtube.com/watch?v=Zn6zAYHImG4

President of Russia, 'Condolences over death of Ilya Glazunov', 9 July 2017: en.kremlin.ru/events/president/news/55020

Pussy Riot, 'Police State', 2017: www.youtube.com/watch?v=oaZl12Z5P7g

Pussy Riot, 'Putin Will Teach You to Love the Motherland', 2014: www.youtube.com/watch?v=gjI0KYl9gWs

Pussy Riot, 'Unicorn Freedom', 2018: www.youtube.com/watch?v=UmceUBd78d0

'Putin criticises painter's sword size', *Stuff*, 29 June 2009: stuff.co.nz/oddstuff/2491381/Putin-criticises-painters-sword-size

Pasmur Rachuiko, 'I like you', Gogol Centre, Moscow, 2019: pasmurr.com/post/2019/11/15/i-like-you-personal-exhibition-engrus

Alex Ulam, 'In Putin's Moscow, an Urban Wilderness Emerges', *Bloomberg*, 17 May 2017: bloomberg.com/news/articles/2017-05-17/liz-diller-and-charles-renfro-talk-about-zaryadye-park

v-a-c.org

Anastasia Vepreva, 'I like you' press release, 2019: akfmo.org/uploads/EN_Press_release_PASMUR_RACHUIKO.pdf

www.zaryadyepark.ru

ACKNOWLEDGEMENTS

Many people have contributed to the making of this book. First of all, Zoe Ross at United Agents, whose belief in this whole weird idea has been both surprising and invaluable. In particular, Zoe's editorial clarity helped me navigate the murk of my own words at various vital stages. Thank you for being on my team!

An equally huge thank you to Sarah Castleton at Little, Brown for taking on *The White Birch* in the first place and for being so caring and responsive throughout a very difficult period for many people. Copy-editor Tamsin Shelton has been everything a writer could hope for: rigorous, encouraging, and with brilliant ideas (especially about barcodes and the history of shorthand). Thank you for helping to iron out some structural issues and picking up on a million minor errors (and some fairly major ones too). Thank you also to Sophie Harris for her gorgeously autumnal cover design, to Linda Silverman for tracking down some elusive images, and to everyone at Little, Brown for helping to make this thing happen.

A number of people have contributed to the text in ways they may not be aware of. Andrew Latimer gave early support to a nascent idea. Angus Carlyle encouraged me to embrace my shortcomings. Without their enthusiasm I would have stopped before I started.

Thank you to Olga Koroleva for conversations about animals and art and trees and Russia, for a wonderful day at Tolstoy's estate, and for putting me in touch with Maria Kapajeva. Thank you to Maria for her incredible work and for taking the time to meet and talk about birches and identity. And thank you to Agenie Shuvalova for numerous joyful and illuminating discussions about art and literature and for her generosity in responding to some early chapters with encouragement and astute criticism.

Thanks to all those who gave their time to meet, including Max Coleman and Ian Edwards at the Royal Botanical Gardens Edinburgh, Valentin Diaconov at Garage Museum of Contemporary Art, Ilya Dolgov, Anna Gidora, Sergei Kishchenko and Dmitry Melkin.

Thank you to everyone who sent me links or photographs or snippets of text, or told me about artworks, books, articles, people, places and a whole array of other bits and bobs that helped inform my research and writing including: Wapke Feenstra, Adel Kim at ZARYA, Taus Makhacheva, Nicoletta Misler, Tanya Shadrick and Sheila Sim. Thanks to Anna Lewington for her knowledge and encouragement and to Hugh A. McAllister for his botanical expertise.

I'm super grateful to Miina Hujala and Arttu Merimaa for being awesome and for letting me tag along on their Trans-Siberian research trip and to HIAP for their contribution to the costs. And to Iona Roisin and Katja Kalinainen for being such excellent travel companions and for helping me, momentarily, see the world through their eyes.

A number of editors have commissioned me to write about Russian art and culture. I'm especially grateful to Una Hamilton Helle at *Becoming the Forest*, who introduced me to Russian black metal, and to Jennifer Higgie at *Frieze* whose support arrived just when it was most needed. Stray sentences and paragraphs from these two articles can be found in chapters III and IV.

Thank you to those who facilitated some of the journeys that enabled my research: Alex Rashevska and Nadya Vatulyova at Pinchuk Art Centre; Simon Mraz and the Austrian Cultural Forum; Elena Kurbatskaya and Cosmoscow; J. B. Pelham and RIBOCA (Riga International Biennial of Contemporary Art).

Thank you of course to Mum and Dad for being such wonderful, supportive parents. Your love and hard work have given me the freedom to write and I'm forever grateful to you both.

Thank you to Edinburgh Central Library for providing a home from home in which to read and write. (And no thanks whatsoever to Richard Branson, for trying to ruin it.)

Above all, thank you to Dr Crystal Bennes, the most intelligent, fun, strange, brilliant person I know, whose ethical compass and passion for knowledge are (thankfully) unsurpassed. Every year with you is lovelier than the last. Thank you for so patiently reading numerous early drafts and for so very gently tearing them to shreds. And thank you for your boundless enthusiasm from the beginning. 'Why on earth do you think this is something you could write about?' you asked. This whole book is my failure to answer your question.